Wildlife
Law & Ethics

A U.S. PERSPECTIVE

EDITORS:

Yolanda Eisenstein and
Bruce Wagman

TORT TRIAL & INSURANCE PRACTICE SECTION

Cover design by Amanda Fry/ABA Design.
Interior design by Betsy Kulak/ABA Design.

Printed in the United States of America.

21 20 19 18 17   5 4 3 2 1

Library of Congress Cataloging-in-Publication Data

Names: Eisenstein, Yolanda, editor. | Wagman, Bruce A., editor. | American Bar
    Association. Tort Trial and Insurance Practice Section, sponsoring body.
Title: Wildlife law and ethics : a U.S. perspective / Yolanda Eisenstein and
    Bruce Wagman, editors.
Description: Chicago, Illinois : American Bar Association, 2017. | Includes index.
Identifiers: LCCN 2017002939 (print) | LCCN 2017003390 (ebook) |
    ISBN 9781634258043 (pbk. : alk. paper) | ISBN 9781634258050 (ebook)
Subjects: LCSH: Wildlife conservation—Law and legislation—United States.
Classification: LCC KF5640 .W55 2017 (print) | LCC KF5640 (ebook) |
    DDC 346.7304/695—dc23
LC record available at https://lccn.loc.gov/2017002939

Discounts are available for books ordered in bulk. Special consideration is given to state bars, CLE programs, and other bar-related organizations. Inquire at Book Publishing, ABA Publishing, American Bar Association, 321 N. Clark Street, Chicago, Illinois 60654-7598.

www.ShopABA.org

*Bruce thanks all the wild animals
that have inspired him to dream,
and the one human who has let him
have those dreams for decades.*

*Yolanda thanks Abram for
sharing a journey like no other.
Also, thank you to Skylar,
our furry companion,
for reminding us of the joys in
the simple things in life.*

Contents

Introduction

Yolanda Eisenstein and Bruce Wagman

~

This is a book about wildlife—the myriad species of animals outside of our direct sphere of influence that populate our planet and that we impact every day through our actions. It is also a book about the law and how it can be used to influence, for better and for worse, the lives of the billions of individual animals we call wildlife. However, unlike other "wildlife law" books that stop at the doors of the courthouse or the legislature, this is a book about the compelling ethical and moral issues that are inextricably intertwined with our legal treatment of wild animals. In approaching the subject and wanting to provide a new and broader perspective than previously attempted, we acknowledge at the outset that the subject matter is much too complex and variegated to be covered in one book by one author. For this reason, we have carefully chosen a few especially illustrative and focused issues that have broad implications for many species and authors who have special knowledge in those areas. The result is a book that is a distinct collection of essays on select areas by some of the most knowledgeable and experienced wildlife lawyers and advocates in the country. It addresses some of the most crucial and topical issues in wildlife law today.

We envisioned a book that was informative but also approachable and understandable, not only to lawyers and educators, but also to the increasing numbers of citizens who care about the future of the wild animals on our planet. We hope that readers find that we have met that challenge.

A Different Approach to Wildlife Issues

While most books covering wildlife law include a survey of international laws, this book takes a different approach—focusing instead on the power of U.S. law to influence wildlife protections around the world. Each chapter demonstrates that, contrary to some perceptions, the United States plays a significant and often unrealized role in international wildlife issues. As authors, we demonstrate this by presenting the issues almost exclusively through the lens of U.S. law. We look at federal and state laws, as well as the policies and procedures that affect the lives of wild animals here and abroad.

As stated, our approach is first to provide the law as a solid background and then to provide social context regarding the circumstances facing all members of the global community. To this end, the book is framed around specific issues (not laws), such as extinction or animals in captivity. By organizing the chapters around these focused areas of influence, we hope to make the related legal complexities understandable and avoid becoming too focused on specific animals or the acts of certain industries or individuals. Once the issues are laid out, each chapter includes one or more case studies. The case studies are based on both public reporting and related legal materials that demonstrate the tensions arising in this area and how the law has been applied, or manipulated, to serve desired ends. For lawyers, the case studies include helpful detail in footnotes providing references for further research. For lay readers, the cases are clearly presented in a hopefully enjoyable and easy to comprehend manner. The facts and relevant laws in each case speak volumes about the threats to wildlife, such as the competition for habitat, the pollution of the oceans, climate change, and the exploitation of species themselves.

Finally, the essays include considerations that are inherent in our legal treatment of animals as property. The book's contributors provide meaningful insights into the moral dilemmas and conflicts that accompany legal decisions that greatly affect the lives of wild animals.

The Acts of Individuals

In our work as lawyers and advocates we often hear the questions: "What can I do personally to help animals in the wild? What actions can I take that will truly make a difference?" Wild animals, unlike companion animals, are usually in distant lands or public parks rather than in our own backyards. This fact makes our ability to help seem beyond the reach of an individual or local lawyer. The reality is much different. After reading this book, no one should see his or her role in wildlife protection as limited or nonexistent. By understanding the issues and the laws, it is clear how the products we buy, the entertainment we choose, and the votes we cast have a direct impact on wildlife and the environment.

Acknowledgments

The editors readily acknowledge that they are biased observers of the issues they have presented. It is impossible to be completely objective when speaking from the perspective of experience as a wildlife advocate. Nonetheless, we believe that we have achieved an objective format, and the situations discussed are presented accurately. The threats to wildlife are substantial and deserve reflection as well as reporting.

We are grateful to our authors for their contribution to this interesting and profound text. The breadth and depth of their experience and knowledge are reflected in their biographies and even more in the authoritative work they have presented in this book. As lawyers and animal advocates we could not have envisioned a more relevant and important book about wildlife law. We hope you agree.

—Yolanda Eisenstein and Bruce Wagman

About the Editors

Yolanda Eisenstein is an attorney with an animal law practice in Dallas, Texas, and an adjunct professor of animal and wildlife law at SMU Dedman School of Law. Eisenstein is the author of *Careers in Animal Law* and *The American Bar Association Legal Guide for Dog Owners* and a contributor to *Animal Cruelty: A Multidisciplinary Approach to Understanding*. In addition, she has written numerous articles and speaks regularly on animal law and animal protection issues. She is former chair of the ABA TIPS Animal Law Committee and served two terms as chair of the State Bar of Texas Animal Law Section. She serves on the board of the Texas Humane Legislation Network, a nonprofit organization that lobbies for the passage of animal protection legislation in Texas.

~

Bruce Wagman is a partner in Schiff Hardin's San Francisco office, with an almost exclusive focus on animal law matters, including litigation, legislative drafting and counseling, education, and private consultation. He has been active in animal law since 1992. He is a coeditor of the casebook *Animal Law Cases and Materials* and coauthor of *A Worldview of Animal Law* and publishes and speaks regularly on various animal law topics. He has been teaching animal law since 1996 and currently teaches on a rotating basis at three Bay Area law schools.

Wagman's clients include numerous animal protection organizations as well as private individuals. He has worked on behalf of birds, cats, chickens, chimpanzees, cows, deer, dogs, dolphins, ducks, elephants, elk, gorillas, horses (domestic and wild), lions, mice, monkeys, pigs, sharks, turkeys, whales, and wolves, on myriad issues including the use of animals in entertainment, biomedical research, and animal agriculture/food production; animal cruelty; and wildlife protection and control, as well as individualized cases involving animal custody, dangerous dog defense, and injuries to, and caused by, animals. Wagman has focused significant time on issues involving the retirement of chimpanzees and their placement in sanctuaries, as well as wild horses, horse abuse cases, and the slaughter of American horses for food.

About the Authors

Anna Frostic is senior attorney for wildlife and animal research for The Humane Society of the United States' Animal Protection Litigation department. Frostic received her law degree from University of the Pacific, McGeorge School of Law, following her undergraduate studies in biological anthropology at the University of Michigan. Since 2008, Frostic's career in animal law has concentrated on the protection of threatened and endangered species that are unsustainably hunted for sport, exploited for commercial entertainment, sold in the exotic pet trade, and used for invasive biomedical research. Her major accomplishments include successfully petitioning the U.S. Fish and Wildlife Service to extend Endangered Species Act protections to captive chimpanzees, prohibiting harmful biomedical research, and eliminating the interstate pet trade; a federal False Claims Act petition challenging illegal chimpanzee breeding at a Louisiana lab that led the federal government to discontinue funding the facility's chimpanzee research; a successful petition to list African lions under the Endangered Species Act, prohibiting the import of lion trophies; a petition to the U.S. Department of Agriculture that resulted in a prohibition on using infant tiger cubs for interactive experiences with members of the public; filing complaints with state and federal agencies based on undercover investigations of four roadside zoos that resulted in eleven exotic animals being seized and sent to sanctuary; and a victorious federal court trial and appeal in defense of Ohio's dangerous wild animal law.

~

Ralph Henry is director of animal protection litigation at the Humane Society of the United States and an adjunct professor at George Mason

University School of Law where he teaches a course on animal law and
policy. His past and present work in animal law has focused on protection of threatened and endangered species, marine mammals, animals
trapped and farmed for their fur, and other wild animals subjected to
cruel and unnecessary suffering. Henry has represented animal protection and conservation organizations in litigation affecting vulnerable
wildlife species, including cases concerning the delisting of gray wolves
from the Endangered Species Act, the import of polar bear hunting trophies into the United States, the killing of sea lions protected under the
Marine Mammal Protection Act in response to predation on endangered
salmon, the false advertising of animal fur products made from highly
exploited wildlife species, and the widespread practice of live-finning of
shark species that are protected internationally due to their vulnerability
to extinction. Henry received his law degree from the Georgetown University Law Center, where he was managing editor of the Georgetown
International Environmental Law Review and president of a chapter of
the Student Animal Legal Defense Fund. Prior to practicing law, Henry
received an undergraduate degree in biological sciences from the University of Maryland and studied the physiological bases of animal behavior.

~

Peter LaFontaine is a campaigns manager with the International Fund
for Animal Welfare (IFAW), based in Washington, D.C. He helps to
lead IFAW's state and federal efforts to safeguard elephants, rhinoceros,
and other species threatened by illegal wildlife trafficking, and he is also
engaged in wildlife cybercrime prevention, strengthening international
trade agreements, and climate change advocacy. He was a coauthor of
a 2015 rulemaking petition to list the African elephant as Endangered
under the US Endangered Species Act. LaFontaine graduated with hon-
ors from Washington University in St. Louis.

Prior to joining IFAW, Peter was the energy policy advocate for the
National Wildlife Federation (NWF), where he coordinated NWF's tar
sands campaign and guided federal strategy to prevent coal exports in
the Pacific Northwest and Intermountain West; in previous roles Peter
campaigned on a range of issues including offshore drilling and natural
resources adaptation. Peter began his career in conservation as a natural-

ist with the Cottonwood Gulch Foundation, a nonprofit geared toward experiential learning and wilderness ethics in the American southwest.

~

Kristen Monsell is a staff attorney in the Oceans Program at the Center for Biological Diversity where she works to protect imperiled marine species and their habitats. Prior to joining the center, she was a wildlife staff attorney at The Humane Society of the United States and an Assistant Attorney General in the Natural Resources Section of the Oregon Department of Justice. Monsell has litigated cases on a variety of ocean issues, including cases to protect whales and sea turtles from getting tangled up in fishing gear, prevent the expansion of dirty fossil fuel development in our oceans, stop offshore fracking, and secure Endangered Species Act protections for Arctic seals whose sea ice habitat is melting because of climate change. She has drafted several rulemaking petitions, including one that helped establish ship speed limits off the East Coast of the United States to prevent critically endangered North Atlantic right whales from getting run over by ships. Kristen graduated cum laude from Lewis & Clark Law School in 2009, and received her bachelor's degree from St. Lawrence University in 2004.

~

Joan E. Schaffner is an associate professor of Law at the George Washington University Law School. She received her B.S. in mechanical engineering (magna cum laude) and J.D. (Order of the Coif) from the University of Southern California and her M.S. in mechanical engineering from the Massachusetts Institute of Technology. In addition to teaching civil procedure, sexuality and the law, and remedies, she directs the GW Animal Law Program and has presented on animal law panels at conferences worldwide. Professor Schaffner is the author of *Introduction to Animals and the Law* (Palgrave MacMillan 2011), is a coauthor and editor of *A Lawyer's Guide to Dangerous Dog Issues* (ABA 2009) and *Litigating Animal Law Disputes: A Complete Guide for Lawyers* (ABA 2009), and is author of several book chapters including "Blackfish and Public Outcry: A Unique Political and Legal Opportunity for Fundamental Change to the Legal Protection of Marine Mammals in the United

States" in *Animal Law and Welfare: International Perspectives* (Springer 2016); "Animal Cruelty and the Law: Permitted Conduct" in *Animal Cruelty: A Multidisciplinary Approach* (Carolina Academic Press, 2d ed. 2016); and "Valuing Nature in Environmental Law: Lessons for Animal Law and the Valuation of Animals" in *What Can Animal Law Learn from Environmental Law?* (ELI 2015). She is active in various organizations including serving as past chair, ABA TIPS Animal Law Committee; founding chair, American Association of Law Schools Section on Animal Law; and fellow, Oxford Centre for Animal Ethics. In August 2013 Professor Schaffner received the Excellence in the Advancement of Animal Law Award from the American Bar Association, Tort Trial & Insurance Practice Section.

1

On the Path to Extinction

Ralph Henry, with a case study by Anna Frostic

~

O f the four billion species estimated to have lived on the Earth over the last three and a half billion years, some 99 percent are gone.[1] An unkind truth of life on our planet is that extinctions happen; they are a natural function of life. But species extinction is not something we humans are accustomed to contemplating—the last mass extinction occurred some sixty-five million years ago when dinosaurs roamed the planet, and outside of such catastrophic events individual extinctions are usually few and far between. Unfortunately, that is no longer true today. Scientists believe that we are in the middle of the world's sixth mass extinction. The past five mass extinctions on Earth were caused by huge natural disasters like chains of volcanic eruptions and collisions with meteors. But the modern mass extinction is not being caused by nature itself, it is being caused by humans.

The current rate of extinction is astounding—we are losing species at a rate that is at least 100 (and possibly up to 10,000) times faster than ever

---

1. Michael J. Novacek, *The Biodiversity Crisis: Losing What Counts* (2001).

before in human existence.[2] Some reports indicate that we have lost more than half of the world's wildlife species in the last forty years, and will have lost two-thirds of our wild animals by the year 2020.[3] In that time-frame, species like the Javan tiger, Yangtze River dolphin, golden toad, Zanzibar leopard, West African black rhino, and Pyrenean ibex, among many others are believed to have become extinct. Several recently extinct species were found in the United States, such as the Tecopa pupfish, Caribbean monk seal, Po'ouli (a Hawaiian bird also known as the black-faced honeycreeper), and blue pike. Evidence points to human activities, including poaching, overfishing, and other direct exploitation; deforesta-tion and other habitat destruction; and emissions of greenhouse gases and pollutants that poison the land, water, and air, as the primary sources of this deadly trend. Indeed, of the 477 vertebrates that have gone extinct since 1900, only nine would be expected to have been lost under natural rates of extinction absent human influence.[4]

Some see our impact on nonhuman life in the natural world as itself being cause to take action to combat extinction, believing that the wild creatures that inhabit the Earth along with us have their own intrinsic value, and that we have an obligation to protect them from the threats to their survival that we humans create. But the fact that humans have become the primary driver of destructive changes to natural processes throughout the world is also entirely self-defeating, given our own depen-dency on well-functioning ecosystems. Our societies, economies, health and well-being rely on the natural resources of the Earth. And as we lose species to extinction, we lose their contributions to so-called "ecosys-tem services"—nutrient cycling and redistribution, water purification, pollination, erosion control, waste consumption and decomposition, carbon sequestration, and other activities that benefit all living organ-isms, including humans. The loss of other species also results in a loss of

---

2. Gerardo Ceballos et al. *Accelerated Modern Human–Induced Species Losses: Entering the Sixth Mass Extinction.* 1(5) Sci. Advances e1400253 (2015).
3. World Wildlife Fund, *Living Planet Report 2016,* http://wwf.panda.org/about_our_earth/all_publications/lpr_2016/; Damian Carrington, *World On Track to Lose Two-Thirds of Wild Animals by 2020, Major Report Warns,* The Guardian, October 26, 2016, https://www.theguardian.com/environment/2016/oct/27/world-on-track-to-lose-two-thirds-of-wild-animals-by-2020-major-report-warns.
4. Ceballos et al. *supra* note 2.

many cultural benefits to humans. Species protection is sometimes seen as reflective of a sense of natural virtue, religious duty, and even national identity (in 1940, Congress enacted a law specifically to protect bald eagles as "a symbol of American ideals of freedom,"[5] and the species is now widely considered a success story of endangered species protection), and we often refer to wild animals and their habitats as integral parts of our heritage and seek to preserve them as an important legacy we leave for future generations. In sum, there are many valid reasons for protecting wildlife species from extinction, including ecological, aesthetic, historical, recreational, scientific, moral, and other concerns and values.

The issues discussed in this chapter are at the forefront of the challenges we face in slowing the mass extinction of species. They are the symptoms of an expanding human footprint in the world. The chapter focuses on several contemporary threats to the survival of species, and how those threats are or could be better addressed by United States law and policy, and particularly the Endangered Species Act (ESA).[6] First, humans now exist in greater numbers and in more places, creating additional opportunity for conflict between human activity and wildlife. We look to the controversial continued ESA listing of gray wolves and the influence of social tolerance on endangered species policy making. Second, the environmentally harmful activities we humans carry out in already-developed areas of the world are having a farther reach than ever before. We examine efforts to protect polar bears, as well as efforts to limit their protection, under the ESA based on projected loss of their sea ice habitat due to climate change. Finally, humans are racing to extract commercial value from natural resources in the developing world, which contains some of the most biodiverse areas on Earth. We examine the impact to great apes in Africa and Southeast Asia of extractive industries, such as coltan mining and palm oil production, and the potential to address trade in the resulting products directly and indirectly through legislation in the United States. The issues discussed in this chapter are clearly not the only causes of species endangerment, but they are among those threats most deserving of our attention. Global efforts to address

---

5. 16 U.S.C. § 668.
6. 16 U.S.C. § 1531, *et seq.*

the rapid extinction of species are needed and this chapter looks primarily at the role of the United States and the ESA in solving some of challenges we face in the future.

Saving species from extinction and protecting their wild places is crucial for the sustainability of our natural world. As more species are lost, so too are our options for future discovery and learning in order to ensure that we can protect our planet. If we do not want the vast major-ity of species on the planet (potentially including our own) to go the way of the dinosaur, quite possibly within the next century, we need to act quickly and resolutely to address the most significant and emerging human-caused threats of extinction.

United States Laws Relating to Endangered Species

In the United States, many federal wildlife laws affect species threat-ened with extinction. Our earliest federal wildlife law, the Lacey Act of 1900, restricts movement in interstate and international commerce of wild animals and their parts that were taken, transported, or sold in violation of other federal, tribal, foreign, or state laws.[7] Thus, the Lacey Act helps to prevent U.S. citizens from profiting from poaching and other illegal activities involving wildlife. Other federal wildlife laws, such as the Marine Mammal Protection Act,[8] Migratory Bird Treaty Act,[9] Wild Bird Conservation Act,[10] Rhinoceros and Tiger Conservation Act,[11] and Bald and Golden Eagle Protection Act[12] protect certain types of species, including several endangered species, from a variety of harms. Further-more, the welfare of endangered species that are held in captivity for purposes of public exhibition is regulated to some degree by the federal Animal Welfare Act.[13] The application of several of these laws to wildlife

---

7. 16 U.S.C. § 3371, *et seq.*
8. *Id.* § 1361, *et seq.*
9. *Id.* § 703, *et seq.*
10. *Id.* § 4901, *et seq.*
11. *Id.* § 5301, *et seq.*
12. *Id.* § 668, *et seq.*
13. 7 U.S.C. § 2131, *et seq.*

species is discussed in other chapters of this book. But the only federal law with the primary purpose of establishing a coordinated program to prevent the extinction of wildlife species is the ESA.

The ESA is "the most comprehensive legislation for the preservation of endangered species ever enacted by any nation."[14] Beginning in 1966, Congress enacted three successive federal statutes, culminating in the passage of the ESA in 1973 "to provide a means whereby the ecosystems upon which endangered species and threatened species depend may be conserved, [and] to provide a program for the conservation of such endangered species and threatened species . . ."[15] Thus, by its plain language, the ESA is intended not only to protect endangered species from direct harms, but also to require implementation of proactive measures to conserve these species and their habitats.

Among those proactive measures is the ESA's directive to the U.S. Fish and Wildlife Service (USFWS) and National Marine Fisheries Service (NMFS) to encourage other countries to adopt their own regulatory schemes to safeguard endangered species, to provide funding and loan personnel to other countries to facilitate protection of endangered species, and to conduct law enforcement investigations and research to protect endangered species abroad.[16]

The principal application of the ESA to a particular species is triggered by the "listing" of that species as either "threatened" or "endangered" pursuant to Section 4 of the Act, often in response to a petition by wildlife protection advocates to the USFWS or NMFS, federal agencies

---

14. Tenn. Valley Auth. v. Hill, 437 U.S. 153, 180 (1978).

15. 16 U.S.C. § 1531(b).

16. 16 U.S.C. § 1537(d). The ESA also serves as the United States' implementing legislation for certain international agreements dedicated to protecting vulnerable species worldwide. By example, the ESA mandates implementation of the Convention on Nature Protection and Wildlife Preservation in the Western Hemisphere, a treaty intended "to protect all native plants and animals from extinction" that was signed (but not implemented) over thirty years prior to enactment of the ESA. Most notably, the ESA implements the Convention on International Trade in Endangered Species of Fauna and Flora (CITES). CITES is commonly viewed as the preeminent international treaty for the protection of endangered species. And yet, as its name suggests, CITES is focused exclusively on international trade and is not a comprehensive conservation scheme that seeks to address all factors contributing to the extinction of species. (For example, because it focuses on trade only, CITES does not control or have any effect on in-country treatment or exploitation of any species.)

charged with implementing the law (the jurisdiction of each depends on the nature of the environment in which the species is found). The ESA defines an "endangered species" as one "which is in danger of extinction throughout all or a significant portion of its range."[17] A "threatened species" is "any species which is likely to become an endangered species within the foreseeable future throughout all or a significant portion of its range."[18] Many of the statutory protections of the ESA apply only to endangered species, but can be extended to threatened species by the USFWS or NMFS. In 1978, the agencies promulgated a "blanket rule" extending to all species listed as threatened the protections generally afforded to endangered species, unless one of the agencies issues a "special rule" specific to the threatened species when it is listed.[19] While a "special rule" may thus have the effect of significantly reducing protections for a threatened species, such rules must nonetheless "provide for the conservation of such species."[20] Species that are not yet listed as threatened or endangered, but which are proposed for listing, or that are designated as candidates for study and consideration for listing, can also receive some protections. In the case of a domestic species, the Services are also required to designate "critical habitat" for the species concurrently with a listing.[21] Critical habitat is defined as any occupied or unoccupied area "essential to the conservation of the species" and any occupied area that "may require special management considerations or protection" with respect to the listed species.[22]

Once a species is listed under the ESA, the Act generally confers upon the species two types of benefits: protections intended to prevent the species from further risk of extinction, and efforts intended to restore the species to a point at which it has recovered and is no longer in need of protection. In other words, the goals of the ESA are to counteract species

17. *Id.* § 1532(6).
18. *Id.* § 1532(20).
19. *See* 50 C.F.R. § 17.31(a) (2000).
20. 16 U.S.C. § 1533(d).
21. *Id.* § 1533(a)(6)(C).
22. *Id.* § 1532(5)(A)(i).

imperilment and to promote species recovery, to the point where species do not need to be on the ESA lists.

In terms of preventing extinction, Section 9 of the ESA makes it unlawful for any person to "take any such species within the United States."[23] The term "take" includes "to harass, harm, pursue, hunt, shoot, wound, kill, trap, capture, or collect, or to attempt to engage in any such conduct."[24] This prohibition applies to both intentional and unintentional harms, as well as certain forms of habitat modification. Section 9 also prohibits the import or export of a listed species under certain circumstances, including when it was taken in violation of the Act, regardless of where the take occurred.[25] The prohibitions in Section 9 of the ESA apply to all private and governmental actors. There are exceptions to the prohibitions of Section 9, however, for activities deemed not to be inconsistent with the conservation of the species, including activities that are intended to enhance the survival of the species, such as regulated captive breeding, where the ultimate goal is to introduce new members of the species to the wild.[26] Section 7 of the ESA adds further restrictions on actions undertaken or permitted by the federal government, by prohibiting federal actions that would further jeopardize the existence of the species or adversely modify any critical habitat.[27] Section 7 also requires federal agencies to consult with the USFWS or NMFS in order to mitigate harms to listed species, where the federal government's actions or authorizations might negatively impact those species.[28]

In terms of restoration of the species, Section 4 of the ESA requires the USFWS and NMFS to develop and implement "recovery plans" for listed species.[29] The purpose of recovery planning under the Act is to go beyond reversing the species' tumble toward extinction, and to increase the species' population and range to ensure viability of the species in

---

23. *Id.* § 1538(a)(1).
24. *Id.* § 1532(19).
25. *Id.* § 1538(a)(1).
26. *Id.* § 1539.
27. *Id.* § 1536(a)(2).
28. *Id.*
29. *Id.* § 1533(f).

the future, up to and including removal from listing based on statutory criteria for delisting. The ESA requires that recovery plans describe "site-specific management actions" necessary to restore the species, establish "objective, measurable criteria" for the point at which the species will be deemed recovered and can be removed from the list, and set benchmarks for progress in implementing the plan, including time and cost estimates and assessable "intermediate steps" on the road to recovery.[30] In addition to recovery planning under Section 4 of the Act, tucked among the consultation requirements in Section 7 is an affirmative obligation on federal agencies to "carry[ ] out programs for the conservation of endangered species and threatened species."[31]

The existing legal landscape for protection of endangered species in the United States is extensive; and yet a common criticism of our endangered species protection policy—and particularly the ESA and its implementing regulations—is that, while it has enjoyed success in preventing extinctions, it has not often succeeded at recovering species. However, any failures of the ESA are more likely due to practical and political obstacles to implementing the law, rather than due to the construction of the Act. As discussed below, the ESA is too often implemented to address the symptoms of, and underutilized in addressing the most significant causes of, species imperilment. Current federal law protecting endangered species may need to be amended or supplemented to address emerging and more complex and broad-ranging threats to species survival. Specific laws targeting the root causes of destruction and exploitation of species and their habitats (e.g., through trade restrictions, limits on greenhouse gas emissions, or product labeling requirements) would enhance the United States' existing laws and regulations designed to protect endangered species.

---

30. *Id.*
31. *Id.* § 1536(a)(1).

Crying Wolf: Social Tolerance as a Limiting Factor in Gray Wolf Recovery

The gray wolf is an icon of America's wilderness. Highly intelligent and social, wolves are family oriented, pair for life, raise their pups using extended family groups, and have inspired Americans for centuries. Wolves connect us to nature, directly and indirectly. They drive tourism and economic prosperity for the states that have significant wolf populations, as well as those from which wolf tourists originate. They promote and sustain the natural functions of the ecosystems they inhabit. The ecological benefit of this keystone species is staggering—gray wolves counteract the negative impacts of overpopulation of prey species, have an important moderating influence on other predator species, and protect and facilitate ecosystem health. Wolves are one of our nation's most effective and important protectors of biodiversity in the environments in which they are found. And we nearly killed them all.

Beginning more than a century ago, westward expansion and overall growth of human populations in the United States led to increasing concern over conflicts with wolves. These societal concerns ultimately triggered government-sponsored bounty programs and other human persecution of the species that resulted in mass extermination of wolf populations. The species was nearly eliminated from the landscape of the contiguous United States. Despite significant and laudable efforts to recover wolf populations throughout the lower forty-eight states—primarily via protections and recovery efforts implemented as a result of the designation of the species for protection under the ESA—the species still only occupies as little as 5 percent of its historic range.[32] And yet, many individuals continue to exhibit extreme animosity toward wolves. Indeed, you can easily purchase a bumper sticker that proudly states "smoke a pack a day" next to a picture of wolves in the crosshairs of a gun scope from hunting outfitters.[33] A recent billboard campaign in eastern Washington sponsored by an anti-wolf group indicated that wolves kill

32. 68 Fed. Reg. 15,804, 15,805 (Apr. 1, 2003); Virginia Morell, *Wolves at the Door of a More Dangerous World*, 319(5865) Sci. 890–92 (2008).
33. Timber Butte Outdoors, Smoke a Pack a Day, http://www.timberbutteoutdoors.com/TBO Store/Clothing-smokeapackaday.html.

humans, suggesting that children might be "next on their menu," despite the fact that there has been only one fatal attack on a human by a wild wolf in the United States (which occurred in Alaska) since the beginning of the twentieth century.[34]

Whether or not the species is deserving of further legal protection and efforts at continued recovery of more numerous or broader ranging populations depends largely on what is viewed as the real goal of our endangered species policy. If our goal is simply to restore some minimal wolf presence in currently occupied regions and to revisit the issue of providing protection when the last remaining individuals of the species are again at the doorstep of extinction, then the goal has been met. But if our aim is to recover wolf populations to a level and range that are large enough to secure their existence indefinitely, then protections are still needed. If the goal is to return wolves to their natural role in the ecosystems that have historically depended on them and could continue to benefit from them, then work at range expansion is far from complete.

Within governmental ranks, federal and state wildlife managers have taken a very narrow view of the recovery goal for wolves, and have proposed removing ESA protections for wolves for more than a decade, with an acknowledged intent to subject wolves to state regulations that seek immediate population reductions throughout all corners of the species' current range. While government officials have espoused various scientific and legal arguments that the species is no longer in danger of extinction, unsuccessful efforts to remove ESA protection for wolves pursuant to such arguments (due to rejection by wolf scientists and the courts) have led the government to embrace the concept of social intolerance for wolves as a rationale for eliminating legal protection for the species. Human conflicts with wolves, both verifiable and merely perceived, have become a focal point in wolf protection policy.

Wolves are not alone in this regard. Though the discussion outlined here focuses on wolves as a point of illustration, many vulnerable species face increasing conflicts with expanding human presence and influence

---

34. Kirk Johnson, *Study Faults Efforts at Wolf Management*, N.Y. Times (Dec. 3, 2014), http://www.nytimes.com/2014/12/04/us/washington-state-study-faults-efforts-at-wolf-management .html?_r=0.

in their habitats. A key to successful endangered species policy in the future will be addressing these conflicts and their sources, and in particular, devising strategies to address social intolerance for vulnerable species. It is clear that negative societal views toward maintaining extant species on the landscape cannot be ignored. But should we allow such views to drive policy decisions with respect to species protection, or should we establish and implement species protection policy with a goal of fostering a level of social tolerance necessary to prevent species imperilment? The history underlying enactment of the ESA and the case law interpreting it establishes that Congress intended the law to protect other living creatures even if some segment of the population questions or does not fully appreciate their value, and even if they offend or disrupt human desires and decisions with respect to their existence and the preservation of their habitats.[35] However, as increasing conflicts with wildlife are an inevitable result of mounting human impact on the natural world, the question of the role of social tolerance in endangered species policymaking will be pressed to the forefront.

Human Intolerance of Predator Species and Its Impact on Wolf Populations

Wolves were once abundant throughout most of North America, but the superstitions about and fears of the species held by European settlers, as well as both real and perceived conflicts between wolves and human activities, gave rise to unregulated poisoning, trapping, and shooting of wolves.[36] The widespread killing of wolves was further spurred on by government-sponsored bounty and eradication programs. By example, in 1909, the New Mexico legislature enacted a bounty law, which authorized counties to levy an annual property tax in order to maintain a "Wild Animal Bounty Fund" that paid out $15 per dead wolf (equivalent to nearly $400 today).[37] The federal government was also involved—the U.S. Biological Survey, predecessor of the USFWS, hired professional

---

35. *See* Tenn. Valley Auth., 437 U.S. at 180 (1978).
36. 68 Fed. Reg. 15,804, 15,805 (Apr. 1, 2003).
37. Edward. A. Fitzgerald, *Lobo Returns from Limbo*: New Mexico Cattle Growers Ass'n v. U.S. Fish & Wildlife Service, 46 NAT'L RESOURCES J. 9, 12 (2006).

wolf hunters and trappers to respond to livestock depredation claims by utilizing steel-jawed traps, poison baits, gassing wolf dens, shooting, and delimbing and decapitation by roping to kill wolves.[38] In fact, the last two wolves in Yellowstone National Park were killed by park rangers in 1926, who were simply doing their assigned jobs.[39]

By the middle of the twentieth century, wolves had been eliminated from the contiguous United States, with the exception of a small population in the northeastern corner of Minnesota. Seizing on the momentum of the environmental protection movement, federal protections for gray wolves began in 1967 when they were protected under the Endangered Species Preservation Act,[40] the precursor to the ESA, which was enacted in 1973. To implement these statutory protections, the USFWS split gray wolves into four subspecies—one in the western Great Lakes region, one in the northern Rocky Mountain region, one in the southwestern United States, and one in portions of Texas, New Mexico, and Mexico.[41] But in 1978, after determining that the gray wolf "formerly occurred in most of the conterminous United States and Mexico [, and] [b]ecause of widespread habitat destruction and human persecution, the species now occupies only a small part of its original range in these regions," the USFWS reclassified gray wolves as endangered at the species level throughout the contiguous United States, except for the remnant Minnesota population which was listed as a threatened species.[42]

The USFWS developed recovery plans for the gray wolf as required by the ESA, but chose to focus on three "core" recovery areas—the northern Rocky Mountains, the western Great Lakes, and the southwestern United States. In 1994, the USFWS designated areas around Yellowstone National Park and in the Bitterroot Range in central Idaho to facilitate reintroduction of experimental populations of wolves,[43] and the agency introduced more than sixty wolves to these areas between 1995 and

38. *Id.*
39. Bradford C. Lister, Carl N. McDaniel. *The Wolves of Yellowstone.* Ecology 7: Predation (Apr. 17, 2006), http://www.bioinfo.rpi.edu/bystrc/pub/artWolves.pdf.
40. P.L. 89-669, 80 Stat. 926 (Oct. 15, 1966).
41. 39 Fed. Reg. 1171 (January 4, 1974); 41 Fed. Reg. 17736 (April 28, 1976); 41 Fed. Reg. 24064 (June 14, 1976).
42. 42 Fed. Reg. 29527 (June 9, 1977); 43 Fed. Reg. 9607 (Mar. 9, 1978).
43. 59 Fed. Reg. 60252 (Nov. 22, 1994); 59 Fed. Reg. 60266 (Nov. 22, 1994).

1996.[44] Countless wildlife advocates were supportive of the reintroduction effort, but many opponents of reintroduction felt that wolves had been forced upon them. Despite the fact that wolves had already begun to disperse into northern Idaho and Montana—a small pack of eight wolves denned in Glacier National Park in northwestern Montana in 1986— opponents to reintroduction took to calling all wolves in the area "Canadian wolves," which allowed them to characterize them as an unwelcome nonnative intruder on the American landscape.[45]

With additional dispersal of reintroduced wolves, expansion of wolves in Minnesota, and additional migration of wolves from Canada, opportunities for conflict with human activities increased. However, many of the loudest claims of conflict have been based on perception and trepidation rather than fact. Ranchers have claimed that wolves attack and kill their livestock at unacceptable levels. But wolves account for less than 1 percent of all livestock losses—the vast majority of livestock losses are attributable to disease, illness, birthing problems, extremes of weather, accidents, and error in livestock operations.[46] Indeed, more livestock are lost to other animals, such as coyotes, mountain lions, and even stray dogs than are lost to wolves.[47] In lobbying in 2013 to open a public wolf hunt for the first time in many decades, wolf opponents in the Michigan legislature cited a recent spike in livestock loss reports in the state. However, a closer look at those reports revealed that over 60 percent of the recent claims, and nearly half since 1996, were made by a single farmer. The farmer left his farm unattended with piles of dead cows lying around, intentionally left deer legs in his truck bed to bait wolves, neglected to maintain exclusion fencing, and starved guard donkeys that the state had provided him at taxpayer expense (he accepted a plea deal in 2014 over

44. Rocky Barker, *Twenty Years Ago Today, 4 Wolves Were Released into Idaho. What If It Never Happened?* IDAHO STATESMAN (Jan. 14, 2015), http://idahostatejournal.com/news/local/years-ago -wolves-were-released-in-idaho-what-if-it/article_210b3a2c-9c90-11e4-ac2a-6f6ad49fa2a0.html.
45. *Id.*; JIM YUSKAVITCH, IN WOLF COUNTRY: THE POWER AND POLITICS OF REINTRODUCTION, 58 (2015). (quoting Ron Gilflet, founder of the Idaho Anti-Wolf Coalition, as stating that "the only way to manage Canadian wolves in Idaho is to get rid of them").
46. USDA, National Agricultural Statistics Service (NASS), Agricultural Statistics Board, *Cattle Death Loss* (May 12, 2011), http://www.nass.usda.gov/Publications/Todays_Reports/reports/ catlos11.pdf.
47. *Id.*

charges for the mistreatment of the donkeys).[48] Similarly, hunters have claimed that wolves kill elk and other prey at unacceptable levels and are harming the populations of game species. Science and fact have indicated otherwise. In the northern Rocky Mountains for example, wildlife officials in the states of Idaho, Montana, and Wyoming all reported stable or increasing elk herds and hunter success rates for elk in the years where wolf populations in those states recently peaked.[49] Additionally, scientists studying the peculiar and well-noted elk population declines in the Yellowstone area have determined that other explanations, including human-caused factors, outweigh the impact of wolves on elk.[50] Predator numbers are primarily driven by the availability of their prey, which in turn is controlled by the availability of food and pressure from human-caused mortality, not the other way around. Indeed, larger populations of wolves coexisted with elk and other species now prized as game for centuries before humans eliminated wolves from the landscape. After wolf reintroduction, and continuing to the present day, it has become increasingly apparent that a person's level of intolerance for wolves depends largely on that person's vocational, recreational, and other interests, and his or her perception and perhaps fear of what a future of living with wolves will bring, rather than on objective and accurate information on actual wolf conflicts.

Unfortunately, the USFWS's narrow focus on a few core wolf recovery areas, which combined include only about 30 percent of existing suitable habitat for a species listed under the ESA throughout the con-

48. John Barnes. *Cattle Farmer John Koski, Divisive Symbol in Michigan Wolf Hunt, to Plead in Animal Neglect Case.* MLive (Apr. 15, 2014), http://www.mlive.com/news/index.ssf/2014/04/cattle_farmer_john_koski_divis.html; John Barnes. *Tour the Farm with More Wolf Attacks than Anyone in Michigan's Upper Peninsula.* MLive (Nov. 4, 2013), http://www.mlive.com/news/index.ssf/2013/11/john_koski_part_1_tour_the_far.html#incart_river_default.
49. Rob Chaney. *2013 hunting preview: Game Populations on the Rise in Western Montana.* THE MISSOULAN (Sept. 26, 2013), http://missoulian.com/lifestyles/recreation/hunting-preview-game-populations-on-the-rise-in-western-montana/article_d9e499be-2651-11e3-abfc-0019bb 2963f4.html; Laura Lundquist. *F&G: Wolves Not Causing Most Elk Losses.* TWIN FALLS TIMES NEWS (July 31, 2010), http://magicvalley.com/news/local/wood-river/f-g-wolves-not-causing-most-elk-losses/article_64d3fe91-1afd-5794-b5a0-62129c6f11ca.html; Ralph Maughan, *Wyoming Has a Near Record Elk Hunt.* THE WILDLIFE NEWS (Mar. 26, 2014), http://www.the wildlifenews.com/2014/03/26/wyoming-has-a-near-record-elk-hunt/.
50. Christie Wilcox. *Why Are Yellowstone's Elk Disappearing?* DISCOVER MAGAZINE (Apr. 14, 2014), *available at* http://discovermagazine.com/2014/may/16-elk-vanishing-act.

tiguous United States,[51] caused predictable frustrations for both wolf supporters and detractors. While wolf advocates grew increasingly frustrated
at the lack of coordinated effort toward further geographic expansion
and recovery of the species, wolf opponents—chiefly livestock owners
and to a lesser degree (at least initially) members of the hunting community—living in core recovery areas became increasingly frustrated
that they had to adapt to growing wolf populations while ranchers and
hunters in unoccupied areas of wolves' historical range did not. Further,
the USFWS's wolf recovery plans, some of which are now almost three
decades old, were never updated as the best available science evolved on
the sustainability of wolf populations. Indeed, the current recovery goals
for wolves in the northern Rocky Mountains region are so outdated that
they were established years prior to reintroduction; the recovery plan
questions whether the species will even be able to gain a foothold in the
region. That question has been indisputably and affirmatively answered,
since the species has now established itself there.[52] Of all the ESA-listed
species not to have a comprehensive and updated listing-wide recovery
plan, it would surely be a surprise to many that it is a species as iconic
and controversial as the gray wolf, which was among the first species ever
listed under the ESA in the early 1970s. At the turn of the twenty-first
century, as wolf population numbers in the core recovery areas began to
approach, and then exceed, the minimum recovery goals set forth in the
USFWS's static recovery plans, many members of the public were left to
wonder about the agency's ultimate goals for the species. Pressure began
to mount for the USFWS to shed or at least redefine its role in continuing
the effort to restore wolves, particularly in the northern Rocky Mountains and the western Great Lakes regions.[53]

---

51. Center for Biological Diversity, *Making Room for Recovery*, 1, 3, Fig. 3 (Nov. 2014), http://
www.biologicaldiversity.org/campaigns/gray_wolves/pdfs/Making_Room_for_Recovery_print
.pdf.
52. USFWS. *Northern Rocky Mountain Wolf Recovery Plan* (Aug. 3, 1987), http://www.fws.gov/
mountain-prairie/species/mammals/wolf/NorthernRockyMountainWolf RecoveryPlan.pdf.
53. Beginning in the mid- to late-1990s, many stakeholders and local politicians argued that
wolf expansion should be halted, but the most dramatic move against continuing recovery under
the ESA came in the form of a lawsuit by ranchers that sought a declaration that reintroduction
was illegal in the first place, and that wolves should be rounded up and sent to Canada. A federal
district court initially agreed. Wyoming Farm Bureau Federation v. Babbitt, 987 F. Supp. 1349 (D.
Wyo. 1997) (ruling in favor of ranchers and ordering removal of reintroduced wolves). A federal

Efforts to Remove Protections for Wolves in Response to Actual and Perceived Conflicts

Beginning in 2000, the USFWS commenced efforts to reduce federal protections for wolves under the ESA, and in April 2003 the agency promulgated a final rule reducing ESA protections for wolves throughout the "lower 48" contiguous United States, with the exception of a small area in the southwestern region of the country.[54] The USFWS's 2003 rule was challenged by conservation and animal protection groups in two separate federal courts, one in Oregon and one in Vermont, both of which rejected the rule and issued orders vacating it.[55] These two courts took issue with the Service's decision to treat large areas of unoccupied viable wolf habitat the same as areas of occupied wolf habitat based only on progress toward recovery in the occupied areas. The Oregon court rejected the USFWS's determination that unoccupied areas within wolves' historic range were not a significant portion of the species' range warranting full protection under the ESA, even though large portions of that unoccupied area had formerly been occupied by wolves and remained suitable to sustain a wolf population.[56] Similarly, the Vermont court held that the USFWS could not reduce protections for wolves in unoccupied areas by lumping those areas together with occupied areas where wolves had increased in numbers and USFWS claimed the species to be recovered. Regardless of the merits of the USFWS's finding that the size of the wolf population in occupied areas was large enough that the species was not in immediate danger of becoming extinct in those areas, the court found that in including the unoccupied areas, the USFWS had effectively ignored its

---

appellate court overturned that decision. Wyoming Farm Bureau Fed'n v. Babbitt, 199 F.3d 1224 (10th Cir. 2000). For examples of the rhetoric addressing the reduction of still-recovering wolf populations during this time, *see, e.g.*, Jerry Miller, *Send the Wolves Back*, IDAHO POST REGISTER (Jan 18, 1998); Defenders of Wildlife, *Farm Bureau Delegates Give Death Sentence to Yellowstone Wolves* (Jan. 15, 1999), http://www.defenders.org/press-release/farm-bureau-delegates-give-death-sentence-yellowstone-wolves; Florangela Davila, *Gray Wolves' Return Hailed as Success, But Court Fight Continues*, SEATTLE TIMES, June 4, 1999, at A1.

54. 68 Fed. Reg. 15804 (Apr. 1, 2003).

55. Defenders of Wildlife v. Sec'y, U.S. Dep't of the Interior (Oregon Wolves), 354 F. Supp. 2d 1156, 1158–59 (D. Or. 2005); Nat'l Wildlife Fed'n v. Norton (Vermont Wolves), 386 F. Supp. 2d 553, 557 (D. Vt. 2005).

56. Defenders of Wildlife v. Sec'y, U.S. Dep't of the Interior (Oregon Wolves), 354 F. Supp. 2d at 1167–69.

duty to apply the requirements for delisting under the ESA to all unoc-cupied areas that represented significant portions of the species' historical range.[57]

Almost immediately upon rejection of the 2003 rule, the states of Michigan and Wisconsin sought permission from the USFWS to engage in otherwise unlawful killing of wolves,[58] under a special permit avail-able under Section 10 of the ESA only for actions which "enhance the propagation or survival" of the protected species.[59] The states' theory was that if they were permitted to kill some wolves, specifically those determined to be a threat to livestock, it would increase social toler-ance for continued federal protection of wolves in general. The USFWS granted the permits, stating that if it did not give the states permission to kill some of these wolves "public support for wolf recovery and wolf reintroduction programs will likely erode and individuals will resort to illegal killing . . ."[60] Thus, the USFWS's purported legal justification for approving the permits under the ESA was that the killing of some wolves would enhance the species' likelihood of survival.

To be clear, increasing social tolerance is not the only theory on which hunters, and the USFWS in turn, have relied in claiming that regulated killing can help save a species on the brink of extinction.[61] Hunting pro-ponents have long argued that American hunters should be permitted to kill endangered animals if the money they pay to local governments or wildlife management programs for the opportunity to do so will be used to promote species conservation.[62] However, conservationists have argued

---

57. Nat'l Wildlife Fed'n v. Norton (Vermont Wolves), 386 F. Supp. 2d at 565–66.

58. *See* 70 Fed. Reg. 54401 (Sept. 14, 2005).

59. 16 U.S.C. § 1539(a)(1)(A).

60. Humane Soc'y of U.S. v. Kempthorne, 481 F. Supp. 2d 53, 58 (D.D.C. 2006) *vacated sub nom.* Humane Soc. of U.S. v. Kempthorne, 527 F.3d 181 (D.C. Cir. 2008).

61. In fact, the debate over whether hunters should be permitted to kill members of the world's most vulnerable species had probably never raged as fiercely as it did in response to the killing of a well-known African lion, named Cecil, by a U.S. trophy hunter in Zim-babwe in 2015. Brian Clark Howard, *Killing of Cecil the Lion Sparks Debate Over Trophy Hunts*, NAT'L GEO. (July 28, 2015), *available at* http://news.nationalgeographic.com/2015 /07/150728-cecil-lion-killing-trophy-hunting-conservation-animals/.

62. *See, e.g.*, Safari Club International, *Conservation Facts—General Talking Points* (Dec. 19, 2015), https://www.safariclub.org/docs/default-source/dc-office/sci-conservation-facts---general-talking -points.pdf?sfvrsn=0 (including particular focus on hunting of lions and elephants in Africa).

that legalizing the hunting and trade of endangered species can both encourage and facilitate harmful poaching of those species and devalue the importance of conservation efforts in the perception of local governments and the general public.[63] The USFWS has adopted the so-called "pay-to-play" rationale in issuing import permits for sport-hunted trophies in the past,[64] but recently has exhibited more precaution in doing so, prohibiting import of trophies where it has determined that foreign management regimes in countries that allow hunting of the animals are insufficient to conserve the species.[65]

Even the specific argument that the government can permit hunters to kill ESA-listed animals in order to reduce human conflicts with the species was not a novel one at the time Michigan and Wisconsin requested permits to kill endangered wolves. In 1991, a federal court rejected a proposal by the USFWS to allow hunting of ESA-listed grizzly bears

---

63. *See, e.g.*, David M. Lavigne et al., *Sustainable utilization: the lessons of history*, in The Exploitation of Mammal Populations 251, 260 (Victoria J. Taylor et al. eds., 1996); Valerius Geist, *How Markets in Wildlife Meat and Parts, and the Sale of Hunting Privileges, Jeopardize Wildlife Conservation*, 2(1) Conserv. Biol. 16 (Mar. 1988).

64. In 2003, the Bush Administration published a proposal to expand the issuance of permits for import of sport-hunted trophies of foreign endangered species, as an incentive to encourage conservation of these species in the wild. 68 Fed. Reg. 53327 (Sept. 10, 2003). That proposed policy has never been finalized. Still, USFWS has approved sport hunting of endangered species under this theory. *See* 70 Fed. Reg. 52310, 52315 (Sept. 2, 2005) (authorizing captive breeding and sport hunting of three endangered antelope species at U.S. ranches based on a finding that such activities have "contributed significantly to the conservation of these species."), *vacated by* Friends of Animals v. Salazar, 626 F. Supp. 2d 102 (D.D.C. 2009).

65. *See* USFWS, *Service Announces Decisions on Import of Sport-Hunted Trophies to Further Conservation of Rhinos and Elephants: Authorizes Imports with Clear Conservation Benefits, Denies Those Without* (March 26, 2015), http://www.fws.gov/news/ShowNews.cfm?ID=56D54860 -AEA6-0EEE-73467FE9B00499F0 (issuing permits for import of two sport-hunted black rhinoceros trophies from Namibia, but prohibiting imports of any elephant trophies from Zimbabwe). In December 2015, USFWS issued a final rule listing lion subspecies under the ESA and establishing protections for African lion populations for the first time. *See* USFWS, *Endangered Species Act Listing Protects Lions in Africa and India, Director's Order Strengthens Wildlife Import Restrictions for Violators of Wildlife Laws* (Dec. 21, 2015), http://www.fws.gov/news/ ShowNews.cfm?ref=endangered-species-act-listing-protects-lions-in-africa-and-india-&_ID =35403. In a companion rule, USFWS indicated that it will prohibit imports of African lion trophies unless an enhancement finding can be made for the relevant country's management program—and the agency specifically noted that it is doubtful that such a finding could be made for South Africa, where U.S. hunters obtain over 90 percent of their African lions trophies. *Id.*; *see also* Safari Club International, *How The New U.S. Rules Will Affect Lion Trophy Importation Into The U.S.* (Dec. 28, 2015), https://www.safariclub.org/detail/news/2015/12/28/ how-the-new-US-rules-will-affect-lion-trophy-importation-into-the-US.

to address human-grizzly conflicts.[66] The court rejected the USFWS's assertion that "a limited hunt of the grizzly bear creates a wariness of humans, which protects the bears by confining them to their range and reducing bear-human conflicts, and which, in the long run, promotes the conservation and recovery of the species."[67] And as early as 1984, a federal court enjoined a USFWS proposal to let hunters kill ESA-listed wolves in Minnesota, concluding that "reduc[ing] the level of wolf-human contact" through a hunting program was not permitted under the ESA.[68] These cases concerned populations of species listed as threatened (not endangered) under the ESA, so the legal rulings were based on provisions of the ESA found in Section 4(d) of the Act that apply only to threatened species.[69] However, because those provisions provide equivalent or potentially even less protection than the ESA's coverage of endangered species, animal advocates argued that the same logic should apply to endangered species in the case of the Michigan and Wisconsin permits.

In 2006, a federal court invalidated the Michigan and Wisconsin Section 10 permits, and the USFWS was enjoined from allowing any further killing of endangered gray wolves based on a rationale that the killing would increase human tolerance for the species.[70] The court indicated that it was "confounded by" "the notion you kill the wolves to save the wolves," and held that allowing endangered wolves to be killed, purportedly to "foster [ ] greater social tolerance for wolves," runs counter to the

---

66. Fund for Animals, Inc. v. Turner, No. CIV. A. 91-2201(MB), 1991 WL 206232 (D.D.C. Sept. 27, 1991).

67. *Id.* at *7 (The court further stated that "the [ESA], as currently interpreted, does not authorize hunting whenever it would be a sound conservational tool. Congress has specifically limited the hunting of a threatened or endangered species to extraordinary cases of population pressures, and the Court is constrained to enforce that legislative restriction.").

68. Sierra Club v. Clark, 577 F. Supp. 783, 790 (D. Minn. 1984) (the court noted, but rejected as inconsistent with the plain language of the ESA, USFWS's arguments "that a sport season is needed to enhance the value of the wolf in the eyes of the public"), *aff'd in part and rev'd in part on other grounds*, 755 F.2d 608 (8th Cir. 1985).

69. 16 U.S.C. § 1533(d) ("Whenever any species is listed as a threatened species . . . the Secretary shall issue such regulations as he deems necessary and advisable to provide for the *conservation* of such species." [emphasis added]). The term "conservation" is defined in the ESA as only included "regulated taking" "in the extraordinary case where population pressures within an ecosystem cannot be otherwise relieved." 16 U.S.C. § 1532(2).

70. Humane Soc'y of U.S. v. Kempthorne, 481 F. Supp. 2d at 58.

plain language, intent, and legislative history of the ESA.[71] The court rejected the USFWS's decision to appease what the agency itself identified as "intolerant stakeholders" by authorizing some killings in an effort to reduce illegal killings, calling the agency's reasoning "a labyrinthian analysis that does not comply with the text of the [ESA] on its face."[72]

Does the 2006 federal court ruling on the Michigan and Wisconsin wolf removal permits shut the door on consideration of social tolerance in endangered species policy decisions? Far from it—regardless of the court's questioning of the logic behind the USFWS's invocation of social tolerance as a rationale for killing an endangered species, the ESA itself has been increasingly under attack and it may be directly or indirectly altered by Congress, or new interpretations of the Act by the USFWS might survive legal challenges in the future. For example, even though multiple efforts by the USFWS to delist wolves were turned away by the courts between 2007 and 2010, Congress stepped in and legislatively delisted wolves in Idaho and Montana in a rider slipped into an appropriations bill in 2011.[73] Congress did this even though the normal process for listing or delisting a species under the ESA involves a detailed rulemaking process conducted by the USFWS, with input from experts, stakeholders, and the public—the process that was established by Congress when it enacted the ESA.[74] However, because it is a congressionally mandated process, it is also one that Congress can alter with a vote. Thus, Congress can override that process by amending the ESA or by enacting superseding laws specific to certain circumstances (as in the case of the 2011 appropriations rider).[75] It did just that in 2011 when it delisted the

---

71. *Id.* at 54, 62–63 (The court noted that it could think of only one circumstance where the intentional killing of an endangered animal might qualify as enhancing the species' survival, and that was "where an individual wolf had mange or some other communicable disease that could ultimately result in the death of other *wolves*.").

72. *Id.* at 63.

73. P.L. 112-10 § 1713, 125 Stat. 38 (April 15, 2011).

74. 16 U.S.C. § 1533(b).

75. Several conservation groups filed lawsuits to overturn the 2011 appropriations rider, alleging that Congress violated constitutional separation of powers principles by requiring USFWS to enforce its delisting rule in the face of a federal court ruling that the delisting rule was unlawful. Alliance for the Wild Rockies v. Salazar, 800 F. Supp. 2d 1123 (D. Mont. 2011), *aff'd* 672 F.3d 1170 (9th Cir. 2012). The court rejected these claims, holding that Congress acted appropriately when it changed the law with respect to wolves—thus, Congress had not crossed the line and

Idaho and Montana wolves. This marked the first time in history that a species, as opposed to a specific permit or project, was removed from the ESA by legislation rather than by agency rulemaking.

The USFWS itself appears to be undeterred by the 2006 Michigan and Wisconsin wolf removal permits ruling or its past decisions. On June 13, 2013, the USFWS published a proposed rule that would remove ESA protections for wolves throughout the contiguous United States, except for the Mexican wolf subspecies in the southwest.[76] In justification of this broad delisting rule, the USFWS asserts that unoccupied portions of wolves' range should not be considered in the listing decisions because the ESA's mandate that listings include "significant portions" of a species' range refers only to "the range in which a species currently exists,"[77] and the unoccupied portions of wolves' historic range are "unsuitable" habitat because of "a lack of tolerance for wolves."[78]

The USFWS's new justifications for broad delisting of wolves are in stark contrast to the obligations and limitations under the ESA that the agency stated when it originally listed wolves (and for decades thereafter). At the time of their listing, the current range of the gray wolf was a remote segment of northern Minnesota, but the USFWS made clear in listing the species throughout the contiguous United States that while there "appear[ed] to be no serious problems that could result in the immediate extirpation of the species in [northern Minnesota]" the ESA's command to recover species required a broader listing that included the species'

directed the Executive Branch to take action in contravention of an act of the Judicial Branch. Rather, it avoided the separation of powers by simply making new law which simultaneously rendered the prior judicial decision moot by changing the law. *Id.*

76. 78 Fed. Reg. 35,664 (June 13, 2013). Mexican wolves are an especially vulnerable subspecies of gray wolf that is genetically and legally distinct from the broader population of the North American gray wolf. *See* USFWS, Final Rule: Endangered Status for the Mexican Wolf, 80 Fed. Reg. 2488, 2488-89 (Jan. 16, 2015). Mexican wolves were completely extirpated from the United States by 1942. *Id.* at 2491. In order to facilitate return of Mexican wolves to a portion of their range in central Arizona, New Mexico, and northwest Texas, USFWS began a captive-breeding program in 1998 using the last seven Mexican wolves known to exist in the wild. *Id.* at 2491–92. This fragile reintroduced "experimental population" is managed separately under Section 10(j) of the ESA, 16 U.S.C. § 1539(j), and USFWS has not included this subspecies in its efforts to delist all other gray wolves in the contiguous United States.

77. 78 Fed. Reg. 35,673 (June 13, 2013).

78. *Id.* at 35,680.

entire historic range.[79] And ironically, the USFWS rejected low social tolerance as a reason for withholding ESA protections for wolves when choosing to list the species. The separate threatened listing for wolves in Minnesota met resistance from officials in the state, including the governor and the legislature, which passed a resolution calling for "complete declassification of the wolf in Minnesota," arguing that "hardship was resulting from wolf depredations" and therefore it was appropriate for "the State to have exclusive control of its resident wolf population."[80] Despite this resistance, the USFWS concluded that Minnesota officials' concerns about human conflicts with wolves were not among those factors "that may legally be considered in determining the classification of a species under the Endangered Species Act."[81]

How Should Social Tolerance of Wildlife Be Treated in Conservation Policy?

Some scientists, including noted wolf biologists, have questioned the accuracy of the USFWS's recent conclusions about social tolerance, casting strong doubt on the Service's use of tolerance levels as a basis for delisting of wolves in unoccupied areas of the species' range. These scientists directly responded to the USFWS's June 2013 proposed delisting rule by citing to a wealth of recent scientific study on humans' attitudes toward wolves, which indicate that people in unoccupied areas of wolf range are more tolerant of wolves than people in currently occupied areas.[82] The scientists reference over five dozen relevant articles published on the issue since 2000—articles that the USFWS did not address in its proposed rule. The scientists note that there is empirical evidence indicating that people in several states containing adequate habitat to support self-sustaining wolf populations generally support wolf recovery, and conclude

79. 43 Fed. Reg. 9,610–11 (Mar. 9, 1978).
80. 43 Fed. Reg. 9,608 (Mar. 9, 1978)
81. *Id.*
82. Jeremy T. Bruskotter et al. *Removing Protections for Wolves and the Future of the U.S. Endangered Species Act (1973).* 7 CONS. LET. 401–7 (2013) (the author-scientists include researchers and academic experts on wolf behavior and ecology, and on human values, attitudes, and behaviors relating to natural resources and their impact on wildlife management policy).

that "it is simply factually inaccurate to claim that lack of human toler-ance makes these unoccupied areas unsuitable for wolves."[83]

Many other voices in the conservation and wildlife protection com-munity argue that social tolerance should not be a factor at all in deci-sions concerning the recovery of endangered species. Some wolf advocates have continued to push for additional reintroduction of wolves in unoc-cupied areas of their range without consideration of social tolerance for the species in those areas. By example, WildEarth Guardians filed a law-suit challenging a December 2007 decision of the National Park Service (NPS) not to reintroduce wolves into Rocky Mountain National Park as part of the agency's effort to reduce the burgeoning elk population in the park. WildEarth Guardians felt that a naturally sustaining popula-tion of wolves should be introduced in the park, despite NPS's concerns that such an alternative faced a lack of support from coordinating agen-cies, concerns by neighboring communities, and the high potential for human-wolf conflicts. The courts ultimately ruled in favor of the agen-cy.[84] In July 2010, the Center for Biological Diversity filed a petition with the USFWS asking the agency to promulgate a national wolf recovery plan for wolves. The petition requested that wolves be introduced or their populations bolstered in "at least seven interconnected regions" through-out the continental United States, including currently unoccupied areas such as the southern Rocky Mountains and New England.[85] Notably, these proposals do not consider whether humans occupying the areas at issue would accept wolves on the landscape, or whether reintroduction might lead to suffering on the part of wolves if left to be regulated by state and local wildlife officials whose management decisions may be swayed by citizens who are intolerant of wolves. While many conservationists might argue that endangered species policy decisions must be based only on science and the needs of the species, is it fair to ask whether such policy decisions will be effective (let alone ethical) if a species is restored

---

83. *Id.*

84. WildEarth Guardians v. National Park Service, 703 F.3d 1178, 1181–82 (10th Cir. 2013).

85. Center for Biological Diversity, *Petition for a National Recovery Plan for the Wolf* (Canis lupus) *in the Conterminous United States Outside the Southwest under the Endangered Species Act* (July 20, 2010), http://www.biologicaldiversity.org/species/mammals/northern_Rocky_Mountains_gray_wolf/pdfs/GrayWolfNationalRecoveryPlanAPAPetition.pdf.

to an area where it will likely be subjected to cruel treatment and potential overkill in the region?

Social tolerance has already played a role in decision-making processes concerning wolves by state government actors. In 2011, in seeking to add wolves to Michigan's list of game species so that they could
be hunted immediately upon federal delisting, Michigan legislator Tom
Casperson made the claim that wolves had repeatedly shown up outside a
day care center in the state's Upper Peninsula, threatening children while
they played outside. The claim was repeated in a letter to Congress urg-
ing delisting of the species. However, when it came to light that the story
was largely fabricated, Casperson issued a formal apology on the floor of
the legislature.[86] Thereafter, Michigan voters overwhelmingly rejected the
establishment of a wolf hunt in voting on two referenda on the subject
in the November 2014 election.[87] Undeterred, the state legislature passed
another law to permit hunting of wolves after delisting. This final law was
initially upheld by the Michigan Court of Claims, with one judge referencing the "Big Bad Wolf" of the Little Red Riding Hood fable, but the
law was recently struck down by the Michigan Court of Appeals.[88] The
drama surrounding wolf hunting policy in Michigan shows the difficult
nature of assessing social tolerance for a species—with elected members
of the legislature and appointed members of state administrative agencies
pushing for a hunt at the same time that Michigan voters rejected a hunt
at the ballot box.

Adrian Treves, a professor at the University of Wisconsin, and a coauthor
of the paper responding to the USFWS's 2013 proposed rule mentioned
previously, has conducted multiple studies on wolf tolerance in Wisconsin.

---

86. Jonathan Oosting, *Michigan Senator Apologizes for Fictional Wolf Story in Resolution: I am
Accountable, and I am Sorry.* MLive (Nov. 7, 2013), http://www.mlive.com/news/index.ssf/
2013/11/michigan_senator_apologizes_fo.html; Nate Hopper. *Today in Fables: Man Actually Cries
Wolf.* ESQUIRE (Nov. 8, 2013), *available at* http://www.esquire.com/news-politics/news/a25790/
michigan-state-senator-who-cried-wolf/.

87. CBS News, *Michigan Voters Reject Laws Favoring Wolf Hunting* (Nov. 5, 2014), http://detroit
.cbslocal.com/2014/11/05/michigan-voters-reject-laws-favoring-wolf-hunting/.

88. Keep Michigan Wolves Protected v. State of Michigan, Mich. Ct. of Claims, No. 15-000087-
MZ, Opinion and Order (July 10, 2015) at 1 (upholding the law); Keep Michigan Wolves Protected v. State of Michigan, Mich. Ct. of Appeals, No. 328604, Per Curiam Opinion (Nov. 22,
2016), *available at* http://publicdocs.courts.mi.gov:81/OPINIONS/FINAL/COA/20161122_
C328604_21_328604.OPN.PDF.

In a study published in 2009, Treves and his colleagues measured attitudes to livestock compensation payments programs for wolf depredation among over 1,350 state residents, including those who voluntarily contributed funds to such programs and those likely to receive compensation through those programs. Study respondents reported that the existence of compensation programs increases tolerance for wolves. The authors found that support for compensation programs remained high among recipients regardless of the ESA status of wolves and whether the species is subject to hunting, but that most donors to compensation programs opposed killing wolves in general and over 25 percent unconditionally rejected a wolf hunt. This suggests that as a species' protected status decreases, motivation of donors to participate in compensation programs declines, while recipients' desire to continue to benefit from compensation programs remains high.[89] In a more recent study published in 2015, Treves and colleagues conducted focus group surveys among farmers and hunters in Wisconsin's wolf range to gain a more in-depth understanding of attitudes towards wolves. The study notes that participants had generally favorable views toward hunting and other lethal control measures for wolves. However, this study also revealed that neither negative attitudes toward wolves nor the inclination to poach wolves decreased after wolves were removed from protection under the ESA and hunting was allowed. To the study's authors, the results suggested that lethal control measures, at least in the short term, may be ineffective for increasing tolerance of wolves, contrary to the position of the USFWS.[90] More broadly, the results of both of these surveys, and others, suggest that public tolerance should be treated as a target of policy decisions rather than a basis for them.

In communities where public tolerance for wolves is low and an impediment to furthering recovery goals for an ESA-listed species, programs that will actually address the concerns underlying negative attitudes must be important components of endangered species protection policy if it is to be effective. A recent Washington State University study using twenty-five years of data assessed the effects of wolf mortality on reducing livestock dep-

89. Adrian Treves et al. *The Price of Tolerance: Wolf Damage Payments after Recovery.* 18(14) Bio-divers. Conserv. 4003–21 (2009).

90. C. Brown-Nunez et al. *Tolerance of Wolves in Wisconsin: a Mixed-Methods Examination of Policy Effects on Attitudes and Behavioral Inclinations.* 189 Biol. Conserv. 59–71 (2015).

redations in Idaho, Montana, and Wyoming, and found that killing wolves in response to livestock depredation events can actually increase the risk that wolves will prey on livestock in the future.[91] Together with the results of the 2015 attitudinal study discussed above, these results suggest that other means of addressing negative attitudes toward wolves besides lethal control measures should be promoted. Compensation programs—the expenses of which are now primarily borne by state governments, but which have been funded by conservation groups in the past (Defenders of Wildlife has paid out over $1 million to ranchers in the western United States for livestock losses cause by wolves)—are one such tool. However, recent advances in our understanding of wolf behavior and efforts at implementing new nonlethal control methods have illuminated the value of other tools, such as use of range riders, guard dogs, llamas and donkeys, deploying light and sound emitting devices, hazing with nonlethal ammunition, erecting portable fencing and fladry, and other altered animal husbandry practices, which have all proved highly effective in deterring wolf depredations, and thereby addressing underlying causes of low tolerance for wolves.[92]

---

91. R. B. Wielgus & Kaylie A. Peebles, *Effects of Wolf Mortality on Livestock Depredations*, PLoS One (Dec. 3, 2014), http://dx.plos.org/10.1371/journal.pone.0113505; *see also* Warren Cornwall, *Why Killing Wolves Might Not Save Livestock*. Nat'l Geo. (Dec. 3, 2014) *available at* http://news.nationalgeographic.com/news/2014/12/141203-wolves-hunting-livestock-ranchers-endangered-species-environment/.

92. Wolves are opportunistic hunters, which means that they seek out the weakest or disadvantaged prey animals (*i.e.*, those that are injured, diseased, or separated from a herd), and will avoid engaging in more difficult or challenging kills if easier prey is generally available. Nonlethal control methods take advantage of wolves' natural wariness to engage in dangerous (for the wolves) activities. Because of this wolf trait, range riders (individuals hired to monitor a herd on the range), and animals that exhibit natural guardianship tendencies (like herding dogs, llamas, donkeys, and aggressive steer breeds), can successfully ward off wolves from livestock herds. Disruptive stimuli (such as visual and acoustic devices intended to scare wolves) can be used to repel wolves from livestock, and aversive stimuli (such as bean bag shells, rubber bullets and other nonlethal ammunition, and bait containing lithium chloride or other ill-tasting but not especially harmful substances) can condition wolves to avoid areas where livestock are maintained. Additionally, livestock operators should eliminate wolf attractants, such as carcasses of dead livestock. Nonlethal control measures are well-described in several guides produced by state wildlife managers and conservation groups. *See, e.g.*, Western Wildlife Outreach and Washington Dept. of Fish and Wildlife, *Living with Livestock and Wolves—Livestock Non-lethal Conflict Avoidance: A Review of the Literature* (Sept. 2014), http://wdfw.wa.gov/conservation/gray_wolf/livestock/wolf_livestock_conflict_avoidance_literature_review_11_2014_final_submitted_version.pdf; Defenders of Wildlife, *Livestock and Wolves: A Guide to Nonlethal Tools and Methods to Reduce Conflicts*, 2d ed. (2016), *available at* http://www.defenders.org/publication/livestock-and-wolves-guide-nonlethal-tools-and-methods-reduce-conflicts (produced in consultation with conservationists, biologists, academic researchers, government agency personnel, and livestock producers).

In September 2015, amid a raging debate over whether wildlife officials in the State of Washington have been too quick to kill wolves on
report of depredations by ranchers, wolf advocates and a sheep rancher
who has claimed more livestock losses than any other rancher in the state
(in response to which the state Department of Fish and Wildlife contro-
versially shot the breeding female of the Huckleberry wolf pack in northeast Washington) reached a tentative agreement on a partnership that one
Washington official called "amazing."[93] Under the deal, wolf advocacy
organizations involved in an eighteen-member wolf advisory group established by the state will publicly support the rancher's return to graze his
sheep flock in wolf country, where grazing land leases and feed for his
sheep are less expensive, and in return the rancher will work with wolf
advocates to craft a plan to protect his sheep with nonlethal measures.
Regardless of whether this tentative agreement is ultimately maintained,
the future of wolf recovery in the United States may depend on efforts
like this. In a world where human conflicts with wildlife, including the
most vulnerable of species, are ever increasing, the question of whether
and how social tolerance for species should affect and be affected by
wildlife management and protection policy will be increasingly common
and increasingly difficult.

~

Hardly anyone would dispute that chief among the goals of endangered
species policy must be prevention of extinction, and recovery of species
currently in jeopardy of extinction. But if we are to achieve these goals in
a meaningful and lasting way, we cannot begin to implement protections
for a species after it has become threatened or endangered with extinction. Indeed, Congress clearly intended that protection against future
jeopardy of species be an integral component of the ESA. Yet far too often
species protection measures are implemented at a point where dramatic
action is needed; and dramatic action may be, and often is, upsetting to
humans whose lives are immediately affected by such action.

---

93. Don Jenkins. *Rancher-Environmentalists Make Tentative Pact on Wolves.* CAPITAL PRESS (Sept.
4, 2015), http://www.capitalpress.com/Livestock/20150904/rancher-environmentalists-make
-tentative-pact-on-wolves.

Policy decisions with respect to endangered species protection and recovery should not be directly driven by public attitudes toward the species. This is clearly evident in the tortured history of wolf persecution and protection in the United States—social tolerance for wolves has varied dramatically over time and in different communities, and intolerance better tracks political trends and individuals' perceptions and fears than objective measures of the conservation status of the species and actual conflicts with humans. However, public attitudes toward vulnerable wildlife species cannot be ignored. We must reengage our endangered species policy in a contemporary way, by implementing proactive measures that promote harmonious coexistence with vulnerable species, and these measures should responsibly address and prevent conflicts while fully rejecting and protecting against unfounded antipathies.

On Thin Ice: Climate Change and Its Impact on Polar Bears

Polar bears, like giant pandas, bluefin tuna, northern spotted owls, and many other threatened and endangered species, have come to symbolize the fragility of the ecosystems in which they live. Indeed, it is the frailty of the polar bear's ecosystem that was the primary factor in its designation as a threatened species under the ESA in May 2008. Recent and widespread images of starving, marooned, and orphaned polar bears are a stark reminder of the dwindling sea ice and consequent loss of access to prey, mates, maternal denning sites, migratory pathways, and other resources the bears need to sustain their existence. Scientists have done their best to ring alarm bells over increasing and undisputed carbon emissions and rising global temperatures, but the effects of climate change often seem distant from our daily lives, and thus are easy to ignore. That distance is bridged to some degree in the case of polar bears, by the images broadcasted around the world that show that their habitat is literally melting from underneath them, and how they are struggling, and often failing, to survive. Regardless of the debate over the proper approach to address climate change, the threat to the existence and lives of polar bears is undeniable.

The list of species that the ESA has brought back from the brink of extinction is long and impressive. Indeed, although few species have fully recovered, thanks to the ESA we have been able to stave off hundreds of extinctions. But can this landmark legislation really tackle a problem as vast as climate change, the factors contributing to which are ill-defined and certainly not concentrated among a few sources? The authors of the ESA sought primarily to tackle problems they viewed as being within our grasp here in the United States, such as pollution, overexploitation, conflict with invasive species, and rampant development. Certainly, the Act's protections and restrictions have been utilized to benefit species and their habitats that are found outside the United States, particularly by limiting the actions of our own governmental entities and citizens when they impact other areas of the globe. But can the tools the ESA provides be applied to issues like greenhouse gas (GHG) emissions and rising ocean temperatures? Based on executive strategy pronouncements of the Bush Administration when polar bears were listed under the ESA in 2008, this would seem unlikely. In announcing the ESA listing of polar bears, Secretary of the Interior Dirk Kempthorne stated: "I want to make clear that this listing will not stop global climate change or prevent any sea ice from melting. Any real solution requires action by all major economies for it to be effective. That is why I am taking administrative and regulatory action to make certain the ESA isn't abused to make global warming policies."[94]

The "administrative and regulatory action" Secretary Kempthorne was referencing included a Special Rule promulgated under Section 4(d) of the ESA that expressly prevents the listing of polar bears from forcing restrictions on GHG-emitting activities, despite the fact that most scientists accept such activities as the primary driving force behind the global warming process that is threatening polar bears with extinction. The Bush Administration did not hide its motivations for the Special Rule—Secretary Kempthorne's official announcement of the polar bear listing specifically sought to reassure the oil and gas extraction industry

94. Press Release, Department of Interior, *Secretary Kempthorne Announces Decision to Protect Polar Bears under Endangered Species Act* (May 14, 2008), http://www.fws.gov/ news/ShowNews .cfm?ID=ECB61DD1-0D74-1D7B-4A67E9B51FB1626B ("USFWS, Polar Bear Listing Press Release").

by noting that the special rule would "allow[ ] us to continue to develop our natural resources in the arctic region . . ."[95] Predictably, conservation groups sued over these limited measures, claiming that the listing did not go far enough and that the Special Rule should be overturned.[96] From the other side, the State of Alaska under then-Governor Sarah Palin, hunting groups, and the ranching industry sued, claiming that the entire listing should be thrown out.[97] In all, over ten different lawsuits were filed over the listing, and there were many intervenor litigants on both sides, including animal protection groups and the oil and gas extraction industry.[98] The newly elected Obama Administration chose to defend the Bush Administration's actions on polar bears (though it has taken a different path on the issue of climate change more generally). All of the lawsuits were eventually consolidated, and a federal court ultimately upheld both the threatened listing and the Special Rule.[99]

Polar bears are by no means the only vulnerable species affected by climate change. Since the polar bear was listed under the ESA, there have been efforts to designate the Pacific walrus, the American pika (a rabbit relative), and several penguin and seal species as threatened or endangered based on threats caused by a warming climate. But the polar bear may become a primary storyteller when it comes to human understanding of, and response to, the impacts of climate change on wild animals, especially given the dire outcomes predicted for the species in the relatively near future from climate change and habitat modeling. Scientists now estimate that if Arctic sea ice continues its melting trend, the worldwide polar bear population will decline by two-thirds by 2050, and will be near extinction by the end of the twenty-first century.[100] Unfortunately, as

---

95. *Id.*

96. Ctr. for Biological Diversity, et al. v. Salazar, et al., No. 08–1339 (N.D. Cal. Mar. 10, 2008).

97. State of Alaska v. Salazar, et al., No. 08–1352 (D.D.C. Aug. 4, 2008); Safari Club Int'l, et al. v. Salazar, et al., No. 08–1550 (D.D.C. Sept. 8, 2008); California Cattlemen's Ass'n, et al. v. Salazar, et al., No. 08–1689 (D.D.C. Oct. 2, 2008); Conservation Force, et al. v. Salazar, et al., No. 09–245 (D.D.C. Feb. 9, 2009).

98. *In re Polar Bear Endangered Species Act Listing and § 4(d) Rule Litigation*, 794 F. Supp. 2d 65, 77–8 (D.D.C. 2011), *aff'd* 720 F.3d 354 (D.C. Cir. 2013).

99. *Id.*

100. John Roach, *Most Polar Bears Gone by 2050, Studies Say*, NAT'L GEO. NEWS (Sept. 10, 2007), http://news.nationalgeographic.com/news/2007/09/070910-polar-bears.html (citing the findings

a chiefly foreign species—more than 85 percent of polar bears live outside the United States, in Arctic regions of Canada, Greenland, Norway, and Russia—polar bears may be among the most difficultly situated species for the United States to protect through implementation of a domestic policy scheme like the ESA. However, as human activities continue to have an increasingly global reach with respect to impacts on the environment, including by dramatically changing the world's climate, we should continue to ask whether our endangered species policy provides opportunities to address such impacts to the most vulnerable inhabitants of the planet.

Human Contribution to Climate Change and the Destruction of Polar Bear Habitat

There is now near universal scientific consensus that global climate change is occurring at much higher rates as compared to historical trends and that anthropogenic sources of GHGs (primarily carbon dioxide) are a primary cause. The Intergovernmental Panel on Climate Change (IPCC)—an international body created by the United Nations Environment Programme (UNEP) open to all United Nations member countries (of which there are 195 at present time)—reviews and assesses the most recent scientific, technical, and socioeconomic information related to global climate change. In 2014, the IPCC released its Fifth Assessment Report. The report concludes that "[h]uman influence on the climate system is clear, and recent anthropogenic emissions of green-house gases

---

of the U.S. Geological Survey in studies conducted to assist USFWS in its decision as to whether listing of polar bears was warranted under the ESA). According to USFWS, the Geological Survey has, as recently as 2014, "corroborated the climate threat . . . through Bayesian network modeling." USFWS, *Draft Polar Bear Conservation Management Plan*, at 11 (July 2, 2015), http://www.fws .gov/alaska/PDFs/PBRT%20Recovery%20Plan% 20Book.pdf (citing T. C. Atwood et al., Evaluating and ranking threats to the long-term persistence of polar bears. U.S. Geological Survey Open-File Report 2014–1254, 114 p. (first published Jan. 9, 2015), http://dx.doi.org/10.3133/ ofr20141254). The 2014 USGS Open-File Report concluded, *inter alia*, that "[f]rom 2002 to 2013, the extent of summer sea ice decreased at a rate of 14 percent per decade . . . [and,] the Arctic may be functionally ice-free (i.e., < 1.0 M km^2) in summer within 10–15 years, and perhaps sooner." *Id*. at 2 (internal citations omitted).

are the highest in history."[101] Among GHGs, carbon dioxide is the most significant heat-trapping gas emitted today. Before the industrial revolution, the amount of carbon dioxide in the atmosphere was below 300 parts per million (ppm), but now that level has increased to nearly 400 ppm, which is significantly higher than the 350 ppm that scientists say is needed to avert the worst effects of climate change.[102] According to the IPCC, the oceans are where most of the heat in the climate system is eventually trapped, with oceans storing over 90 percent of the amount of bioaccumulated energy in the last forty years.[103] Thus, it should be no surprise that increase in ocean temperatures, sea level rise, and surface ice melt are among the most immediately measurable impacts of climate change.

For polar bears, sea ice loss due to climate changes is the primary threat to the species' long-term survival. Polar bears are evolutionarily adapted to, and dependent upon, sea ice—they use the ice as a platform from which to hunt seals and other prey, find mates, and give birth to and raise their young. The current global population of polar bears is loosely estimated to be between 20,000 and 25,000 individuals occupying a circumpolar range in five countries in the Northern Hemisphere—the United States (Alaska), Canada, Denmark (Greenland), Norway, and Russia.[104] Unlike many other species vulnerable to extinction, overall polar bear numbers may be stable at the present time, with only some populations currently decreasing.[105] However, the outlook for polar bears in the foreseeable future is grim. Scientists estimate that the worldwide polar bear population will decline by more than two-thirds by 2050 and will be near extinction by the end of the century, almost exclusively due to sea ice loss as the result of climate change.[106]

---

101. IPCC, *Climate Change 2014: Synthesis Report*, at 2 (2015), http://www.ipcc.ch/ pdf/assessment-report/ar5/syr/SYR_AR5_FINAL_full.pdf.
102. NOAA, *Earth System Research Laboratory, Global Monitoring Division, Trends in Atmospheric Carbon Dioxide*, http://www.esrl.noaa.gov/gmd/ccgg/trends/.
103. IPCC, *Climate Change 2014: Synthesis Report, supra* note 101, at 4.
104. USFWS, *Draft Polar Bear Conservation Management Plan, supra* note 100, at 5.
105. IUCN/SSC Polar Bear Specialist Group, *Summary of Polar Bear Population Status 2014*, http://pbsg.npolar.no/en/status/status-table.html.
106. Steven C. Amstrup, Bruce G. Marcot, & David C. Douglas. *Forecasting the Range-wide Status of Polar Bears at Selected Times in the 21st Century*, U.S. Geological Survey (2007).

In January 2007, the USFWS issued a proposed rule to list the polar bear as a threatened species under the ESA.[107] The proposed listing was premised upon the agency's findings that polar bears are threatened by projected sea ice melt, making the polar bear one of the first species to be proposed for protection under the ESA based primarily on threats directly related to climate change. Although the proposed rule identified the primary threat to the species as habitat modification due to warming oceanic and atmospheric temperatures, the proposed rule conspicuously contained no mention of GHG emissions. Because of the controversial basis for the listing, the USFWS opened multiple rounds of public comment, held three public hearings, and actively sought input from other federal agencies, state and tribal officials, polar bear range countries and other stakeholders, and scientific peer reviewers. Among those entities the USFWS contacted was the United States Geological Survey (USGS), which collected and analyzed scientific data and developed models to augment the information available to the USFWS in reaching a final determination. In May 2008, in response to a court order requiring that the agency issue a decision without further delay, the USFWS published a final rule listing the polar bear as a threatened species under the ESA.[108]

Efforts to Limit Regulation of Greenhouse Gas–Emitting Activities That Harm Polar Bears

The USFWS's May 2008 final rule repeatedly acknowledged the role of climate change in diminishing polar bear sea ice habitat during its discussion of its rationale to list the polar bear as threatened. Nevertheless, USFWS did not propose to regulate activities that generate GHG emissions through the mechanisms available in the ESA for limiting harm to species covered by the Act. Cognizant of concerns from politically powerful GHG-producing industries, the USFWS proactively sought to ensure that the activities of these industries would not be regulated through the ESA to mitigate their impacts to Arctic ecosystems. Simultaneous with publication of the ESA listing rule, the USFWS announced it would

---

107. 72 Fed. Reg. 1064 (Jan. 8, 2007).
108. 73 Fed. Reg. 28212 (May 15, 2008).

take several steps "to make sure the ESA is not misused to regulate global climate change."[109]

The first step the USFWS took to prevent the ESA from being used as a tool to address climate change as related to species endangerment was specific to polar bears. The agency published a Special Rule under Section 4(d) of the ESA to immunize most GHG-emitting activities from the requirement that they not cause harm to polar bears[110] (in the context of the ESA, "harm" includes habitat modification or degradation that impairs essential behavioral patterns, including breeding, feeding, and sheltering).[111] The Special Rule eliminates the ordinary prohibition on harming polar bears as long as such harm is incidental to, but not the purpose of, an otherwise lawful activity in any part of the United States except for Alaska. In effect, the Special Rule forecloses any claim that a source of GHG emissions outside of Alaska should be restricted under the ESA because it is harming polar bears by contributing to the destruction of their habitat. The ability to promulgate special rules to reduce the ordinary protections for ESA-listed species exists only for threatened species and not for those listed as endangered, which fact provides cause to wonder whether the USFWS decided that the species should be listed as threatened rather than endangered based on the availability of regulatory flexibility to address the concerns of the oil and gas extraction and other GHG-emitting industries rather than the species' actual imperilment status.

The USFWS's next effort at limiting the ESA's use as a tool to address climate change was applicable to all federal actions that may affect ESA-listed species. At the same time as it issued the final polar bear listing rule, the USFWS issued a formal policy memo to its staff to instruct that GHG emissions do not trigger the "consultation" requirement under Section 7 of the ESA.[112] Under Section 7 of the ESA, any federal agency taking action that may affect an ESA-listed species, such as the issuance of a permit for operation of a power plant, must consult with the USFWS

109. USFWS, *Polar Bear Listing Press Release, supra* note 94.
110. 73 Fed. Reg. 28306 (May 15, 2008), *codified at* 50 C.F.R. § 17.40(q).
111. 16 U.S.C. § 1532(19) (definition of "harm").
112. USFWS, *Expectations for Consultations on Actions that Would Emit Greenhouse Gases* (May 14, 2008), http:www.fws.gov/policy/m0331.pdf ("USFWS Greenhouse Gas Consultations Memo").

(or NMFS in the case of some marine animals) to determine if the action is likely to jeopardize the species.[113] As an initial matter, the policy memo indicated that USFWS staff should not determine that consultation is required "unless it is established that the emissions from the proposed action cause an indirect effect to listed species or critical habitat."[114] Thus, the agency appears to concede that some GHG-emitting activities should be subject to consultation. However, the memo thereafter proceeds to announce that it is the USFWS's position that "the best scientific data available today do not allow us to draw a causal connection between GHG emissions from a given facility and effects posed to listed species or their habitats, nor are there sufficient data to establish that such impacts are reasonably certain to occur."[115] The memo purports not to foreclose all consultations on GHG production, but the USFWS shifts the burden to the federal agency approving the GHG-emitting activity to request consultation if it "believes it may have a compliance duty under Section 7 for its programs or actions."[116] The memo also asserts that the policy could change in the future as new data on GHG-emitting activities are developed, but there is no trigger for review of the policy as the facts and science with respect to GHG production evolves. In effect, the USFWS has prohibited its staff from making individualized determinations as to the need for consultation regarding impact of GHG production for all future federal agency actions.

Shortly after the USFWS's Special Rule for polar bears was published, conservation organizations challenged it in federal court.[117] The conservation groups argued that even though the USFWS may provide special rules for threatened species that are not coextensive with the protections afforded to endangered species, Section 4(d) nonetheless requires that these rules must be "necessary and advisable to provide for the conservation of such species,"[118] and the USFWS cannot promulgate a special rule

---

113. 16 U.S.C. § 1536.

114. USFWS, *Greenhouse Gas Consultations Memo, supra* note 112.

115. *Id.*

116. *Id.*

117. *In re* Polar Bear Endangered Species Act Listing and 4(d) Rule Litigation, 818 F. Supp. 2d 214 (Oct. 17, 2011).

118. 16 U.S.C. § 1533(d).

for which the primary purpose is to avoid addressing the principal cause of the species' imperiled status. The court ruled in favor of the USFWS, stating that the court must be most deferential to agency judgments on issues that are "at the frontiers of science," and held that the USFWS "reasonably concluded that its Special Rule provides for the conservation of the polar bear even if it does not reverse the trend of Arctic sea ice loss," by focusing on the "direct impacts to individual bears and their habitats" that it can control.[119] The court indicated that it was sympathetic to the conservation groups' frustration over the lack of a strong mechanism to combat the effects of global climate change, but indicated that it could not find that the USFWS had acted arbitrarily or capriciously in determining that the ESA did not provide a useful means of alleviating "the particular threat to the polar bear" in this case. The court's decision upheld the USFWS's Special Rule under a very deferential standard of review, and should not be read to preclude the agency from taking a different approach (i.e., using the ESA to restrict climate change-inducing activities) in other circumstances, or as the science and/or threat of climate change evolves. Nonetheless, it continues to be the USFWS's position that the ESA "was never intended to regulate global climate change"[120] and should not be used to restrict GHG production, despite the evidence that it is global climate change, and GHG production in particular, that is affecting a large number of species, including the polar bear.

The USFWS is not alone in determining that a statute it is charged with implementing should not be used to address the causes of climate change. In 2003, the U.S. Environmental Protection Agency (EPA) denied a citizen rulemaking petition to regulate GHG emissions from motor vehicles under the Clean Air Act (CAA), principally on the assertion that Congress did not intend for the agency to regulate GHG emissions when it enacted the CAA (although the agency also stated that if it did have authority to regulate GHG emissions under the CAA it would decline to do so).[121] Litigation over the denial eventually made it all the way up to the U.S. Supreme Court where the decision was overturned, with a majority of the justices holding that just because Congress had

---

119. *In re* Polar Bear Endangered Species Act Listing and 4(d) Rule Litigation, 818 F. Supp. 2d at 218–19.
120. USFWS, Polar Bear Listing Press Release, *supra* note 94.
121. 68 Fed. Reg. 52922.

not anticipated climate change as a problem that would be caused by air pollutants when it enacted the CAA does not mean that it could not be a subject of regulation under the statute in the future.[122] In 2007, the Supreme Court concluded that GHGs could fall within the CAA's definition of an "air pollutant" regulated by the law. However, the decision merely determined that the EPA's reason for not regulating GHG emissions from motor vehicles (that it lacked authority to do so) was invalid, and it required the agency to revisit the matter. The EPA subsequently did enact regulation covering GHG emissions and their effect on climate change when it promulgated a rule known as the "Tailpipe Rule" upon concluding that motor vehicle emissions of six specific GHGs "contribute to the total greenhouse gas air pollution, and thus to the climate change problem, which is reasonably anticipated to endanger public health and welfare."[123] The EPA's Tailpipe Rule was upheld by a federal appeals court in 2012.[124]

How Should Impacts of Climate Change on Wildlife Be Treated in Conservation Policy?

Several commentators have agreed with the USFWS's sentiments that GHG emissions should not be regulated under the ESA. By example, at the ABA's March 2009 Annual Conference on Environmental Law, a group of environmental law practitioners that represent the oil and gas industry presented a paper on the polar bear listing (then still in active litigation) and the potential to regulate GHG emissions using the ESA.[125] The authors argued not only that climate change is a global problem in need of a global solution, but that the ESA's regulatory mechanisms "are at best, blunt, cumbersome, litigious and relatively random tools" that could only regulate GHG production in an indirect manner, and that the USFWS and NMFS "are not staffed, funded or otherwise equipped

---

122. Massachusetts v. EPA, 549 U.S. 497 (2007).
123. 74 Fed. Reg. 66,496, 66,499 (Dec. 15, 2009).
124. *Coalition for Responsible Regulation, Inc. v. EPA*, 684 *F.3d* 102 (D.C. Cir. 2012).
125. Jeffrey W. Leppo et al. *The Polar Bear Listing Story: Efforts to Regulate GHG Emissions Using the Endangered Species Act.* American Bar Association, 38th Annual Conference on Environmental Law (Mar. 12–15, 2009), http://www.americanbar.org/content/dam/aba/migrated/environ/programs/keystone/2009/bestpapers/JeffreyLeppo_Keystone2009.pdf.

to monitor, evaluate and manage GHG emissions."[126] These may be fair criticisms, but the fact remains that the ESA has often been used to address activities that only indirectly impact listed species, such as the incidental take permitting of dams that change water flow and quality in the habitats of endangered species[127] or of commercial fishing operations that reduce or redistribute the prey base of an endangered species.[128]

Although they are not without their difficulties and weaknesses, there are opportunities to address climate change through the ESA as it is currently structured. First, the ESA arguably could be a part of a desperately needed invigoration of carbon emissions reduction efforts, though tough decisions would need to be made about what sources and degree of GHG emissions affecting listed species should be regulated through the ESA and how to provide resources for such an effort without distracting from other applications of the Act. Second, we could utilize the ESA's existing framework to facilitate protection of habitats and species recovery planning in a manner that better accounts for the likely impacts of climate change. As our understanding of the underlying science behind climate change and our ability to model its impacts grows, the ESA may prove to be a viable tool for finding creative solutions to reduce and prevent harms to vulnerable species.

---

126. *Id.* at 15.

127. *See* Riverside Irr. Dist. v. Andrews, 758 F.2d 508 (10th Cir. 1985) (requiring site-specific permitting under the ESA for a dam that would divert water away from ESA-listed whooping crane habitat). In the *Riverside Irrigation District* case the court noted: "No one claims that the fill itself will endanger or destroy the habitat of an endangered species or adversely affect the aquatic environment. However, the fill that the Corps is authorizing is required to build the earthen dam. The dam will result in the impoundment of water in a reservoir, facilitating the use of the water in Wildcat Creek. The increased consumptive use will allegedly deplete the stream flow, and it is this depletion that the Corps found would adversely affect the habitat of the whooping crane." *Id.* at 511–12.

128. Greenpeace v. Nat'l Marine Fisheries Serv., 106 F. Supp. 2d 1066, 1077 (W.D. Wash. 2000) (requiring preparation of a biological opinion, which would necessarily include mitigation measures, under Section 7 of the ESA for commercial fishing activity in endangered Steller sea lion habitat). In the *Greenpeace* case, the court noted: "The evidence in the Administrative Record demonstrates that these large fisheries threaten to appreciably diminish the value of critical habitat as a prey resource for Steller sea lions through 'exploitative' and 'interactive' competition for fish," and "although the actual effects of the fisheries and the efficacy of mitigation measures are uncertain, the significant and demonstrated potential negative effects of these large fisheries constitute a clear *threat* to appreciably diminish the value of critical habitat for Steller sea lions." *Id.* at 1077–79, 1084–86.

Although it clearly would be controversial to do so, GHG emissions could be regulated under the ESA, and the effort to do so likely would not grind GHG-emitting activities to a halt as some fear. By example, if the USFWS had not promulgated the Special Rule under Section 4(d) described previously that prevented any regulation of GHG emissions to benefit polar bears, GHG-emitting activities would not be absolutely prohibited. Activities that harm a listed species are generally unlawful under the ESA, but Section 10 of the Act provides for incidental take permits for activities in which the harm to listed species is not the purpose of the activity.[129] Additionally, incidental take authorization for similar activities could be addressed in a programmatic manner. With respect to actions of the federal government, the requirement to engage in consultation under Section 7 of the ESA is only triggered by a finding that the activity "may affect" a listed species, which standard may not be met unless the impact on habitat modification due to climate change is traceable to the action.[130] Furthermore, while Section 7 of the ESA places a duty on federal actors not to "jeopardize" a listed species, the term "jeopardize" means "to engage in an action that reasonably would be expected, directly or indirectly, to reduce appreciably the likelihood of both the survival and recovery of a listed species . . ."[131] Thus, the obligation to avoid activities that would place an ESA-listed species in further jeopardy of extinction may be determined not to implicate many GHG-emitting activities if they do not "appreciably" increase that risk. Therefore, wholesale exemption of GHG production from the ambit of the ESA may be an extreme and unwarranted overreaction to fears about restricting GHG emissions. Rather, application of the ESA to GHG-emitting activities could allow for mitigation of activities that produce GHGs if they individually or collectively do rise to the level of impacting listed species and trigger the ESA's regulatory mechanisms; however, they would surely not affect every GHG-producing activity.

Of course, if very few GHG-emitting activities would rise to the level of action under the ESA at this time, the ESA may not be valuable as a driver of GHG reduction. Further, regardless of how few individual

129. 16 USC § 1539.
130. 50 C.F.R. § 402.14.
131. 50 C.F.R. § 402.02.

GHG-emitting activities the ESA might be applied to, there would still be concern that application of the Act to GHG production would require a significant expansion of agency budgets and staffing, given the sheer number of such activities throughout the country and likely litigation over the many determinations that consultation and permitting requirements are not triggered for most GHG-emitting activities. However, even if the ESA and USFWS are currently ill-equipped to meaningfully combat GHG production, to the extent ESA regulation would make even an appreciable change to the causes of the destruction of listed species' habitats such a goal is surely consistent with the purposes of the Act, and as such the ESA should remain an arrow in the quiver with respect to tackling GHG production as one of several possible tools to address harmful emissions. As is clear from the example of the EPA's Tailpipe Rule discussed previously, while some statutory schemes may not seem at first to provide viable mechanisms to address production of GHGs, growing pressure to tackle the problem of climate change with all tools available may eventually counsel some restrictions under the ESA in the form of mitigation measures in response to consultations over government action under Section 7 of the Act or incidental take permits for private actions issued under Section 10 of the Act.

In addition, separate from the regulation of GHG-emitting facilities, we may be able to utilize the ESA's existing tools for protecting habitats and facilitating species recovery planning to incorporate climate change–focused action into species protection decisions. Even some opponents of using the ESA to regulate GHG production see value in implementation of the Act in other ways to protect species from the impacts of climate change. By example, J. B. Ruhl, a professor at Florida State University's law school, wrote in a widely read and reviewed 2009 article that the USFWS should not attempt to use the ESA to combat GHG emissions, asserting that no matter how swift and effective global GHG reduction measures are implemented, GHG emissions cannot be brought back to below 1990 levels (approximately 350 ppm),[132] as many policy makers and world leaders (including both candidates for the U.S. presidential election in 2012) have set as a goal. Professor Ruhl argues that we will need

---

132. J. B. Ruhl. *Climate Change and the Endangered Species Act: Building Bridges to the No-Analog Future*, 88 B.U. L. Rev. 1 (2008).

to come to accept that some species will go extinct as a result of impacts due to climate change, and that instead of regulating GHG emissions the ESA should be utilized to create a "bridge to the no-analog future" (i.e., a future in which the world's ecosystems will experience changes with which we have no experience),[133] in which we incorporate innovative and adaptive management techniques to address these previously unseen changes. Among those creative efforts Professor Ruhl envisions are: regulating human adaptations to climate changes that would impact listed species, and conducting assisted migrations of climate change-affected species under the "experimental population" provisions of the ESA.

Focusing on protecting species from impacts of climate change, rather than trying to limit the causes of climate change in the first instance, would require a more proactive approach to species recovery planning under the ESA than the USFWS and NMFS have historically committed to, with few notable exceptions. Species at risk of endangerment due to climate change could be listed as threatened earlier, with the understanding that what constitutes the "foreseeable future" for purposes of listings under Section 4 of the ESA will be a longer timeframe with respect to the threats caused by climate change as compared to other threats, especially as we gain greater knowledge of the future impacts of climate change and become better at modeling those impacts.[134] Listing species as threatened earlier may encourage domestic and international recovery planning efforts to begin sooner. Furthermore, listing decisions based on threats posed by climate change might be even more effective if the USFWS would revert back to its 1994 policy emphasizing an ecosystem-focused

---

133. *Id.* at 13.

134. In their decisions to list polar bears, and not to list ribbon seals, USFWS and NMFS considered data projections of up to 100 years, but ultimately both relied on a 45-year timeframe as the "foreseeable future" for determining whether climate change factors counseled protection of these species under the ESA. *In re Polar Bear Endangered Species Act Listing & 4(d) Rule Litig.*, 794 F. Supp. 2d 65, 93–5 (D.D.C. 2011) (upholding use of 45-year timeframe as "foreseeable future" in agreeing to list polar bears); *Ctr. for Biological Diversity v. Lubchenco*, 758 F. Supp. 2d 945, 967–68 (N.D. Cal. 2010) (upholding use of 45-year timeframe as "foreseeable future" in declining to list ribbon seals). However, this timeframe might be longer for future listing decisions if scientific data and modeling capabilities allow for reliable projections beyond that point. *See* 73 Fed. Reg. 28212, 28239-40 (May 15, 2008) (final polar bear listing rule stating that "[t]he 45-year timeframe coincides with the timeframe within which climate model projections are most reliable"); 73 Fed. Reg. 77,264 (Dec. 18, 2008) (proposing to list four penguin species under the ESA based largely on impacts to habitat by climate change, and relying on projections of conditions in Antarctica over the next 100 years).

listing review process that recognizes dramatic habitat modifications are often relevant to the conservation status of many species at the same time.[135] In the context of Section 7 consultations, litigation under the ESA has clearly established that the USFWS has an obligation to strive to "recover" species, not merely to provide enough stopgaps against threats to ensure mere survival of some members of the species.[136] We might also use the existing framework of the ESA to safeguard against climate change–caused stressors, such as severe droughts, warming waters, intensified weather events, loss of mountain top snow pack, migrating prey species, sea level rise, etc. We can use predictive climate impact modeling to identify new habitat, food sources, and other resources necessary for species pushed to the brink by dramatic ecosystems changes caused by climate change. We can work to promulgate policies that prioritize maintenance of genetic diversity in wild populations in order to buttress species against dramatic ecosystems changes that may be caused by climate change.

In December 2013, on the fortieth anniversary of the enactment of the ESA, NMFS scientists published eight research papers in the peer-reviewed scientific journal *Conservation Biology* that addressed the question of how the agency should incorporate climate change into its decision-making under the ESA.[137] Unlike the Section 7 consultation policy memo issued in 2008 by the USFWS, the 2013 NMFS papers reflected an agency understanding that work needs to be done to keep up with emerging science on climate change and because future conditions are not guaranteed. Strategies discussed in the NMFS papers included: incorporating robust climate change modeling in ESA listing decisions; consideration of multispecies and ecosystem-focused approaches to threat reduction; identifying climate-caused shifts in distribution of species and areas that are not used by species today but might be critical refuges in the future; and addressing genetic diversity as an important objective

---

135. 59 Fed. Reg. 34274 (1994).
136. Nat'l Wildlife Fed'n v. Nat'l Marine Fisheries Serv., 534 F.3d 917 (9th Cir. 2008); Gifford Pinchot Task Force v. U.S. Fish & Wildlife Serv., 378 F.3d 1059 (9th Cir. 2004).
137. NMFS, *A Changing Climate for Endangered Species* (December 2013), http://www.nmfs .noaa.gov/stories/2013/12/12_4_2013climate_and_the_esa.html (NMFS website announcing publication of the articles). The articles are published in Volume. 27, Issue 6, of Conservation Biology, and are available at http://onlinelibrary.wiley.com/doi/10.1111/ cobi.2013.27.issue-6/issuetoc.

of recovery planning to allow species to adapt to changing conditions. NMFS's effort to think creatively with a purpose of ensuring that the ESA remains effective in the face of a changing climate is an effort that should be modeled by the USFWS.

In a concerted effort to find real solutions to the imperilment of polar bears, the five polar bear range states met in Greenland in September 2015 to provide updates on each country's management plan for the species and to adopt the first Circumpolar Polar Bear Action Plan (CAP).[138] The threat of climate change was discussed repeatedly throughout the multiday meeting, providing hope that serious and impactful multilateral action to combat the issue might be implemented soon. However, while the recently published CAP officially recognizes climate change as the primary threat to polar bears and proposes that range states adopt adaptive management techniques to respond to its adverse effects on the species, the CAP principally encourages monitoring and evaluation of climate change indicators and impacts rather than proposing action items to combat the problem. Indeed, the only specific "actions" related to climate change proposed in the CAP are to: (1) "Consider the cumulative effects of climate change and human activities on polar bear subpopulations and habitats when making management decisions using tools such as predictive modeling;" and (2) "Investigate how climate change effects vary among subpopulations on both temporal and spatial scales and incorporate this knowledge into management actions."[139]

Separate from the CAP, the polar bear range states have all agreed to play an active role in negotiations under the United Nations Framework Convention on Climate Change to finalize a post-2020 climate change agreement aimed at limiting global temperature rise to 2°C or less.[140] To this end, all of the range states have already submitted their Intended Nationally Determined Contributions (INDCs), identifying post-2020 targets for GHG emissions reductions.[141] Furthermore, as members of the

138. Naalakkersulsut (Greenland), 2015 Polar Bear Range States Meeting, http://naalakkersuisut.gl/en/Naalakkersuisut/Departments/Fiskeri-Fangst-og-Landbrug/Isbjorn.
139. Polar Bear Range States, *Circumpolar Action Plan: Conservation Strategy for the Polar Bear*, at 56 (September 2015), http://naalakkersuisut.gl/~/media/Nanoq/Files/ Attached%20Files/Fiskeri_Fangst_Landbrug/Polarbear%202015/CAP/CAP%20Book.pdf.
140. *Id.* at 55.
141. *Id.*

Arctic Council, the polar bear range states have approved a Framework
for Action on Enhanced Black Carbon and Methane Emission Reductions, which may have beneficial impacts to Arctic environments with
respect to specific short-lived climate pollutants.[142]

On the home front, our federal government produced a Draft Polar
Bear Conservation Management Plan (Draft CMP) on July 2, 2015.[143]
The Draft CMP is intended to "serve as the United States' contribution
to" the CAP,[144] and thus similarly focuses on research and analysis when
it comes to the impacts of climate change on polar bears, and maintains
the USFWS's repudiation of GHG emission regulation under the ESA.
Indeed, the recovery goals established by the plan sound more like an
effort at managed decline of the species rather than real recovery or sustainability plan (the Draft CMP establishes that the "carrying capacity"
for the species is a minimum of 500 bears in each of four regions or 15
percent of the current population).[145] However, the USFWS's press release
announcing publication of the Draft CMP is remarkably different than
the press release it issued in announcing the 2008 listing rule for the species. In fact, the agency's press release on the Draft CMP mentions GHG
emissions at least five times, whereas the draft listing rule did not mention GHGs at all.[146] The release states at the outset that the "[s]ingle-most
important step" to protecting polar bears "is decisive action to address
Arctic warming."[147] And so, despite the dire projections for the species
that led to its listing under the ESA in the first place, the USFWS offers
a glimmer of hope: "the long-term persistence of polar bears may be possible if global greenhouse gas emissions are stabilized at or below" currently projected levels.[148] Hopefully these are signs that the USFWS, now
and under future presidential administrations, is warming to the idea of
using the ESA to help address an overheating world.

---

142. *Id.*
143. USFWS, *Draft Polar Bear Conservation Management Plan, supra* note 100.
144. USFWS, *Press Release: Fish and Wildlife Service and Partners Announce First Conservation Management Plan for Polar Bear* (July 2, 2015), http://www.fws.gov/news/ShowNews.cfm?ID =4FB1AB4D-D753-E538-66AA14ADFF963403 ("USFWS, Draft CMP Press Release").
145. USFWS, *Draft Polar Bear Conservation Management Plan, supra* note 100, at 6-7.
146. USFWS, *Draft CMP Press Release, supra* note 144.
147. *Id.*
148. *Id.*

~

It seems certain that climate change will dramatically change our planet in the near future. The result will surely be a radical reshuffling of current ecosystems and dramatic impacts to the species living within them. To arbitrarily dismiss the ESA as a potential tool for regulating GHGs as a primary driver of climate change, or as a potential tool for protection of climate-affected endangered species and their habitats wholly apart from GHG regulation, would be to deny the ESA the landmark role it has played through the first forty years of its existence as a complex and robust regulatory scheme that can be wielded as a hammer when necessary but also utilized in nuanced ways to facilitate creative and lasting solutions to complicated problems.

Some experts view the extinction of the polar bear as a foregone conclusion; still others insist that only international efforts will prevent that from happening. However, we should not bend over backward to make the ESA irrelevant. All imperiled species affected by climate change should be subject to meaningful recovery and conservation planning, lest we stand in the way of letting the polar bear and other endangered species help teach us what we must do to combat the daunting threat of climate change to the natural world.

Mining and Monocultures: How Extractive Industries Are Endangering Great Apes (A Case Study)

*"The conquest of the earth, which mostly means
the taking it away from those who have a different
complexion or slightly flatter noses than ourselves, is
not a pretty thing when you look into it too much."*

Heart of Darkness, Joseph Conrad (1902)

More than a century ago, Joseph Conrad wrote an alluring and controversial tale of an imperial journey up the Congo River by a European ivory trading company. Today, the ever-increasing demand for energy and consumer products continues to fuel the plundering of natural resources in Africa, Asia, and globally. In addition to the impacts that such activities have on local people (from economic impacts to human rights abuses), resource extraction constitutes a severe threat to the conservation of humans' closest living relatives, the great apes.

Global Demand for Forest Resources Puts Great Apes in Peril

Four species of great apes are found in Africa (the chimpanzee, bonobo, eastern gorilla, and western gorilla) and two species in Asia (the Sumatran orangutan and the Bornean orangutan). They often share their forest ecosystems with other imperiled species, such as tigers, leopards, rhinoceroses, elephants, gibbons, or sun bears. Humans share 98.4 percent of their genetic code with chimpanzees and bonobos, meaning that these three species are more closely related to each other than they are to other apes.[149] All great apes—including humans, for we are in the great ape family—share similar cognitive, emotional, and cultural capacities, including the ability of self-recognition, numerical skills, use and comprehension of symbolic language systems, problem-solving skills, understanding the mental states of peers, behavioral and emotional pathologies, and cultural behavior patterns that differ by geographic region.[150]

---

149. The Chimpanzee Sequencing and Analysis Consortium, *Initial Sequence of the Chimpanzee Genome and Comparison with the Human Genome*, 437 NATURE 69–87 (September 1, 2005); Michael Gross, *Homo gets a Panning*, 13(12) CURRENT BIOL. 464–5 (June 17, 2003); Ann Gibbons, *Bonobos Join Chimps as Closest Human Relatives*, SCIENCE (June 13, 2012), http://news .sciencemag.org/plants-animals/2012/06/bonobos-join-chimps-close-human-relatives.

150. *See, e.g.,* Brian Hare et al., *Do chimpanzees Know What Conspecifics Know?*, 61(1) ANIMAL BEHAV. 139–51 (2001); Max Planck Institute for Evolutionary Anthropology, *Primate Cognition*, http://www.eva.mpg.de/psycho/primate-cognition.php; Sana Inoue & Tetsuro Matsuzawa, *Working Memory of Numerals in Chimpanzees*, 17(23) CURRENT BIOL. R1004–5 (December 4, 2007); Amy S. Pollick & Frans B.M. de Waal, *Ape Gestures and Language Evolution*, 104(19) PROC. NAT'L ACAD. SCI. 8184–9 (May 8, 2007); Alicia P. Melis et al., *Chimpanzees Recruit the Best Collaborators*, 311 SCI. 1297–1300 (March 3, 2006); Brian Hare et al., *Tolerance Allows Bonobos to Outperform Chimpanzees on a Cooperative Task*, 17(7) CURRENT BIOL. 619–23; Francys Subiaul et al., *Do Chimpanzees Learn Reputation by Observation? Evidence from Direct and Indirect Experience with Generous and Selfish Strangers*, 11(4) ANIMAL COGNITION 611–23 (March 21, 2008); G. A. Bradshaw et al., *Building an Inner Sanctuary: Complex PTSD in Chimpanzees*, 9(1) J. TRAUMA

Much academic discussion has surrounded the anthropological debate regarding why our common ancestors moved out of the forests into savannahs and gave rise to the human lineage;[151] however, there is no doubt that humans continue to be heavily dependent on forest ecosystems not only for sustenance, but for myriad raw materials that supply our modern lifestyle.

In tropical forests in Asia and Africa, viable habitat is dwindling rapidly and ape populations have plummeted over the last century. According to the United Nations Food and Agriculture Organization, millions of hectares (thousands of square miles) of forest in Africa and Asia are lost each year.[152] While climate change and local energy demands certainly play a role in the loss of forests, industrial logging, commercial and artisanal mining, and agricultural land conversion are driving forces of habitat loss for great apes (and the many other species that exist in these biodiversity hotspots).[153]

The U.S. demand for technology like cellphones, tablets, laptops, printers, cameras, videogame consoles, and even electric cars contributes to the destruction of tropical forests through the mining of the precious metals needed for these devices. Similarly, personal care products and processed foods sold in thousands of retail outlets across the United States contain palm oil or derivatives thereof, the vast majority of which is produced by destroying primary rainforest habitats for great apes. This case study will discuss the impacts of mining and palm oil plantations on great ape conservation and the legal landscape that impacts this global supply chain.

& DISSOCIATION 9–34 (2008); Stephen J. Lycett et al., *Phylogenetic Analyses of Behavior Support Existence of Culture Among Wild Chimpanzees*, 104(45) PROC. NAT'L ACAD. SCI. 17588–92 (Nov. 6, 2007); Michael Krutzen et al., *Culture and Geographic Variation in Orangutan Behavior*, 21(21) CURRENT BIOL. 1808–12 (Nov. 8, 2011).

151. *See, e.g., Ardipithecus ramidus*, SCI. (2009), *available at* http://www.sciencemag.org/site/feature/misc/webfeat/ardipithecus/.

152. *See* United Nations Food and Agriculture Organization, *Global Forest Resource Assessment 2015*, http://www.fao.org/3/a-i4808e.pdf.

153. *See* IUCN Primate Specialist Group Action Plans, http://www.primate-sg.org/action_plans/.

Consumer Nations and Range States Are Failing to Adequately Protect Apes from Extractive Industries

Great ape habitat in Africa overlaps significantly with reserves of valuable minerals, metals, and hydrocarbons, and the extractive industries continue to grow to meet global demand.[154] Pristine rainforests are disappearing as the acres of land converted to commercial exploration and production rise rapidly. This commercial activity has both direct impacts (e.g., deforestation, emissions and other environmental waste, noise, water mismanagement, and road building) and indirect impacts (e.g., bushmeat hunting and poaching in previously impenetrable forests) on apes and their habitats.

For example, the Democratic Republic of the Congo (DRC) is the only country where bonobos exist and is one of the few remaining strongholds of chimpanzee and gorilla habitat in Africa. It also holds a significant portion of the world's reserves of columbite-tantalite (coltan), a metallic ore that can hold a high electrical charge and allows for the "miniaturization" of electronic products like cellphones.[155] Coltan is mined by cutting down patches of trees (either on a smaller scale by artisanal miners or on an industrial scale), digging into the soil, and removing the ore from shallow deposits.[156] It is estimated that the subspecies of eastern lowland gorillas in the DRC (Grauer's gorillas) has suffered a 77–93 percent decline in the last two decades, and one of the primary causes of this decline is mining for coltan and associated bushmeat hunting.[157] The extraction and production of this valuable resource is also linked to human rights abuses and the funding of armed militias,

---

154. Arcus Foundation, *State of the Apes: Extractive Industries and Ape Conservation* (2013), http://www.stateoftheapes.com/.

155. Sabrina J. Smith, *The Conflict Mineral: Coltan Mining in DR Congo and Australia*, THE STRATEGIST (July 22, 2013), *available at* http://www.aspistrategist.org.au/the-conflict-mineral-coltan-mining-in-dr-congo-and-australia/.

156. Ewan Sutherland, *Coltan, the Congo and Your Cell Phone* (April 11, 2011), http://web.mit.edu/12.000/www/m2016/pdf/coltan.pdf.

157. Andrew Plumptre et al., *Status of Grauer's Gorilla and Chimpanzees in Eastern Democratic Republic of Congo: Historical and Current Distribution and Abundance* (2015), http://albertinerift.wcs.org/Wildlife/Apes/Grauers-Gorillas.aspx. *See also* Wildlife Conservation Society, *New Report Documents Shocking Collapse of Gorilla Subspecies During 20 Years of Civil Unrest* (April 4, 2016), http://newsroom.wcs.org/News-Releases/articleType/ArticleView/articleId/8675/New-Report-Documents-Shocking-Collapse-of-Gorilla-Subspecies-During-20-Years-of-Civil-Unrest.aspx.

fueling the ethnic conflict that has persisted in this region for decades.[158] Recently the DRC and Uganda have even indicated a desire to allow oil exploration in or around Virunga National Park (Africa's first protected parkland and home to the few remaining mountain gorillas, another subspecies of eastern gorilla).[159] Great apes are enormously affected by this environmental disturbance and violent conflict.

In some cases resource extraction leads to total destruction of forest habitats; however, even when extraction results in limited deforestation, the practice routinely has dramatic indirect impacts on apes and other species. Roads are often built to access previously inaccessible areas of forest, and the roads persist long after a site is emptied of its mineral reserves, leading to increased interaction between humans and apes and creating transit routes for poachers.[160] Hundreds of chimpanzees, gorillas, and bonobos are killed each year to feed humans working in and around forests and to sell in the profitable bushmeat trade; and, because there is little meat on an infant ape, these vulnerable individuals are captured alive after their families are killed, and sold into the pet and entertainment trades in Africa and abroad.[161] The United Nations Great Ape Survival Project estimates that from 2005 to 2015, well over 20,000 great apes (more than four individuals per day) have been lost due to poaching and illegal trade.[162] In addition to the devastating impacts on wild ape populations, this poaching and trade is related to the emergence

---

158. United Nations Report of the Panel of Experts on the Illegal Exploitation of Natural Resources and Other Forms of Wealth of the Democratic Republic of the Congo (2001), http://www.srwolf.com/reports/UNCONGO.pdf.

159. Melanie Gouby, *Democratic Republic of Congo Wants to Open Up Virunga National Park to Oil Exploration*, THE GUARDIAN (March 16, 2015), http://www.theguardian.com/environment/2015/mar/16/democratic-republic-of-congo-wants-to-explore-for-oil-in-virunga-national-park; European Parliament, *Prevent Irreversible Damage to Virunga National Park, Says EP* (Dec. 17, 2015), http://www.europarl.europa.eu/news/en/news-room/20151210IPR06855/Prevent-irreversible-damage-to-Virunga-National-Park-says-EP. *See also* https://savevirunga.com/.

160. IUCN, *Regional Action Plan for the Conservation of Western Lowland Gorillas and Central Chimpanzees 2015–2025* (2014), http://static1.1.sqspcdn.com/static/f/1200343/26274825/1433108664180/WEA_English_corrected.pdf?token=8PTWOr%2Be4BFGuNJcVN3lw%2BHEhLY%3D.

161. Great Ape Survival Partnership, *Stolen Apes—The Illicit Trade in Chimpanzees, Gorillas, Bonobos and Orangutans. A Rapid Response Assessment.* United Nations Environment Programme (2013), http://www.un-grasp.org/stolen-apes-report/.

162. *Id.*

of infectious diseases, such as Ebola virus, which can be transmitted to humans who handle meat or other parts from apes.[163]

Mining also affects orangutan habitat in Southeast Asia (specifically, on the islands of Borneo and Sumatra, the only remaining places where orangutans persist).[164] However, a far larger concern for orangutan conservation is the conversion of rainforest to palm oil plantations.[165] Palm oil, derived from the pulp of the fruit of just a few species of palm trees, is the most widely used vegetable oil in the world; similarly, palm kernel oil is derived from the seed of the oil palm fruit and is used in cosmetics and personal care products.[166] Because production of these oils is highly profitable, thousands of acres of primary rainforests and peatlands that orangutans depend on have been destroyed (first through the logging of valuable hardwood trees and then by burning to clear the land) and replaced with monocultures of palms.[167] After forest habitat (such as that in the Leuser Ecosystem in Sumatra, one of the most biologically diverse places on Earth) is converted to palm plantations, orangutans who have been displaced are frequently killed when they are caught in palm oil fields searching for food (and infants captured when their mothers are killed).[168] It is estimated that at least 50,000 orangutans have died as a result of palm oil deforestation in the last two decades, resulting in a population decrease of 50 percent and a habitat loss of 80 percent in the last decade alone.[169]

---

163. CDC, *Facts about Bushmeat and Ebola*, http://www.cdc.gov/vhf/ebola/pdf/bushmeat-and-ebola.pdf.

164. ERIK MEIJAARD & SERGE WICH, *Extractive Industries and Orangutans*, in STATE OF THE APES: EXTRACTIVE INDUSTRIES AND APE CONSERVATION (Arcus Foundation, 2013), http://www.stateoftheapes.com/reports/extractive-industries-and-orangutans/.

165. UNEP, *The Future of the Bornean Orangutan: Impacts of Change in Land Cover and Climate* (2015), http://issuu.com/ungrasp/docs/unep_ou_eng_20150629.1.compressed.

166. The Orangutan Project, *What is Palm Oil?*, http://www.orangutan.org.au/palm-oil.

167. Orangutan Foundation International, *The Effects of Palm Oil*, https://orangutan.org/rainforest/the-effects-of-palm-oil/; Indra Nugraha, *Indonesia Seeks Re-Do on Court Decision Absolving Company for Haze-Causing Fire*, Mongabay (Jan. 12, 2016), http://news.mongabay.com/2016/01/indonesias-environment-czar-to-personally-oversee-rematch-with-bmh/.

168. ERIC ARNHEM ET AL., *The Bigger Picture: Indirect Impacts of Extractive Industries on Apes and Ape Habitat*, in STATE OF THE APES: EXTRACTIVE INDUSTRIES AND APE CONSERVATION (Arcus Foundation, 2013), http://www.stateoftheapes.com/themes/indirect-impacts/; Patrick Rouxel, *Green: Death of the Forests*, http://www.aljazeera.com/programmes/witness/2012/03/201231483446653151.html.

169. IUCN Red List, *Bornean Orangutan*, http://www.iucnredlist.org/details/17975/0; IUCN Red List, *Sumatran Orangutan*, http://www.iucnredlist.org/details/39780/0.

But despite the documentation and publication of this environmental catastrophe, the U.S. demand for palm oil and palm kernel oil is met almost entirely from Indonesia and Malaysia (where Bornean and Sumatran orangutans are found).[170] Palm oil is regularly used by American food product companies as a vegetable oil in snack foods like ice cream, chocolate, potato chips, margarine, and canned soups, in part because of efforts to reduce unhealthy trans fats in foods (although there is ample evidence that palm oil is high in unhealthy saturated fats).[171] Palm oil is also routinely found in personal care products from soaps to cosmetics—indeed, the twenty-first century has seen a marked increase in imports of palm oil to the United States, with current consumption rates increasing more than eight-fold from their 1999 levels (to 1.2 million metric tons in 2015).[172]

In 2004 the Roundtable on Sustainable Palm Oil (RSPO) was established in an effort to develop a certification scheme to ensure that palm oil (a renewable resource in theory) is produced in a sustainable manner.[173] RSPO, which is led in part by major industrial palm oil producers, has been criticized by environmental groups for failing to ensure that palm oil is in fact produced without deforestation (for example, by planting oil palm in already degraded land).[174] However, the United Nations Great

---

170. *See, e.g., Rainforest Action Network, Conflict Palm Oil: How U.S. Snack Food Brands Are Contributing to Orangutan Extinction, Climate Change and Human Rights Violations* (2013), http://www.ran.org/_conflict_palm_oil_how_u_s_snack_food_brands_are_contributing_to_orangutan_extinction_climate_change_and_human_rights_violations.

171. *See* Sanjay Basu et al., *Palm Oil Taxes and Cardiovascular Disease Mortality in India: Economic-Epidemiologic Model,* The BMJ 347 (2013), http://www.bmj.com/content/347/bmj.f6048.short ("Palm oil contains approximately 49 g saturated fat per 100 g oil, as opposed to 17 g in peanut oil, 16 g in soybean oil, and 7 g in canola/rapeseed oil").

172. *See* Index Mundi, *United States Palm Oil Domestic Consumption Per Year,* http://www.indexmundi.com/agriculture/?country=us&commodity=palm-oil&graph=domestic-consumption. Fortunately, while palm oil is also used internationally as a biofuel, the U.S. Environmental Protection Agency has determined that palm oil does not meet the federal definition of a renewable fuel. *See* EPA, *Notice of Data Availability for Renewable Fuels Produced from Palm Oil Under the Renewable Fuel Standard* (2012), https://www.epa.gov/renewable-fuel-standard-program/learn-more-about-notice-data-availability-noda-renewable-fuels.

173. Roundtable on Sustainable Palm Oil, http://www.rspo.org/about.

174. Voices for Biodiversity, *Consumer Groups Slam Greenwashing in Sustainable Palm Oil Marketing,* http://voices.nationalgeographic.com/2013/08/08/consumer-groups-slam-greenwashing-in-sustainable-palm-oil-marketing/; Denis Ruysschaert & Helga Rainer, *From Process to Impact of a Voluntary Standard: The Roundtable on Sustainable Palm Oil,* State of the Apes (2015), http://www.stateoftheapes.com/themes/from-process-to-impact-of-a-voluntary-standard/.

Ape Survival Partnership recently called on the conservation community to collaborate more closely with oil palm developers to find a sustainable strategy to protect great apes from this agro-industry before it is too late.[175]

Campaigns to raise awareness and pressure corporations to adopt zero-deforestation policies for their palm oil supply chain have made some progress, but legislative reform and improved enforcement could more effectively address the devastating impacts the U.S. market has on orangutan survival.[176] For example, the Supreme Court of Indonesia recently upheld an unprecedented $25.6 million verdict against a palm oil company for the illegal burning of the Tripa peatland, critical habitat for orangutans.[177] More recently, the President of Indonesia announced a moratorium on new oil palm concessions, though it remains to be seen how stringently this moratorium will be enforced.[178] However, illegal deforestation remains an enormous problem that often goes without punishment (although conservation organizations have begun using drones to try to identify such activity in real time).[179]

Similarly, the capacity of African range states to quell the exploitation of great apes is limited, and international efforts are often necessary (especially if armed militias or corrupt officials are complicit in the poaching of wildlife). For example, the Secretariat of the Convention on International Trade in Endangered Species of Fauna and Flora (CITES) and INTERPOL recently worked with the government of Guinea to

175. Marc Ancrenaz et al., *Palm Oil Paradox: Sustainable Solutions to Save the Great Apes* (UNEP / GRASP, 2016) http://www.un-grasp.org/united-nations-report-calls-for-conservation-to-collaborate-with-palm-oil-industry/.

176. One particularly notable campaign is that of two Girl Scouts who set out to get the famous cookies to stop using palm oil that is not sustainably harvested. *See* Melissa Cronin, *Girl Scouts Demand Sustainable Palm Oil for Cookies to Save Orangutans*, https://www.thedodo.com/girl-scouts-demand-sustainable-433365522.html.

177. Hans N. Jong, *Record Fine Against Plantation Company Upheld*, THE JAKARTA POST (Sept. 13, 2015), http://m.thejakartapost.com/news/2015/09/13/record-fine-against-plantation-company-upheld.html.

178. *See* Philip Jacobson, *How Effective Will Indonesia's Palm Oil Permit Freeze Really Be?* MONGABAY (May 4, 2016), https://news.mongabay.com/2016/05/effective-will-indonesias-palm-oil-permit-freeze-really/.

179. Conservation Drones, *Drone Footage of Fire Aftermath in Peatlands of Tripa, Sumatra, Indonesia* (June 26, 2013), http://conservationdrones.org/2013/06/26/drone-footage-of-fire-aftermath-in-peatlands-of-tripa-sumatra-indonesia/.

investigate and arrest the former Guinea wildlife director who was alleg-edly involved in corruption and fraudulent issuance of export permits for wild apes, including some sent to China for use in zoos.[180] (See Chapter 5 on captive animals for more detailed information on the use of endan-gered species in substandard zoos).

What Can the United States Do to Minimize Destruction of Great Ape Habitat in Africa and Asia?

Since 2008, the United Nations program for Reducing Emissions from Deforestation and Forest Degradation (REDD) has improved the capac-ity of developing countries to assess and monitor the scope of their for-est cover and provided economic incentives for activities that preserve forests and store carbon.[181] Incorporating REDD principles into a bind-ing international agreement to address climate change—for example, by allowing industrialized nations to offset their carbon footprint by donat-ing money towards forest conservation projects—would likely have a significant impact on the economics that currently motivate destructive activities like land conversion for palm oil plantations and other resource extraction.

The U.S. must also take action at the national level to address the American role in resource consumption that is pushing great apes to the brink of extinction. All great apes are listed as endangered under the ESA, which (along with international restrictions under CITES) protects them from unsustainable trade, but the ESA does not extend extrater-ritorially to directly protect wild apes from being killed or their habitats destroyed.[182] In 2000, Congress passed the Great Ape Conservation Act to fund programs for increased enforcement capacity to protect habi-tat, minimize poaching and trafficking, and to increase public awareness and educate communities within African and Asian range states on the

---

180. CITES, *Great Apes*, https://www.cites.org/eng/prog/ape.php.
181. *See* United Nations REDD Programme, http://www.un-redd.org/.
182. 50 C.F.R. § 17.11; 16 U.S.C. § 1538. Note that most ape range states already have enacted laws prohibiting the killing of great apes, but such laws are often not properly enforced.

threats to great ape survival.[183] While these conservation laws are imperative, less traditional strategies are also needed to address this conservation
crisis.

Federal law can operate to the benefit of great apes through corporate
reform. For example, the Dodd-Frank Act of 2010 required manufacturers to certify that their purchases of potential "conflict minerals" (and
the metals smelted from them) do not come from sources involved in
funding war crimes and human rights abuses in the DRC.[184] That simple
reporting requirement has had a significant impact on the coltan market
to the benefit of great apes, although it has been criticized as being overly
restrictive.[185]

Another strategy that could significantly impact the U.S. consumption of products produced through destruction of great ape habitats is
federal labeling and advertising law. For example, regulations promulgated pursuant to the federal Food, Drug, and Cosmetic Act require that
for packaged food, the ingredient list must include each individual oil
ingredient "declared by its specific common or usual name."[186] However,
the rate of compliance with this requirement is not clear and the Food
and Drug Administration does not require premarket approval of ingredient lists to ensure compliance.[187] Currently, there are no parallel federal labeling requirements for disclosing palm oil on cosmetic packages,
allowing palm oil to be labeled simply as vegetable oil.[188] Further, derivatives of palm oil (such as Vitamin A palmitate) and other undecipherable
chemical components found in palm oil (such as sodium laureth sulfate
and stearic acid) can be found on ingredient lists for food, cosmetics,

---

183. U.S. Fish and Wildlife Service, *Great Ape Conservation Fund*, http://www.fws.gov/international
/wildlife-without-borders/great-ape-conservation-fund.html.

184. U.S. Securities and Exchange Commission, *Disclosing the Use of Conflict Minerals*, http://
www.sec.gov/News/Article/Detail/Article/1365171562058.

185. Sudarsan Raghavan, *How a Well-Intentioned U.S. Law Left Congolese Miners Jobless*,
WASHINGTON POST (Nov. 30, 2014), https://www.washingtonpost.com/world/africa/how-a
-well-intentioned-us-law-left-congolese-miners-jobless/2014/11/30/14b5924e-69d3-11e4-9fb4
-a622dae742a2_story.html.

186. 21 C.F.R. § 101.4(b)(14).

187. As evidenced through warning letters issued by the FDA, multiple manufacturers have failed
to properly label palm oil on food ingredient lists in recent years. *See* http://www.fda.gov/iceci/
enforcementactions/warningletters/.

188. *Compare* 21 C.F.R. § 701.3 *with* 21 C.F.R. § 101.4(b)(14).

and household products.[189] Thus, it is nearly impossible for consumers to have confidence that the food or personal care products they purchase are sourced without contributing to deforestation of orangutan habitat (unless the company has explicitly adopted a policy to such extent).[190]

Moreover, it is generally prohibited under federal law for well-intentioned companies to make clear on the front of a package that food products do not contain any palm oil. In the 1980s the American Soybean Association petitioned the U.S. Food and Drug Administration to require that food products be explicitly labeled as containing palm oil as a source of saturated fat.[191] That campaign appears to have been largely motivated by protecting the profit margins of domestic companies by making it less desirable to include imported oils rather than raising awareness about the environmental implications of palm oil production. While the FDA never adopted such a requirement, after Congress adopted the Nutrition Labeling and Education Act of 1990, the FDA adopted regulations generally prohibiting products from being advertised as containing "no palm oil" (reasoning that such a claim suggests, perhaps misleadingly, that the product is low in saturated fat).[192] These types of "implied nutrient content claims" can now only be used if the agency specifically approves them before use.[193]

Thus, under current U.S. law it is difficult for food companies to proactively advertise that their products do not contain palm oil, and it is easy for personal care product manufacturers to obscure the environmental, conservation, and animal welfare impacts of ingredients in

---

189. World Wildlife Fund, *Which Everyday Products Contain Palm Oil?*, http://www.worldwildlife.org/pages/which-everyday-products-contain-palm-oil.

190. *See, e.g.,* Dr. Bronner's, *Palm Oil from Ghana*, https://www.drbronner.com/ingredients/fair-trade-around-the-world/palm-oil/.

191. Sonja Hillgreen, *On the Farm Front*, UPI (April 15, 1988), http://www.upi.com/Archives/1988/04/15/ON-THE-FARM-FRONT/3386577080000/; Food Product Design, *The Truth about Palm Oil*, http://www.foodproductdesign.com/bgpl/FPDamerpalm6.pdf.

192. 56 Fed. Reg. 60421, 60423 (Nov. 27, 1991). *But see William J. Moxley v. Hertz*, 216 U.S. 344, 350 (1910) (in the context of a dispute about whether adding palm oil to oleomargarine constitutes artificial coloring, the Supreme Court noted that "Palm oil is perfectly wholesome, is readily digested, and has long been used as an article of food in countries where it is produced. Palm oil was successfully employed in oleomargarine prior to May, 1902, and is a proper constituent of oleomargarine.").

193. 21 C.F.R. § 101.69.

cosmetics and household cleaners. Congress could take action, whether through improved labeling requirements or financial reporting mandates, to greatly improve transparency over the use of palm oil and palm oil derivatives in products. However, such legislation would need to be drafted carefully so that it did not discriminate against Indonesian and Malaysian oil producers (in order to defend against any potential challenge before the World Trade Organization, as happened with the U.S. effort to label tuna as dolphin-safe and has recently been suggested in the context of a proposed tax on palm oil in France).[194] If such reform was achieved, educated consumers could shape the market to decrease demand for palm oil produced through deforestation and the attendant animal cruelty.

~

Great ape populations have suffered dramatically in the last century, primarily as a result of human population growth and the environmental destruction inherent in facilitating a modern consumer lifestyle for billions of people in America, China, and other major economies. In order to ensure that great apes are conserved for future generations, it is imperative that the United States take action to address its direct and indirect impacts on ape habitat, both through international cooperation and domestic demand reduction efforts.

194. World Trade Organization, *United States—Measures Concerning the Importation, Marketing and Sale of Tuna and Tuna Products*, https://www.wto.org/english/tratop_e/dispu_e/cases_e/ds381_e.htm. *See also* Reuters, *French Assembly Adopts Softer Tax on Palm Oil Used in Food* (March 18, 2016), http://uk.reuters.com/article/france-palmoil-idUKL5N16P500; Reuters, *French Parliament Rejects New Palm Oil Tax Proposal* (Oct. 27, 2016), http://uk.reuters.com/article/environment-palmoil-tax-idUKL8N1CX4G7.

2

The Tragedy of Trade

Peter LaFontaine

~

iophilia, as the naturalist E. O. Wilson described it, is the phenom-
enon of life connecting to life, in particular of humans' inherent
feeling of connection to other species. Biophilia helps explain why a
seventh grader in Atlanta can tell you that his favorite animal is a Ben-
gal tiger, and why the recent discovery of water on Mars made grown
adults celebrate in a NASA robotics center thirty-five million miles away.
Our affinity with the rest of the natural universe is not something that
national borders, or even atmospheres, can constrain, and so it stands to
reason that we often seek to protect imperiled species far from our homes.
In the last century this impulse has helped to inform our legal systems,
resulting in international wildlife conservation treaties and domestic laws
that safeguard animals irrespective of geopolitical proximity.

Biophilia has a dark side; however, and many creatures that elicit
our wonder have also suffered the consequences of those most human of
impulses—greed and materialism.

As a case study in these concepts, we examine how Americans have
sought to protect, and to possess, one of this planet's most iconic animals:

the African elephant. Our defensive efforts have not always been effective, nor have they always been consistent, but in the last forty years U.S. citizens and regulators have shouldered a considerable responsibility to help shield the planet's largest land animal from extinction, and we have made considerable headway toward this goal. These successes, however, are seriously threatened by a new wave of poaching, precipitating weighty legal and policy decisions not just in the United States but around the globe.

North America, of course, is not the decisive battleground in this fight to save the elephant. African environmental agencies and, more immediately, local wildlife rangers are on the front lines, in the true sense of that term, and African communities suffer costs of poaching that few Americans will ever experience. However, this is not at odds with the concept of biophilia as a driving force; indeed, both the modern ecotourism economy and traditional ways of life are crucial exemplars of it. If contemporary Africa is to protect the assets of the old system and reap the benefits of the new one, it must remain a continent with space for both humans and wildlife.

It is ultimately the success or failure of officials and citizens from South Africa to Kenya (and even China and Thailand) that will determine whether elephants have a place in the wild in the decades ahead. Nonetheless, American laws and policies can help to advance this cause. We owe it to our planet and its inhabitants to make that effort.

Illegal Wildlife Trade: An Overview

Between fossil fuel–driven climate change on the one hand, and agricultural and industrial takeovers of wildlife habitat on the other, it is easy to recognize that Earth has become a difficult place to live for most nonhuman animals. Another driver of extinction, though, pulses below most people's radar: global commerce. Trade in exotic wildlife products is not new—Macbeth's three witches presumably did not scavenge a tiger's entrails in the Scottish lowlands—but it has reached colossal volumes in the last century and can aptly be listed alongside the other major threats to biodiversity.

Just how colossal? The U.S. government estimates the illegal wildlife trade to be worth about seven to ten billion dollars each year—not counting the profits from unreported and unregulated fishing, which could push that figure as high as $33 billion (and other sources report much higher ceilings).[1] This places wildlife trafficking in rarified criminal air, ranking behind only narcotics, counterfeiting, and human trafficking on the list of the most lucrative illegal activities.[2] The legal wildlife trade is far higher; according to the monitoring organization TRAFFIC, legal commerce was worth ten times that amount, $323 billion in 2009.[3]

Regardless of their legal status, nonnative wildlife products (i.e., parts or derivatives from an animal from another part of the world) are bought and sold in every country on Earth and for just about every use a person could imagine: culinary, artistic, medicinal, sartorial, religious, and more.[4] Vietnamese apothecaries grind rhinoceros horns into tea for an (unfounded) catchall cure for everything from hangovers to cancer. Bolivian macaws and iguanas are taken from the rainforests to become suburban pets in Milwaukee. Chinese entrepreneurs steep tiger bones in wine for a pricey aphrodisiac. French craftsmen turn tortoise shells into combs and narwhal tusks into cane handles. Baboon meat and sturgeon roe grace dinner plates in Cameroon and Belarus. African elephant ivory is turned into crucifixes for Filipino priests and bangles for Japanese fashionistas. Practically any species is available for the right price, and as trade increasingly moves online in the new millennium, the prospective audience continues to expand exponentially. You would be hard-pressed to find a bleaker outgrowth of globalization: "medicines" that save no one,

---

1. *See* Lyanna Sun Weiler & Pervaze A. Sheikh, Cong. Research Serv., RL34395, International Illegal Trade in Wildlife: Threats and U.S. Policy (2013).
2. *See* Marina Ratchford et al., International Fund for Animal Welfare, Criminal Nature: The Global Security Implications of the Illegal Wildlife Trade 4 (2013).
3. TRAFFIC. http://www.traffic.org/trade (last visited Dec. 1, 2015).
4. What is "legal" and what is "illegal" is determined by an (increasingly thorny) calculus of domestic and international interests. Common sense would argue for weighting *sustainability* heavily in this equation—that is, that governments should set wildlife trade policy based on whether ecosystems can bear the costs. This is rarely the case in the real world, and sustainability concerns rarely determine policy outcomes, even in the United States, which is generally considered ahead of the pack in this regard. Animal welfare concerns play a similarly underwhelming role in policy making. This means that there can be similar impacts from legal and illegal wildlife trade, at least as it pertains to environmental costs.

a pet trade that picks the forests clean, carved ivory elephants on mantel-pieces taking the place of living ones on the plains. But it is globalization all the same, a sector worth billions of dollars.

With so much money at stake, governments are beginning to pay attention. Partly, this is due to the emergence of a new class of traf-ficker, one with strong ties to organized criminal syndicates and mili-tant groups, and the recognition that poaching undermines development goals by fostering corruption, criminality, and unsustainable resource extraction. Partly, though, it also appears to be a genuine acknowledg-ment of the existential threat poaching now poses to biodiversity—the rich variety of life on Earth. Whatever the motivation, numerous bodies ranging from the European Union to the G-8 to the United Nations Security Council have pledged to help stamp out the crisis. The U.S. federal administration under President Obama made the poaching issue a centerpiece of its environmental agenda, allocating millions of dollars to antipoaching efforts and promising policy changes at home and abroad. In international law, CITES (the Convention on International Trade of Endangered Species of Flora and Fauna)[5] continues to wield significant influence in this sphere, four decades after its inception. The 181 member countries of this international accord use CITES as a forum to regulate cross-border trade in thousands of species (and their parts and products), and calls grow stronger by the month for the Convention to increase protections for hard-hit animals like elephants and rhinos.

It is too soon to tell whether the various action plans and commitments will be enough to salvage an ever-worsening situation, but this high-level attention is long overdue and should help tilt the balance against traffick-ers and poachers, who until recently could operate far from the spotlight of law enforcement agencies and with relative impunity.

Another major tool that may successfully slow the market for exotic animal parts is the use of market pressure at the consumer level, by reduc-

---

5. "CITES (the Convention on International Trade in Endangered Species of Wild Fauna and Flora) is an international agreement between governments. Its aim is to ensure that international trade in specimens of wild animals and plants does not threaten their survival." CONVENTION ON INTERNATIONAL TRADE IN ENDANGERED SPECIES OF WILD FAUNA AND FLORA, http://www.cites.org/eng/disc/ what.php (last visited July 10, 2016). See page XX of this chapter for further description of CITES workings.

ing the demand for these products in the first place. Regardless of the laws on the books, the consumer appetite for exotic species is a force to be reckoned with, and conservation groups are working feverishly to create wide-ranging public education campaigns that dispel the myths about exotic species and drive home the message that, for many of these animals, time is running out. When the market signals that demand has dried up, the incentive to poach dries up with it.

Case Study: African Elephants

One could be excused for forgetting that your garden variety slug or bullfrog is a wonder of creation, but it takes a cold soul to look at an African elephant without being captivated. It is social, intelligent, expressive, and imposing, drawing our attention not just with its massive body but also with a prehensile trunk, giant ears, and thick tusks rooted solidly in the upper jaw. Those tusks, though, have more admirers than elephants can afford. Since around the time *Homo sapiens* first picked up rocks and sharp sticks, we have been using them to hunt elephants and their forebears—mammoths and perhaps also mastodons—leaving the planet with Neolithic ivory carvings and, as an unfortunate side effect, no more mammoths or mastodons.[6]

Such coordinated pack hunting of large animals is likely one of the things that spurred the human brain's great leap forward, building the capacity for group communication and strategy, but our ancestors' subsequent advances in agriculture and animal domestication may have helped spare elephants the fate of their older pachyderm relatives. As their most dangerous predator moved on to different food sources, elephants maintained strongholds in eastern, central, and southern Africa (*Loxodonta africana* on the savannahs and *Loxodonta cyclotis* in the central forests) and Southeast Asia (*Elephas maximus*), and rough estimates (the only kind, surprisingly for a creature of this size)[7] put the total African

---

6. Climate change was another probable factor in these extinctions.
7. Even the modern era, aerial observations and dung counts place the current "official" estimate between 420,000 and 650,000—demonstrating the difficulty of obtaining an accurate estimate—and some experts say the total population is lower. A new, more comprehensive "Great Elephant Census" is currently underway to provide a closer estimate.

elephant population at around ten million at the turn of the twentieth century.[8] Alongside the agricultural revolution, however, concomitant advances in human weapons technology upgraded the hominid arsenal from flint-tipped spears to poisoned arrows to, eventually, mass-produced semiautomatic 30-round firearms. The new hunting technology would enable people to slaughter elephants on a previously undreamt of scale.

The Poaching Waves

Ivory, being visually attractive and easy to carve, has been a favorite material of craftsmen since humans' first primitive whittlings, and before the development of plastics and other synthetic replacements, ivory was not just a medium for artists, it was a main component in everything from dice to billiard balls, combs to piano keys. As a result, demand for elephant tusks has been widespread around the globe for eons. Africa and Southeast Asia are the longest-standing hubs of commerce, but there has been trade in Japan and China for hundreds of years, and ivory products gained eventual ubiquity in Europe and the United States in just the last few centuries.

Long after newer materials displaced the use of ivory for more commonplace items, consumers have sought luxury goods for which ivory was used, such as jewelry and ornately carved statues. Consumer demand, coupled with growing access to international markets, led to poachers targeting West, Central, and East African elephant populations on a broad scale in the 1970s, ultimately outstripping the species' capacity to reproduce.

"Poaching" is the unsanctioned hunting of animals that belong to another person or entity. As the colonial era in Africa gave way to self-rule in many countries, the concept of state ownership of natural resources, including wildlife populations, was codified across the continent. Like many wildlife species, elephants are wide-ranging and do not respect national boundaries, but they are still considered the property of whichever government's territory they happen to be passing through. The defi-

---

8. *Great Elephant Census: A Paul G. Allen Project, Conservation,* http://www.greatelephantcensus .com/ background-on-conservation/ (last visited July 10, 2016).

nition of poaching, therefore, is broad enough to encompass the acts of both the local villager who illegally hunts an elephant for its meat, as well as the profiteer whose sole targets are an elephant's tusks.

By the mid-1980s, decimated by the poaching wave of the last fifteen years, a record low of around 300,000 African elephants remained.[9] Habitat loss, the bushmeat trade, and retaliatory killings (elephants are notorious crop raiders) were factors in this plummet, but the overwhelming majority of these deaths were ivory-driven.[10]

Traders heavily targeted other exotic species during this period as well, and the international poaching crisis that lasted through the 1970s and 1980s had serious consequences for humans as well as animals: Poachers killed hundreds, if not thousands, of wildlife rangers in the line of duty during these decades,[11] and ivory trafficking (given the profits involved) went hand in hand with corruption in many range states and transit nations.[12] Both conservation and governance concerns led CITES parties to enact a ban, in 1990,[13] on international trade in most African elephant ivory.[14]

This ban was largely successful in stemming the tide of poaching, for a time. The CITES member nations soon fatally undermined this success by sanctioning two major ivory stockpile sales—in 1999 and 2009—from four countries in southern Africa to buyers in China and Japan, a decision that stimulated consumer demand, blurred the lines of legality,

---

9. *See* UNEP, CITES, IUCN & TRAFFIC, Elephants in the Dust: The African Elephant Crisis 22 (Christian Nellemann et al. eds., 2013) [hereinafter UNEP et al., Elephants in the Dust].

10. *See id.* at 41. Asian elephants also face poaching pressure, but to a lesser extent than African elephants; habitat loss and other factors seem to be bigger threats to *Elephas maximus. See id.* at 27.

11. *See, e.g.*, Laurel Neme, *For Rangers on the Front Lines of Anti-Poaching Wars, Daily Trauma*, Nat'l Geo. (June 27, 2014), *available at* http://news.nationalgeographic.com/news/2014/06/140627-congo-virunga-wildlife-rangers-elephants-rhinos-poaching/.

12. Range states are countries where a given animal lives; transit nations are countries through which shipments of those animals pass on their way to final markets, or "destination countries."*See* U.N. Off. on Drugs and Crime, *World Wildlife Crime Report: Trafficking in protected species* 19–21 (2016).

13. U.S. Fish & Wildlife Serv., *CITES & Elephants: What is the "global ban" on ivory trade?* (2013), https://www.fws.gov/le/pdf/CITES-and-Elephant-Conservation.pdf.

14. As described in the previous section, CITES, the Convention on International Trade in Endangered Species of Flora and Fauna, is a 181-member multilateral treaty that oversees its eponymous mandate.

and ultimately cracked the floodgates for another catastrophic wave of poaching.[15] Since the second stockpile sale was put in motion, poaching and smuggling rates have climbed once more to levels not seen since the 1990 ban.[16]

Small-scale operators carried out most of the first killing surge in the 1970s and 1980s, but the current market demand has attracted a far more dangerous element to the poaching business: Militant groups, international criminal syndicates, and even terrorist groups like the Lord's Resistance Army and the Sudanese Janjaweed militias occupy central roles in the supply chain. These groups use ivory sales and related industrial-scale activities like bushmeat trafficking and illicit charcoal production to finance their activities.[17] The home-grown element has not gone away—elephant poaching is still a compelling option for many villagers, herdsmen, and other locals, particularly in poverty-stricken regions—but the industry is increasingly dominated by well-connected expatriate actors with semiautomatic rifles, cyanide (commonly used in the process of mining precious metals, repurposed to poison wildlife watering holes), and even some documented cases of rocket launchers and assault helicopters, possibly in coordination with government troops.[18] Traffickers move ivory across oceans in shipping containers by the ton, or in suitcases packed full of sawn-down tusks.[19] It costs little to pay a port inspector to look the other way, and easy money makes corruption inevitable, up and

---

15. *See* Katarzyna Nowak, *Opinion: Irrelevant, Illogical, and Illegal - 24 Experts Respond to Arguments Supporting Legalization of the Ivory Trade,* NAT'L GEO.: A VOICE FOR ELEPHANTS (Oct. 2, 2014), http://voices. nationalgeographic.com/2014/10/02/opinion-irrelevant-illogical-and-illegal -24-experts-respond-to-arguments-supporting-legalization-of-the-ivory-trade/.

16. UNEP ET AL., ELEPHANTS IN THE DUST, *supra* note 9, at 43.

17. UNEP & INTERPOL, THE ENVTL. CRIME CRISIS: THREATS TO SUSTAINABLE DEV. FROM ILLEGAL EXPLOITATION AND TRADE IN WILDLIFE AND FOREST RESOURCES 8, 23, 48–51 (Christian Nellemann et al. eds., 2014)

18. *See, e.g.,* Jeffrey Gettleman, *Elephants Dying in Epic Frenzy as Ivory Fuels Wars and Profits,* N.Y. TIMES, Sept. 4, 2012, at A1; *see also* Associated Press, *In Congo Park, Armed Groups Hunt Elephants,* CHI. TRIB. (Nov. 8, 2015), http://www.chicagotribune.com/news/nationworld/ct-congo -elephants-20151108-story.html.

19. *See* Tom Milliken, *Illegal Trade in Ivory and Rhino Horn: As Assessment to Improve Law Enforcement under the Wildlife TRAPS Project* 8 (2014), https://www.usaid.gov/sites/default/files/ documents/1865/W-TRAPS-Elephant-Rhino-report.pdf.

down the line of command.[20] Few elephant range states and ivory transit nations have avoided allegations of widespread (and often upper-echelon) malfeasance, with near-monthly episodes of ivory stockpiles vanishing from "secure" police warehouses, bribery charges being leveled against top officials, or even smuggling by diplomatic envoys. The ongoing modernization of many African countries bears related ecological costs, too, as rapidly expanding infrastructure enables poachers to access previously roadless regions.

As habitat for elephants and other fauna disappears at record rates, intense poaching adds an immediate and acute threat to the near-term survival of the species itself. Scientists believe that nearly two-thirds of central Africa's forest elephant population disappeared between 2002 and 2011,[21] and overall, the continent-wide elephant population is estimated to be perhaps 420,000.[22] More governments are taking action in response to public outrage at this loss, but the challenges—not least, some officials' stake in poaching profits—make the path to reform a difficult one. It is not a fight that can be won in Africa alone. Experts agree that policy makers must target all three elements of the ivory trade: consumption, trafficking, and poaching. Our window to prevent the worst consequences is closing fast.

The U.S. Market for Ivory

The United States has long been a major player in the ivory trade, and is still one of the world's largest overall markets. In the 1800s, manufacturers in single-industry towns like Ivoryton, Connecticut, and independent craftsmen across the country, imported hundreds of tons of tusks to churn out piano keyboards, statuary, furniture knobs, gun handles, and many other products. It is impossible to accurately quantify the total amount of ivory in the U.S., but a seminal 2008 report found more than

20. *See, e.g.,* Heidi Vogt, *Elephants in Danger: How Kenya's Port of Mombasa Became the World's Hub for Ivory Smuggling,* WALL ST. J. (Nov. 18, 2015), http://www.wsj.com/articles/kenyan -port-is-hub-for-illicit-ivory-trade-1447720944.
21. UNEP ET AL., ELEPHANTS IN THE DUST, *supra* note 9, at 33.
22. *Id.* at 6.

24,000 items for sale in just sixteen American cities.[23] Likewise, it is
hard to say how much of that inventory is illegal, though federal agents
point to major recent seizures in Philadelphia, Chicago, and New York as
emblematic of ongoing American involvement in the trade.[24] Porous U.S.
borders have long allowed traffickers an easy path to American consumers. INTERPOL, the global police agency, estimates that customs and
border agents only interdict about ten percent of all smuggled goods;[25]
the remaining ninety percent make their way into the domestic market.
In the case of the United States, which until recently did not routinely
enforce documentation requirements for ivory products, illegally smuggled ivory that escaped notice at the border had been de facto legal to sell
once it was on store shelves. Put another way, because American ivory sellers were never been required to document their item's legality at the point
of sale, law enforcement agents bore a formidable burden of proof to show
otherwise, and as a result, rarely bothered to pursue any but the most
suspicious sales. Ivory from a hundred years ago sits on shelves next to
carvings from recently poached elephants, with no surefire way to tell the
two apart except expensive and destructive DNA testing. This "laundering" process is an ongoing concern: An investigation by the International
Fund for Animal Welfare (IFAW) estimated that in 2013–2014 alone
nearly 4,000 illegal elephant items may have been imported into the U.S.
and almost 900 were exported.[26] In just one state, California, researchers for the Natural Resources Defense Council found that around fifty
percent of the ivory items for sale appeared to be recently manufactured.[27]
Seemingly reputable businesses are no stranger to the game, either. In
2016 Jonathan Chait, an executive at I.M. Chait Gallery, a prominent
Beverly Hills auction house, pled guilty to federal charges of selling a

23. Daniel Stiles & Esmond Martin, *The USA's Ivory Markets—how much a threat to elephants?*
45 PACHYDERM J. 67, 71 (July 2008–June 2009).
24. *See* Endangered and Threatened Wildlife and Plants; Revision of the Section 4(d) Rule for the
African Elephant (*Loxodonta africana*), 80 Fed. Reg. 145 (proposed July 29, 2015) (to be codified
at 50 C.F.R. pt. 15).
25. Bryan Christy, *Blood Ivory*, NAT'L GEO.: A VOICE FOR ELEPHANTS (October 2012), *available
at* http://ngm.nationalgeographic.com/2012/10/ivory/christy-text.
26. Beth Allgood, Marina Ratchford, & Peter LaFontaine. *U.S. Ivory Trade: Can a Crackdown on
Trafficking Save the Last Titan?* 20(1) ANIMAL LAW 27–78 (2013).
27. *See* Daniel Stiles, *Elephant Ivory Trafficking in California, USA* 15 (2015), http://docs.nrdc.org/
wildlife/files/wil_15010601a.pdf.

million dollars' worth of illegal ivory, rhino horn, and corals. Chait had helped customers smuggle products to China and elsewhere, falsifying customs forms to mask the true nature of the products. Similar examples abound, making it clear that the money—likely millions of dollars annually—is there for anyone willing to break the rules. It is also there for those simply willing to look the other way: A 2015 IFAW "snapshot" survey of the online ivory trade in Hawaii found $1.22 million worth of products for sale, almost none with adequate documentation that they had been legally imported.[28] An investigation of ivory sales within the U.S. auction industry, published by IFAW in 2014, reached similar conclusions about the paucity of documentation (perhaps not incidentally, the I.M. Chait Gallery had been a main subject of this report),[29] as did a 2015 IFAW investigation of the online classified advertising giant Craigs list.org, which found almost $1.5 million in ivory and related items in just a small subset of postings, nearly all undocumented.[30]

In addition to being an overactive market for the purchase of legal and illegal wildlife parts, the U.S. is also home to more trophy hunters than any other country. After the Civil War, intrepid Great White Hunters began to set out en masse from ports in New York and Boston, bound for Africa; just-retired President Teddy Roosevelt made the passage in 1909 and brought back more than ten thousand subjects of the animal kingdom, stuffed and mounted, including a female *Loxodonta* with ample tusks that has been part of the central display in New York City's American Museum of Natural History ever since.

Trophy hunting has, if anything, increased in popularity since then: Between 2003 and 2012, American hunters imported approximately 7,500 dead African elephants as trophies of successful hunts—almost

---

28. Peter LaFontaine et al., Int'l Fund for Animal Welfare, *An Investigation of Hawai'i's Online Ivory Trade* 3, 10 (2016), http://www.ifaw.org/sites/default/files/IFAW-2016-Hawaii-Market-Report.pdf.

29. Int'l Fund for Animal Welfare, *Bidding Against Survival: the Elephant Poaching Crisis and the Role of Auctions in the U.S. Ivory Market* 33 (2014), http://www.ifaw.org/sites/default/files/IFAW-Ivory-Auctions-bidding-against-survival-aug-2014_0.pdf [hereinafter IFAW, *Bidding Against Survival*].

30. *See* Int'l Fund for Animal Welfare, *Elephant vs. Mouse: An Investigation of the Ivory Trade on Craigslist* 13 (2015), http://www.ifaw.org/sites/default/files/IFAW-craigslist-ivory-report-2015.pdf.

half the global total in that period.[31] Groups like the Dallas Safari Club and Safari Club International boast many thousands of paying members and wield considerable political influence.

Limiting Illegal Trade with American Laws

The Endangered Species Act

Roosevelt, a man of contradictions, is also rightly known as one of the great American conservationists; among other accomplishments he is considered responsible for establishing the National Wildlife Refuge system[32] in 1903, in part to protect habitat for the western hemisphere's migratory birds. Three years earlier his predecessor, William McKinley, had signed a key early environmental law—the Lacey Act—that enabled the federal government to enforce the wildlife protection laws of individual states and other nations.[33] The refuge system and the Lacey Act were two of the United States' first forays into environmental protection, but it would be a full seven decades before the Endangered Species Act of 1973 (ESA) boosted safeguards for foreign species once more.[34] For those unfamiliar with the ESA, it is difficult to overstate just how valuable this law has been in protecting wildlife and raising awareness of the problems facing species threatened by human encroachment and exploitation. Widely considered the planet's premier conservation law, the ESA gives the U.S. Fish and Wildlife Service (USFWS, or simply "the Service") and the National Marine Fisheries Service (NMFS) wide-ranging powers to protect "threatened" and "endangered"[35] species, as well as their "critical

---

31. *See* Int'l Fund for Animal Welfare & Humane Soc'y of U.S., Petition to the Secretary of the Interior to list the African Elephant (Loxodonta Africana) as Endangered Pursuant to the Endangered Species Act 68 (2015) [hereinafter IFAW/HSUS ESA Petition].

32. The National Wildlife Refuge system is a division of the Department of the Interior's U.S. Fish and Wildlife Service. It is a network of habitats for thousands of species, including threatened and endangered plants and animals, provides recreational activities for visitors, and helps protect the environment.

33. *See* Lacey Act, 16 U.S.C. §§ 3371–3378 (1900).

34. *See* Endangered Species Act of 1973, 16 U.S.C. § 1531 *et seq.*

35. These terms correspond to different levels of extinction threats, and to the legal protections afforded as a result. Endangered species are granted more protections than threatened species, as the latter are subject to reduction in the protections otherwise provided to endangered species.

habitat" on American soil, and to issue other regulations that minimize the harmful ecological impacts of human activities.

The ESA is often credited with rescuing humpback whales, bald eagles, and hundreds of other species from looming extinction, and experts believe that the Act's deterrent effect has saved countless others from reaching that point.[36] Unlike whales or eagles, the United States' wild elephant population is approximately zero, and the Service's legal jurisdiction does not reach far enough to confront poachers directly.[37] But the other two elements of the ivory trade—trafficking and consumer demand—fall well within these parameters.[38] The ESA provides a means of addressing both by shutting off avenues for illegal shipments and U.S. sales and by stigmatizing ivory as an ignoble product.[39]

It did not take long for the federal government to leverage this crucial law in support of elephants. Three years after the ESA's enactment, in 1976, the USFWS listed the Asian elephant as endangered under the ESA, and in 1978 listed the African elephant as threatened. These decisions were not simply acknowledgments of the species' perilous situation; they also confirmed the idea that ivory purchases by American consumers were helping to drive elephant poaching, and that trade should be limited in response.

---

36. *See* Eva Drinkhouse, *The Endangered Species Act Under Attack: Relentless Riders Rise Again*, LEAGUE OF CONSERVATION VOTERS BLOG (July 11, 2016), http://www.lcv.org/media/blog/the-endangered-species-act.html.

37. The USFWS does have attachés stationed in several African countries to assist local governments with wildlife crime prevention activities, including antipoaching initiatives. All elephants in U.S. zoos, circuses, and sanctuaries are regulated under the U.S. Animal Welfare Act, and some are also covered by the ESA.

38. The ESA is not the only federal law that allows the U.S. government to influence foreign practices. For example, although not to date utilized for elephants, Section 8 of the Fishermen's Protective Act (P.L. 92-219 (85 Stat. 786)), commonly known as the Pelly Amendment, requires the Secretary of Commerce to report to the President when informed of a foreign nation's depletion of an international fishery conservation program. The President, in turn, would authorize the Secretary of the Treasury to prohibit the importation of that country's fish products. In 1978, the Pelly Amendment was expanded from importing certain fish to embargoing foreign wildlife products violating international wildlife conservation programs. The Pelly Amendment has been used to impose sanctions on Taiwan (in 1994) to hold that nation's government accountable for its failure to safeguard rhinos from poaching.

39. This concept cuts both ways: while many consumers strenuously avoid buying products that come from imperiled species, the allure of scarcity may make these same products attractive to less scrupulous shoppers.

According African elephants threatened status enabled the Service to issue a "special rule" to govern the amount and type of legal trade in elephant specimens, both living and dead. The ESA states that special rules must be "necessary and advisable to provide for the conservation of such species."[40] This provision gives the Service some flexibility to narrowly tailor protections for threatened species, as opposed to implementing the broad (and mandatory) restrictions on trade, hunting, and similar activities that are required for endangered species like Asian elephants. In practice, however, the Service claims it has used special rules to "streamline the regulatory process for minor impacts," as an anodyne USFWS factsheet puts it, not necessarily to maximize conservation benefits.[41] This plays out in interesting and occasionally counterintuitive ways. For example, in the case of the 1978[42] special rule for African elephants, Roosevelt's favorite pastime—trophy hunting—was left basically unchecked, under the theory that hunting fees "incentivize" local African communities to protect elephants. Anti–trophy hunting advocates, on the other hand, argue that sport hunting can be disastrous for African elephant herds. Among other problems, hunting targets the biggest and most mature individuals; killing even a single elephant disrupts family bonds; and U.S. trophy hunters in Africa can perpetuate neocolonial conservation practices by reserving game animals and habitat for exclusive use by wealthy foreign hunters, with often limited economic benefits for the communities that live there.[43] More recently, the Service has modified their broad pro-trophy position by restricting elephant trophy imports from all but a few countries, an acknowledgment that factors out of the Service's control, such as shoddy management and corruption in some foreign wildlife management agencies, have compromised trophy hunting programs in

---

40. 16 U.S.C. § 1533(d) (2012).

41. U.S. FISH & WILDLIFE SERV., THE ENDANGERED SPECIES ACT SPECIAL RULES: QUESTIONS AND ANSWERS (2014), *available at* https://www.fws.gov/mountain-prairie/factsheets/ESA%20 SpecialRules%20Factsheet_020714.pdf [hereinafter USFWS, ENDANGERED SPECIES ACT].

42. The Service would slightly amend the special rule in 1982, 1992 and more significantly in 2014.

43. Economists at Large, *The $200 Million Question: How Much Does Trophy Hunting Really Contribute to African Communities?* (2013), http://www.ifaw.org/sites/default/files/Ecolarge -2013-200m-question.pdf.

places like Tanzania and Zimbabwe and contributed to the rapid decline of elephant populations there.[44]

While the Service pursued remedies through the ESA, the CITES parties began to make paper progress at the international level as well. The year prior to the USFWS threatened listing of African elephants in 1978, the CITES parties voted to transfer African elephants from Appendix III to the more-protective Appendix II. Similar to the ESA's "threatened" and "endangered" lists, the CITES "Appendix" structure imposes varying degrees of trade restrictions on wildlife. Species listed under Appendix I (the most highly threatened) are only allowed to be traded internationally under exceptional circumstances; Appendix II species may be traded so long as such trade does not detrimentally impact their survival; and trade in Appendix III species is very lightly controlled. These rules are primarily enforced through a permit system for imports and exports, and through a system of review and potential sanctions imposed by the CITES member parties. In the case of African elephants (at the time listed under Appendix II), this system meant that if an seller or shipper wanted to move ivory on the international market, they needed a CITES export certificate verifying that "the item involved was taken legally and that its export is not detrimental to the survival of the species," as determined by each range state's national scientific and management authorities.[45]

The ESA is the United States' domestic implementing legislation for its CITES obligations, and as a result, the 1978 USFWS special rule meant that ivory shipments to the United States must be accompanied by a CITES export certificate. With such assurances, the Service reasoned, Americans would not be responsible for any further damage to the species:

The Service is aware that there have been questions regarding the validity and substance of some export permits issued relative

---

44. U.S. Fish & Wildlife Serv., *Importation of Elephant Hunting Trophies Taken in Tanzania and Zimbabwe in 2015 and Beyond* (July 10, 2015), http://www.fws.gov/international/pdf/questions-and-answers-suspension-of-elephant-sport-hunted-trophies.pdf.
45. CITES, App. I, Art. III, § 3(a).

to the Convention. At this time, however, there is no basis for restricting the importation of elephant products from any current or future Convention member, so long as the provisions of the regulations are followed. The Service considers that the pledges made by a sovereign nation, when entering into an agreement with fellow countries for the common good of all, are not to be taken lightly, and that any member nation must be assumed to intend to comply fully with the obligations imposed by Article IV and the other portions of the Convention.[46]

As described earlier, despite being listed under both CITES Appendix II (with the attendant "pledges made by sovereign nations") and the ESA, *Loxodonta* was hit incredibly hard by poachers in the 1970s and 1980s. Conservationists warned that the status quo was failing, miserably, to limit trafficking enough to truly protect the species.[47] More action was urgently required.

The African Elephant Conservation Act

The U.S. Congress responded by passing the African Elephant Conservation Act (AfECA) in 1988, which added an additional layer of regulation to ivory imports and exports in this country.[48] With AfECA, Congress made clear that it did not agree with USFWS' earlier vote of confidence in the CITES process, declaring that "[a]lthough some African countries have effective African elephant conservation programs, many do not have sufficient resources to properly manage, conserve, and protect their elephant populations,"[49] and pronounced that "[t]he United States, as a party to CITES and a large market for worked ivory, shares responsibility for supporting and implementing measures to stop the illegal trade in African elephant ivory and to provide for the conservation of the African

46. 43 Fed. Reg. 20503 (May 12, 1978).
47. Ronald L. Orenstein, Ivory, Horn and Blood: Behind the Elephant and Rhinoceros Poaching Crisis 57–59 (2013).
48. 16 U.S.C. §§ 4201–4246.
49. African Elephant Conservation Act of 1989, 16 U.S.C. § 4202(7).

elephant."[50] In enacting AfECA, Congress attempted to fulfill this promise by limiting imports and exports even further.

Though clear in intent, AfECA was complicated in practice. Among other provisions, it required the Service to establish moratoria on imports from elephant range states and intermediary transit countries that did not meet certain standards, and differentiated categories (with various import and export restrictions) of "worked ivory," "raw ivory," trophies, personal effects, commercial, and noncommercial products. Notably, AfECA did not regulate possession or trade of ivory within the United States, and allowed trophy hunting to continue as before.

In 1988, "clear in intent, complicated in practice" is a phrase that could be applied to the entirety of the legal apparatus that governed U.S. trade in African elephants and their parts. Leaving aside entirely the problem that *Loxodonta* products are difficult to distinguish from items made of mammoth ivory (unregulated) and Asian elephant ivory (tightly regulated as an endangered species product), the regime in place after AfECA treated these items differently depending on, among other things, the ivory's age; country of origin; whether it was to be imported or exported; year of import; whether it was originally a sport-hunted trophy; when it was taken from the wild; and whether it was carved or uncarved.[51] Furthermore, the only U.S. law enforcement agents monitoring compliance with the rules were Customs and Border Patrol (CBP) and USFWS border agents. As a result, once a tusk or statue got past that line of defense it was, for all intents and purposes, considered fair game for the U.S. domestic trade.

The problem was not limited to American soil. CITES parties issued a resolution in 1997 that was intended to pressure countries to firmly control their domestic markets.[52] Recently, this resolution has been leveraged to spur compliance with new "National Ivory Action Plans"[53] but for years after its adoption it was mostly window dressing and the United States, like many other consumer countries, failed to fully comply with

---

50. *Id.* at § 4202(8).
51. 16 U.S.C. § 4202(4), § 4223, § 4222(e), § 4244(10).
52. CITES Resolution Conf. 10.10 (Rev. CoP16) (amended March 3–14, 2013).
53. See CITES SC65 Doc 42.2 *National Ivory Action Plans.* https://cites.org/sites/default/files/eng/com/sc/65/E-SC65-42-02_1.pdf.

the directive, countenancing an ungoverned "gray market" in which old, legal ivory was sold alongside newer, recently poached ivory.[54] Also referred to as "parallel markets," this problem made thorough oversight virtually impossible, especially because funding for the USFWS's Office of Law Enforcement has been static since the 1970s. It would take several more years, however, before this fatal flaw in the system became clear.

The CITES Ban

In 1989, shortly after AfECA was enacted (and influenced by this and similar moves in other countries), the CITES parties transferred *Loxodonta* to Appendix I, stopping most international commercial trade in African elephant ivory. It was a contentious change opposed by several influential range states and even the CITES Secretariat, but eventually passed with a provision that allowed for future "downlisting" of healthy populations to Appendix II. The measure had the desired effect: As a result of this transfer to Appendix I, which is commonly referred to as the "CITES ban," ivory prices plummeted around the world, poaching rates bottomed out, and elephant population numbers began to increase over the next decade. Trophy hunting and international shipment of antiques were still permitted under the "ban," (CITES, oddly, does not classify trophies, which can cost tens of thousands of dollars to procure, as a commercial product) but the new rules created a significant protective atmosphere for African elephants.

The rationale for a black-and-white international ban is simple: Ivory buyers respond to laws and peer pressure. Some pro-trade commentators have compared shutting down the ivory trade to the United States' "war on drugs," which has largely failed to quell consumer demand. They argue that, in the presence of laws restricting trade, ivory sales will simply migrate to the black market. However, extensive research suggests that this is a false comparison. In China, the world's number one consumer,

---

54. Douglas F. Williamson, *Tackling the Ivories: The Status of the U.S. Trade in Elephant and Hippo Ivory* 35 (2004), http://assets.worldwildlife.org/publications/425/files/original/Tackling_the_Ivories.pdf?1345757077.

a 2013 IFAW survey found that 60 percent of likely buyers would forego purchases if ivory were illegal, and almost half would do so on the recommendation of a government leader.[55] A 2015 report from National Geographic and GlobeScan is even more emphatic, showing that "even those respondents who are most pro-ivory (current owners and likely buyers) express support for government intervention" and that "support for regulation and stricter enforcement is consistently widespread."[56] In China, gift giving is the most common reason given for ivory purchases, so it follows that an outright illegal gift would make for an awkward exchange. Ivory is not cocaine; demand is entirely dependent on its currency as a publically validated good.

The idea that demand for ivory is elastic was borne out by the immediate aftermath of the CITES ban, as Ronald Orenstein relates in his in-depth volume on the crisis, *Ivory, Horn and Blood*:

> After the [1989] CITES meeting the ivory market went into rapid collapse. Prices in Africa fell as low as $2 per kilogram [from around $250/kg in early 1989]. Ivory, particularly in Western countries, became practically unsellable. In Japan, demand for ivory decreased significantly after an initial surge, and by November 1990 production had fallen by two-thirds. Hong Kong was unable to dispose of more than a fraction of its stocks, and China, its carving industry nearly bankrupt, withdrew its reservation [an official objection to the Appendix I designation] early in 1991.[57]

Ivory purchases did not end completely, but the combination of bad publicity and reduced market presence pushed down demand significantly. Less demand meant lower prices for ivory further up the procure-

---

55. Int'l Fund for Animal Welfare, *Rapid Asia Flash Report: Impact Evaluation on Ivory Trade in China IFAW PSA: 'Mom, I Have Teeth.'* 5 (2013), http://www.ifaw.org/sites/default/files/ifaw -china-ivory-report.pdf.

56. Nat'l Geographic & GlobeScan, *Reducing Demand for Ivory: An Int'l Study* 10 (2015), http:// press.nationalgeographic.com/files/2015/08/NGS2015_Final-August-11-RGB.pdf.

57. RONALD L. ORENSTEIN, IVORY, HORN AND BLOOD: BEHIND THE ELEPHANT AND RHINOCEROS POACHING CRISIS 63 (2013).

ment chain, which disincentivized poaching, and elephant numbers slowly improved for the next sixteen years.

But the recovery did not last. As African elephant populations grew, so did the stockpiles of ivory collected from government "culls," natural deaths, and the occasional seizure of smuggled goods, all of it gathering dust in warehouses. In 1997, seeking to capitalize on their growing inventories, several southern African countries successfully petitioned for their elephants to be "downlisted" from CITES Appendix I to Appendix II, in order to sell fifty tons of ivory to traders in Japan. When the Parties approved a second stockpile sale, to Japan and China, in 2007 (the actual transaction occurred in 2009), the positive antipoaching trends did an about-face. Again, there seems to be a straight line between administrative decisions and the fate of the species: In 2006, the Chinese government had promoted ivory carving to honored status as an "Intangible Cultural Heritage," and the second sale brought 68 tons of ivory to the (now-officially endorsed) carving workshops, nominally overseen by state officials through an easily rigged registration system.[58]

The New York Times summed up the sequence of events that began with the stockpile sales as "a colossal failure."[59] A product that had been censured was now legal and venerated once more, and mass consumer psychology quickly flipped the collective mental switch to "purchase." By 2007, an IFAW survey found that 70 percent of Chinese did not even know that ivory comes from dead elephants.[60] Demand boomed, particularly as the Asian middle class swelled in the early 2000s, pushing ivory prices far higher, and the suppliers snapped back to attention. Speculators began to stockpile ivory in anticipation of a day in the future

---

58. Under the Chinese registration system, all ivory products heavier than 50 g for sale required a card with a photo ID card and basic information about the item. Additionally, only officially licensed facilities were allowed to sell ivory. A 2011 study found that unlicensed and noncompliant facilities outnumbered legal/compliant facilities 6 to 1. GRACE G. GABRIEL, NING HUA & JUAN WANG, INT'L FUND FOR ANIMAL WELFARE, MAKING A KILLING: A 2011 SURVEY OF IVORY MARKETS IN CHINA (2012).

59. Dan Levin, *From Elephants' Mouths, an Illicit Trail to China*, N.Y. TIMES, March 2, 2013, at A1.

60. Gabriel Ge Grace, *Opinion: Elephants Are Not Widgets*, NAT'L GEO.: A VOICE FOR ELEPHANTS (Sept. 24, 2014), http://voices.nationalgeographic.com/2014/09/24/opinion-elephants-are -not-widgets/.

when extinction would spell scarcity, betting that demand would surge even more.[61]

A mere decade later, experts' opposition to further stockpile sales and legal ivory markets is nearly unanimous, but the situation is dire. By 2010, poachers were gunning down an average of one elephant every fifteen minutes, one hundred each day, with roughly 35,000 killed every year.[62] As of 2016 central African forest elephants were in imminent danger of extinction, with over 60 percent of the population poached between 2002 and 2010.[63] *Loxodonta* strongholds remain in South Africa, Botswana, Namibia and a few other southern and eastern African nations with relatively stable governance and conservation programs, but these conditions are not guaranteed to last, and many authorities fear that poachers will infiltrate even these countries after they wipe out elephants elsewhere on the continent.

Rejoining the Fight

Most of this tragedy has occurred out of the public eye until very recently. Ivory and elephant poaching began to spark regular headlines in early 2012, and the U.S. government started to pay newfound attention to the overlap between poaching and national security issues like terrorism at the same time. That year, the federal Senate Foreign Relations Committee invited CITES Secretary General John Scanlon and pioneering elephant biologist Sir Iain Douglas-Hamilton to testify at a congressional hearing on the topic, and the State Department hosted an international roundtable on illegal wildlife trade, with ivory as a focus. Then, in 2013, President Obama traveled to Tanzania and announced an unprecedented Executive Order on the issue,[64] directing the federal agencies to collabo-

61. Stephanie Nebehay, *African Elephants at Risk, Record Ivory Seizures—CITES*, REUTERS (June 13, 2014), http://www.reuters.com/article/us-africa-elephants-idUSKBN0EO1GW20140613.

62. George Wittemyer et al., *Illegal Killing for Ivory Drives Global Decline in African Elephants*, 111 PROC. NAT'L ACAD. SCI. U.S. 13117, 13117–21 (2014).

63. Fiona Maisels et al., *Devastating Decline of Forest Elephants in Central Africa*, 8 PLoS ONE e59469, e59469 (2013).

64. Exec. Order No. 13,648, 78 Fed. Reg. 129 (July 5, 2013).

rate on a new national strategy to combat wildlife trafficking—a strategy that included what the White House termed a "near total ban on the U.S. domestic ivory trade"—alongside promises of increased American financial and technical assistance for wildlife protection in Africa. During the same period, the USFWS also suspended imports of elephant trophies from Tanzania and Zimbabwe, ruling that there was not enough evidence that the trophy hunting programs of these nations actually benefitted the species.[65]

The new regulations were finalized in June 2016 (and went into effect a month later) but required several preliminary steps: First, in February 2014 USFWS Director Dan Ashe issued a Director's Order that (A) required ivory sellers to be able to prove they qualified for the ESA's antiques exemption; and (B) halted all ivory imports except for some musical instruments, museum artifacts, noncommercial "personal items," and scientific and law enforcement specimens.[66] Second, in July 2015 the Service published a proposed rule that would alter the ESA special rule once more, limiting trophy imports from all countries to two specimens (maximum four tusks) per hunter annually; and further limiting exports and interstate commerce.[67] No part of the new rules impacts mere possession of ivory or other elephant products, and noncommercial transactions like repairs of broken items containing ivory and bequests are still allowed.

Unfortunately, the familiar "clear in intent, complicated in practice" description again applies, in some degree, to these new regulatory changes. Due to limitations written into the ESA, the Service is unable to restrict trade in bona fide antiques, and the new rules also allow trade in a wider range of items which have a "*de minimus*" amount of ivory (under 200 grams) and which also meet a set of seven strict criteria.[68] One key criterion is that the item must be demonstrably old—if it is, the reason-

---

65. *See* Notice of Suspension of Imports of Zimbabwe Elephant Trophies Taken in 2014 on or after April 4, 2014, 69 Fed. Reg. 147 (July 31, 2014).

66. U.S. Dep't of the Interior, Director's Order No. 210 (2015), http://www.fws.gov/policy/do210.html.

67. *See* Endangered and Threatened Wildlife and Plants; Revision of the Section 4(d) Rule for the African Elephant (Loxodonta africana), 80 Fed. Reg. 45154 (July 29, 2015). *Final Rule at* 81 Fed. Reg. 36387 (June 6, 2016).

68. 50 C.F.R. pt. 7 (2016).

ing goes, then it cannot be contributing to the current poaching crisis. The burden of proof for each of these exceptions would lie with the seller, which has caused a tremendous amount of backlash from some ivory owners who do not have paperwork for their products. In response the USFWS decided to allow a broad range of articles—including CITES import certificates and "qualified appraisals"—as proof of provenance, but this broad allowance has in turn spurred some conservationists to ask how, exactly, the Service intends to enforce the rule. If an old picture counts as proof, it may be easy to defraud or to provide "evidence" of age that can be easily fabricated—Photoshop as trafficking aid.

The *de minimus* exception is clearly an attempt by the USFWS to minimize opposition and focus law enforcement resources on the worst offenders, but the rulemaking process raised hackles on both sides of the ideological spectrum. The National Rifle Association, for one, has been actively lobbying against these regulations almost from the moment President Obama took the stage in Tanzania, hoping to stall any restrictions on trophy hunting or on sales of ivory-handled guns.[69] Musicians' groups like the League of American Orchestras (LAO) have been generally supportive of the White House's elephant agenda overall, but worked with the Administration to find a compromise short of a total ban, because ivory is found in older instruments like pianos and violin bows that can cost tens of thousands of dollars. Ivory retailers and auctioneers, craftsmen, and a handful of wealthy private collectors have also lobbied to stop implementation of this rule and carve out more exemptions.[70] From a conservation perspective, it can be easier to stomach some of these compromises—the LAO, for example, stresses that instrument manufacturers have not used elephant ivory for decades (and that musicians do not seek out the material, anyway), in stark contrast to the numerous seizures of

---

69. *See* Nat'l Rifle Ass'n, *Latest Update on Proposed Ban on the Domestic Sale of Ivory and Importation of Elephant Trophies*, NAT'L RIFLE ASS'N INST. FOR LEGIS. ACTION (July 18, 2014), https://www.nraila.org/articles/20140718/latest-update-on-proposed-ban-on-the-domestic-sale-of-ivory-and-importation-of-elephant-trophies.

70. *See* U.S. Fish & Wildlife Serv., *Revisions to the Endangered Species Act (ESA) Special Rule for the African Elephant: Questions and Answers* 1 (2016), https://www.fws.gov/international/pdf/questions-and-answers-african-elephant-4d-final-rule.pdf.

fake "antique" ivory carvings for the collectibles markets, or the fog that surrounds the world of gun accessories.[71]

The issue has not gone unnoticed by members of Congress, either, as lawmakers in both the House and Senate have introduced legislation to undermine the proposed regulations and to reinstate trophy imports from Tanzania and Zimbabwe. With titles like the "Lawful Ivory Protection Act," these bills would freeze any attempts at improving or implementing the special rule, and echo broader conflicts between the legislative and executive branches.[72] In a political climate that may be the worst of the modern era, elephant conservation has become a potential victim of the culture wars, despite polls showing that an ivory trade ban is overwhelmingly popular across a broad spectrum of the American public.[73]

In one legal sense, this is a debate that should not even be happening, as the USFWS has yet to fully deploy its most valuable tool—an ESA endangered listing that would close commercial trade in all African elephant products except for antiques (and very limited trophy imports). Such a listing would do away with many of the complications inherent to a mixed system of laws and regulations. According to the U.S. Supreme Court's seminal 1978 decision in *Tennessee Valley Authority v. Hill*, "The plain intent of Congress in enacting [the ESA] was to halt and reverse the trend towards species extinction, whatever the cost. This is reflected not only in the stated policies of the Act, but in literally every section of the statute."[74] Under a strict reading of the ESA, a species *must* be listed as endangered if any of five criteria put it in danger of extinction throughout all or a significant portion of its historic range, even if that range is in a foreign country (1) the present or threatened destruction, modification, or curtailment of its habitat or range; (2) overutilization for commercial, recreational, scientific, or educational purposes; (3) disease or predation; (4) inadequacy of existing regulatory mechanisms; or, (5) other natural

71. *See* League of Am. Orchestras, *Ivory Ban Impact on Orchestras*, LEAGUE OF AM. ORCHESTRAS: ADVOC. AND GOV'T (July 8, 2016), http://americanorchestras.org/advocacy-government/travel-with-instruments/endangered-species-material/ivory-ban-impact-on-orchestras.html.
72. *See, e.g.,* S. 2587, 113th Cong. (2014); H.R. 5052, 1113th Cong. (2014).
73. Azzedine Downes, *Critics Are Wrong, the US is Complicit in the Elephant Poaching Crisis*, INT'L FUND FOR ANIMAL WELFARE (June 24, 2014), http://www.ifaw.org/united-states/news/critics-are-wrong-us-complicit-elephant-poaching-crisis.
74. Tenn. Valley Authority v. Hill, 437 U.S. 153, 180 (1978).

or manmade factors affecting its existence.[75] Additionally, listing determinations must be made "solely on the basis of the best scientific and
commercial data available"[76] and political or commercial considerations
are not supposed to play a role.

By most measures, the African elephant arguably is entitled to endangered listing under any of the five criteria, and it is difficult to build a reasonable case that none of the criteria are met. In March 2016 the USFWS
issued a positive "90-day finding" to a legal petition from IFAW and the
Humane Society of the United States (HSUS) that asked the Service
to uplist African elephants to endangered status. This procedural move
means that the petition was found to be warranted for further evaluation,
clearing the first hurdle for in-depth review and a possible uplisting. A
subsequent petition from the Center for Biological Diversity, which asks
for separate endangered listings for the African forest elephant—*Loxodonta cyclotis*—and savannah elephant—*Loxodonta africana*—subspecies was also given a positive 90-day finding. Both petitions were filed
in early 2015. The USFWS Endangered Species Program's scientists and
staffers are dedicated and capable, but the department is also notori-
ously underfunded and backlogged, which may be one explanation for
the delayed evaluation of the uplisting proposals, but it is also evident
that the Service would prefer to avoid the mandatory trade closures and
trophy hunting restrictions that accompany endangered status. In place
of uplisting, the current special rule revision is the agency's attempt at
compromise.

Compromise it may be, but not all are happy with the outcome:
Although the League of American Orchestras and others have cautiously
welcomed the *de minimus* exemption, the National Rifle Association
and its backers in Congress rejected even this partial olive branch and
have promised to fight it to the end. Additionally, some animal welfare
and environmental groups remain frustrated with the Service's continued allowance of trophy imports and loopholes that may enable some
continued ivory trafficking. Wildlife organizations are also divided over
the question of how much trade is too much: Some groups believe that

---

75. 16 U.S.C. § 1533(a)(1)(A)–(E) (2012).
76. *Id.*

it makes sense to focus on areas (primarily China, Japan, and southeast Asia) where the demand for ivory, and the potential for laundering of new tusks onto the market, is greatest, given the political climate and the numerous other values at stake. Others believe that nothing short of a total ban will bring the poaching crisis to a halt.

There is a moral element to the debate, too, as many animal welfare organizations are trying to quash the very idea that ivory should be a commodity, arguing that we should not celebrate and perpetuate a trade that requires the wholesale butchery of an intelligent species. With the stakes so high for so many, the Service's actions have been caught in a tangle of conflicting opinions and are sure to influence domestic and international laws for years to come.

This is already the case in the United States where, as of the fall of 2016, four state legislatures have passed bills to limit ivory sales, with New York[77] and New Jersey[78] taking this step in 2014, California[79] in 2015, and Hawaii[80] in 2016. Washington state voters overwhelmingly passed a ballot initiative to the same effect in 2015, with more than 70 percent in favor,[81] and Oregonians followed suit in 2016.[82] More dominos may fall soon, as legislation and ballot initiatives are making their way through the pipelines in Massachusetts, Connecticut, and Pennsylvania. In all, more than a dozen states have proposed laws to shut down their ivory markets, and advocates believe this momentum for reform could carry over to the next level by spurring national or global action.

This development within the states can be very helpful, because it fills one of the major gaps in the federal regulations: although the law restricts the cross-border sale of ivory, the USFWS cannot otherwise bar intrastate trade—commerce that occurs within a state's boundaries—in elephant

77. N.Y. Comp. Codes R. & Regs. tit. 6 §§ 175–176 (2014).

78. Act of August 1, 2014, Pub. L. No. 2014 c. 22 (prohibiting the import, sale, purchase, barter, or possession of ivory or rhinoceros horn).

79. 2015 Cal. Stat. § 475.

80. 2016 Hawaii Act 125, SB2647 SD1 HD2.

81. Wash. Initiative Measure No. 1401 (filed 1401), http://sos.wa.gov/_assets/elections/ initiatives/ FinalText_784.pdf.

82. November 18, 2016 General Election Abstract of Votes – Measure 100, http://sos.oregon.gov/ elections/Documents/results/november-2016-results.pdf.

parts, only interstate trade, imports, and exports.[83] Given the limited capacity of CPB and the USFWS Office of Law Enforcement, it is likely that federal agents will focus their attention on higher-profile trafficking cases instead of trying to stamp out the less intense, but overall probably bigger in scale, everyday commerce in tusks and trinkets that occurs in shops and on websites around the country. Unless a seller explicitly advertises to ship their item across state lines, it can be difficult for regulators to preemptively identify and prevent an interstate sale; retailers do not generally inquire where the customer intends to transport their ivory purchase, and state police are not in the business of conducting highway border checks for elephant tusks. It is far more effective to disallow these sales in the first place. With strong state laws on the books, there will be more levels of oversight, more enforcement capacity, fewer consumers willing to take a risk on ivory purchases, and less incentive for traffickers to try to skirt the rules.

Import and export restrictions, too, are key to eliminating illegal trafficking. Unlike shipments headed for Southeast Asia, which have been interdicted by foreign agencies en masse, U.S. Customs inspectors have not caught ivory smugglers docking their goods by the ton in massive shipping containers. Instead, bangles and carvings are mailed, packed in suitcases, shipped in smaller consignments on freight vessels, or in many cases, inadvertently brought in by tourists returning from overseas. Whatever the method of entry, these recently poached items wind up in store windows and online ads, pitched as legal by default. By prohibiting nonantique commercial imports and exports, the USFWS rule changes make border agents' task—determining legal shipments from illegal ones—simpler.

With all of that said, however, there is still a large element of promotion to these laws and regulations. Because enforcement is spotty and expensive, part of the onus for ensuring the spirit of these laws is carried out is on retailers, auctioneers, and other sellers. These integral players should be encouraged to follow the spirit of the law even if the risks

---

83. A further wrinkle, however, is that the federal law preempts state law when it comes to state border controls: Even states like NJ (which banned ivory sales across state lines) must now allow interstate sales of proven antiques and *de minimus* items.

of detection are low, and in that regard an informed consumer class is indispensable. Conservation advocates and other stakeholders have spent years trying to get the message across that "every piece of ivory comes from a dead elephant," and it will help enormously to be able to broadcast the fact that most products are legally off-limits for sale, too. That is why the White House promotes its regulations as "a near-total ban" in public, while quietly allowing some core exemptions. It remains to be seen whether the new rules brighten the line enough to prod consumers into foregoing that purchase of an ivory necklace or statuette, but some major marketplaces and online platforms are already taking steps to comply with, and in some cases surpass,[84] the new laws.

Conclusion

Everyone agrees that unilateral action by the United States is not sufficient. It is the world's second-largest market for wildlife products, but America could shut down 100 percent of its ivory sales, eliminating U.S. "gray markets" entirely, and elephants would still be in peril due to strong consumer demand in China, Japan, Thailand, Vietnam, and elsewhere. However, it is also true that action by the United States puts the spotlight on those regimes to improve their own antitrafficking methods and stigmatize consumption.

There are no guarantees that American pressure will result in reforms overseas but, simply put, the U.S. government cannot credibly ask China (far and away the world's leading ivory market) to crack down on illegal trade unless America is willing to do likewise.[85] The merits of this approach have already been proven: In late September 2015, President Xi Jinping of China and U.S. President Barack Obama jointly pledged to enact "nearly complete bans on ivory imports and exports, includ-

---

84. Etsy/Lauren Engelhardt, *Policy Update: Prohibited Animal Products* (July 22, 2013), https://blog.etsy.com/news/2013/policy-update-prohibited-animal-products/?ref=about_blog_title.
85. Good old fashioned one-upmanship should not be ignored in the geopolitical arena: In 2013, as part of its public awareness effort to spotlight wildlife trafficking, USFWS crushed its 6-ton stockpile of seized, illegal ivory. Just two months later, China's State Forestry Agency crushed 6.1 tons of seized ivory at an event in Guangzhou.

ing significant and timely restrictions on the import of ivory as hunting trophies," and promised to "take significant and timely steps to halt the domestic commercial trade of ivory."[86] The U.S. promise amounts to implementing and maintaining the USFWS proposed rule, but there are few details on the Chinese side of the accord, and the more loopholes that exist in the American system, the less leverage U.S. diplomats will be able to bring to bear in talks with their counterparts. Gaps like the USFWS's *de minimus* exemption, however reasonable-seeming in the context of the U.S. market, thus have ramifications that could extend far beyond American shores. In any single case, it may be practical to allow the sale of an older tusk, figurine, or ivory-handled pistol. In the broader context of international diplomacy, such a loophole may provide a built-in excuse for foreign officials to include less judicious exemptions of their own.

As we weigh how much responsibility Americans bear for the survival of the planet's biggest land mammal, the problem can seem intractable. Private property rights, global trade laws, and numerous other economic and legal considerations come into play, but those concerns must be weighed against these fundamental facts: Forest elephants could face extinction in the wild in the next decade. Savannah elephants may not be far behind.

If the thought of ivory carvings being all that remains of the elephant does not compel us to use extraordinary measures, perhaps we should reconsider the words of Teddy Roosevelt: "Rhetoric is a poor substitute for action, and we have trusted only to rhetoric. If we are really to be a great nation, we must not merely talk; we must act big."

---

86. Press Release, The White House Off. of the Press Secretary, *Fact Sheet: President Xi Jinping's State Visit to the United States* (Sept. 25, 2015), https://www.whitehouse.gov/the-press-office/2015/09/25/fact-sheet-president-xi-jinpings-state-visit-united-states.

3

The Oceans' Limits

Kristen Monsell

~

*"It is a curious situation that the sea, from which life first
arose, should now be threatened by the activities of one form
of that life. But the sea, though changed in a sinister way,
will continue to exist: the threat is rather to life itself."*

Rachel Carson

The oceans cover almost three-fourths of the surface of our planet, and are the world's largest ecosystems. They are home to an astonishing array of life, from microbes and anchovies to great white sharks and blue whales—the largest animals ever to live on earth. The oceans also play a key role in sustaining life on Earth. Indeed, it is said that at least half of the world's oxygen is produced by processes in the oceans, meaning the oceans are responsible for every other breath we take.

Nevertheless, a combination of intentional exploitation, wanton neglect, and lack of awareness, both onshore and offshore, has had a devastating effect on the world's oceans. The whaling industry killed millions of whales for their meat and oils, nearly eliminating them from the oceans; commercial fishing operations are scooping up fish at an unprecedented rate, often obliterating all life within the path of their mile-long nets; the world's overuse of plastic has created a pollution disaster that chokes and drowns sea turtles, seabirds, and other marine life; and carbon emissions are acidifying ocean waters, preventing crustaceans and invertebrates from forming the shells they need for survival and imperiling coral reefs, which support one-third of all ocean life. The situation has become dire, but there is still time to turn it around.

While the issues impacting the oceans are almost as many as the oceans are vast, this chapter focuses on the intersection of conservation and animal welfare and some of the most significant threats that plague our oceans and the wildlife that call it home. This chapter also discusses legal mechanisms that have been, or can be, used to address these threats both domestically and abroad.

The first section discusses commercial whaling, which drove many species of whales to the brink of extinction and spurred domestic and international agreements to protect and recover these majestic creatures, including the International Convention for the Regulation of Whaling, and the formation of the International Whaling Commission, which has prohibited commercial whaling at the global level since 1986. It also discusses efforts taken by the United States, other governments, and nongovernmental organizations to enforce the terms of the Convention. The second section focuses on commercial fishing, and the negative impacts from marine mammals and other species becoming entangled in fishing gear, and overfishing. It also describes tools to address such threats, including the Marine Mammal Protection Act, a statute that generally prohibits any person from killing or harming any marine mammal and establishes a detailed framework for regulating bycatch; the Endangered Species Act, a law that seeks to protect and recover threatened and endangered species and the habitats on which they depend; and the Magnuson-Stevens Fishery Conservation and Management Act, which seeks to prevent overfishing and recover overfished stocks, and contains powerful provisions to influence fishing practices actions abroad. The final section focuses on the pollution of our oceans, and two of the most ubiquitous types of pollution—plastics and greenhouse gases. It also discusses unique efforts to use what are generally thought of as land-based pollution control statutes to force the cleanup of oceans contaminated with plastic pollution, prevent future plastic pollution from entering the oceans by regulating it as a hazardous waste, and protect coastal waters and marine life from acidification.

Pursuant to international agreements, jurisdiction over the oceans and the wildlife and other natural resources found within them often depend on how far they are from land. "Territorial waters" extend up to twelve nautical miles from shore and are regarded as the sovereign territory of the coastal state, including the air space and the seafloor. Foreign ships enjoy the right of passage while traveling through these waters, subject to the laws and regulations adopted by the coastal nation. The "contiguous zone" is the area adjacent to territorial waters and can extend twenty-four nautical miles from shore. In its contiguous zone, a coastal nation can exercise the control required to prevent any infringement on its customs, immigration, and sanitary laws and can enforce violations committed in territorial waters. The "exclusive economic zone" generally extends two hundred nautical miles from shore. A coastal nation has jurisdiction over the exploration, exploitation, conservation, and management of natural resources in its exclusive economic zone. Waters that fall outside these areas are considered the "high seas" and are outside the jurisdiction of any one nation, except to the extent that a nation that has granted a ship the right to sail under its flag generally has exclusive jurisdiction over that ship on the high seas.

Marine species, pollution, and the ripple effects that natural resource extraction can have on ocean ecosystems do not respect or benefit from these boundaries. Remedying the myriad threats to our oceans thus necessitates the cooperation of many countries. It is incumbent upon the United States—with the world's largest exclusive economic zone at 3.4 million square miles and some of the most powerful conservation laws in the world—to stem the impending wave of extinction and turn the state of our oceans around by taking meaningful action and setting an example for other countries as to how to manage waters within their borders, or use domestic legislation to put teeth in international agreements and force countries to act.

Whaling

"You don't need a peg leg or an eye patch."[1] So reads the opening line to the U.S. Court of Appeals for the Ninth Circuit's opinion finding that a conservation organization's efforts to thwart Japanese whaling vessels from killing whales constitute piracy.[2] This opinion is one of the more recent developments in our country's centuries-long, tumultuous relationship with whaling. This section contains a brief discussion on the history and impacts of whaling, as well as efforts to stop this practice that has had a destructive effect on whales internationally.

A Brief History of Whaling and the International Whaling Commission

Humans have been whaling for centuries,[3] and the practice has been dated back to at least 3,000 BCE, and possibly even 6,000 BCE.[4] Early methods of hunting whales included trying to place several boats next to a whale in the hopes of scaring it to shore, or individuals throwing harpoons at whales from small canoes.[5] These early whale hunts resulted in only a few whales being caught each season.[6]

Whales were originally hunted for their meat for food, for their oil for heating and light, and for their teeth for jewelry and tools. New uses discovered for whale products, such as in cosmetics, transmission fluid, pet food, and agricultural feed, coupled with advances in technology, pushed whaling "beyond cultural identity and into the realm of international business" and "brought about the systematic devastation of the major whaling populations on this planet."[7]

---

1. Institute of Cetacean Research v. Sea Shepherd Conservation Soc'y (Cetacean I), 725 F.3d 940, 942 (9th Cir. 2013).
2. *Id.* at 942–43.
3. *See, e.g.*, Japan Whaling Assn'n v. Am. Cetacean Soc'y, 478 U.S. 221 (1986).
4. *Rock Art Hints at Whaling Origins*, BBC NEWS (Apr. 20, 2004), http://news.bbc.co.uk/2/hi/science/nature/3638853.stm.
5. Jack Hadley, *Whaling off the Alaskan Coast*, 47 BULL. AM. GEO. SOC. 905–21 (1915).
6. American Cetacean Soc'y, v. Baldridge, 604 F. Supp. 1398, 1401 (D.D.C. 1985).
7. *Id.*

Specifically, technologies invented during the late nineteenth and early twentieth centuries, including the steam-powered whale-catcher and the exploding harpoon gun, as well as improvements to ships and shore-based processing facilities "transformed whaling" from "a harrowing and perilous profession . . . into a routine form of commercial fishing," and "allowed for a multifold increase in whale harvests worldwide."[8] Indeed, by the 1930s, a ship could "take more whales in one season than the entire American whaling fleet of 1846 which numbered more than 700 vessels."[9] Recent estimates put the number of whales killed from 1900 to 1999 at 2.9 million.[10] When accounting for biomass, this may be the largest hunt in human history, and is certainly one of the most extreme examples of the exploitation of wildlife.[11]

Recognizing that industrialized whaling was having a profound and devastating impact on whale populations across the globe, the United States initiated an international conference on whaling in 1946.[12] The result of that conference was the adoption of the International Convention for the Regulation of Whaling (the Convention) on December 2, 1946, by fifteen nations, including the United States.[13]

---

8. Japan Whaling Ass'n, 478 U.S. at 224.

9. Robert C. Rocha, Jr. et al., *Emptying the Oceans: A Summary of Industrial Whaling Catches in the 20th Century*, 76 MARINE FISHERIES REV. 37–48 (2014) (quoting Lt. Quentin R. Walsh, USCG, 1938).

10. *Id.* at 47.

11. *Id.* at 48.

12. International Court of Justice, Whaling in the Antarctic (Australia v. Japan: New Zealand Intervening), Judgment ¶ 44 (Mar. 31, 2014). Two multilateral treaties regarding whaling preceded the conference—the Convention for the Regulation of Whaling, adopted in 1931, and the International Agreement for the Regulation of Whaling, adopted in 1937. *Id.* ¶ 43. Both treaties prohibited the killing of certain categories of whale and required parties to collect biological information from harvested whales, but did not address overall catch levels. *Id.*

13. *Id.*; 62 Stat. 1716, T.I.A.S. No. 1849 (entered into force Nov. 10, 1948) (recognizing that "the history of whaling has seen over-fishing of one area after another and of one species of whale after another to such a degree that it is essential to protect all species of whales from further over-fishing"). The fifteen original signatories were the United States, Australia, Brazil, Canada, Chile, Denmark, France, the Netherlands, New Zealand, Norway, Peru, the Russian Federation, South Africa, and the United Kingdom. Gale Smith, *The International Whaling Commission: An Analysis of the Past and Reflections on the Future*, 16 NAT'L RESOURCES LAW 543, n.3. (1984). There are 88 member-countries today. IWC, *Membership and Contracting Governments* (last accessed Sept. 2, 2015).

Some countries joined based on their interest in protecting whale populations, while others joined to protect their interests in continued commercial whaling.[14] Accordingly, the Convention sought to "provide a system of international regulation for the whale fisheries to ensure proper and effective conservation and development of whale stocks . . . and thus make possible the orderly development of the whaling industry."[15] To that end, the Convention established the International Whaling Commission (the Commission) to study whales and whaling practices, and to establish a schedule of regulations regarding the "conservation and utilization of whale resources," including harvest limits for various whale species.[16]

Under the terms of the Convention, the quotas established by the Commission are binding on members if accepted by a three-fourths' majority vote.[17] But, like other international treaties, there are no means within the Convention to enforce these quotas; the Commission has no power to impose sanctions for violations and any member-country can file an "objection" to the Commission's amendment of the schedule, exempting itself from a requirement to comply with the quota or any other rules.[18]

For these reasons, and the dual (and often contradictory) goals of the Convention to both conserve whales and ensure a viable commercial whaling industry, harvest levels of whales for most of the twentieth century exceeded sustainable levels. In fact, the Commission initially set intentionally high quotas to help ensure that member countries would not quit the Commission, but even those liberal quotas were exceeded.[19] Under the Commission's scheme, several species were reduced to very low levels, including the blue whale, which scientists estimate was reduced to just one percent of its prewhaling population in the Southern Hemisphere; and the North Pacific right whale of which fewer than thirty

14. Smith, *supra* note 13.
15. *Id.*
16. Art. III, 62 Stat. 1717–1718; Art. V, 62 Stat. 1718–9.
17. Art. III, 62 Stat. 1717; Japan Whaling Ass'n, 478 U.S. at 224.
18. Art. IX, 62 Stat. 1718-1720; Japan Whaling Ass'n, 478 U.S. at 224–25.
19. Gerry J. Nagtzaam, *The International Whaling Commission and the Elusive Great White Whale of Preservationism*, 33 Wm. & Mary Envtl. L. & Pol'y Rev. 375, 401 (2009).

individuals remain today.[20] Some local subpopulations of whales appear to have been completely eliminated.[21]

In the 1970s, the United States and the United Kingdom began pushing for a ten-year moratorium on whaling to allow whale populations to recover, officially proposing such amendment to the Commission in 1972, and then again in 1973 and 1974.[22] The motion failed, but the idea of a moratorium continued to gain traction as more nonwhaling countries joined the Commission, more scientific evidence emerged about the depleted state of whale stocks, and education campaigns addressed the plight of whales. All of these efforts led to significant public pressure to reduce whaling.[23] The ultimate effect of all of this opposition culminated in 1982 with the Commission's vote to impose a moratorium on all commercial whaling beginning in 1986.[24] The moratorium, though broad in scope, contained express exceptions for aboriginal whaling and whaling for scientific research pursuant to a permit issued by a member-country to its nationals.[25]

Japan, Norway, and Russia filed objections to the moratorium based on their belief that the purpose of the Convention was to promote and maintain both whales and the whaling industry, not to ban whaling completely.[26] Canada quit the Commission immediately after the moratorium went into effect, and Iceland left the Commission in 1992. Iceland rejoined the Commission in 2002, filing a reservation to the commercial ban.[27] By the time the Commission implemented the moratorium on

20. Rocha, *supra* note 9 at 47; B. M. Allen & R. P. Angliss, *Alaska Marine Mammal Stock Assessments, 2013: North Pacific Right Whale* (Eubalaena japonica): *Eastern North Pacific Stock,* NOAA-TM-AFSC-277 (May 2013).
21. Philip J. Clapham, Alex Aguilar, & Liela T. Hatch, *Determining Spatial and Temporal Scales for the Management of Cetaceans: Lessons from Whaling,* MAR. MAMM. SCI. 24:183–202 (2008).
22. Nagtzaam, *supra* note 19 at 408.
23. *Id.* at 408–416.
24. *Id.* at 417; Japan Whaling Ass'n, 478 U.S. at 227.
25. Nagtzaam, *supra* note 19 at 417; Metcalf v. Daley, 214 F.3d 1135, 1138 (9th Cir. 2000).
26. Nagtzaam, *supra* note 19 at 417; Japan Whaling Ass'n, 478 U.S. at 227.
27. A "reservation" is not expressly provided for in the Convention, but is a concept recognized in international law that allows a country to exclude or modify the legal effect of certain treaty provisions as applied to that country. *See* Art. 2.1.d of the Vienna Convention on the Law of Treaties, Vienna, May 23, 1969. As such, Iceland's reservation to the moratorium on commercial whaling when it rejoined the Commission had the same effect as if Iceland had lodged a timely objection to the moratorium.

commercial whaling, at least 2,870,291 whales (99 percent of the overall twentieth century total of 2,894,094) had been killed by industrial whaling methods.[28] Hundreds of whales are still killed each year pursuant to the objection and reservation filed by Norway and Iceland, respectively, and by Japan pursuant to scientific research permits.

The United States' Actions to Limit Whaling

Congress enacted the Whaling Convention Act in 1949 to implement the Convention.[29] The Whaling Convention Act prohibits whaling in violation of the Convention, the Schedule, or any whaling regulation adopted by the Secretary of Commerce, and prohibits the possession, transport, purchase, sale, import, and export of whale products taken in violation of the Convention or its implementing regulations.[30] Then, in 1971, in an effort to provide the United States with leverage to force other countries to comply with international agreements, Congress enacted the Pelly Amendment to the Fishermen's Protective Act of 1967.[31] Although the Pelly Amendment was primarily intended to address Denmark's fishing practices that were depleting North Atlantic salmon in violation of the International Convention for the Northwest Atlantic Fisheries, the Pelly Amendment protects whales as well.[32]

Specifically, the Amendment directs the Secretary of Commerce to certify to the President when "nationals of a foreign country, directly or indirectly, are conducting fishing operations in a manner or under circumstances which diminish the effectiveness of an international fishery conservation program."[33] Upon receiving a certification, the President "may direct the Secretary of the Treasury to prohibit . . . the importation into the United States of any products from the offending country."[34] The Pelly Amendment then makes importation in violation of that prohibi-

---

28. Rocha, *supra* note 9.
29. 16 U.S.C. §§ 916, *et seq.*
30. *Id.* § 916c.
31. 22 U.S.C. § 1978.
32. Japan Whaling Ass'n, 478 U.S. at 224 (citing 117 Cong. Rec. 34752 (1971) (remarks of Rep. Pelly); H.R. Rep. No. 92-468, at 6 (1971)).
33. 22 U.S.C. § 1978(a)(1).
34. *Id.* § 1978(a)(4).

tion unlawful.[35] The Amendment also requires the Secretary to "promptly investigate any activity by foreign nationals that . . . may be cause for certification" and "promptly conclude" those investigations.[36] Once a certification has been issued, the President may prohibit the import of any product from an offending country, not just importation of the particular wildlife species covered by the treaty.[37] However, conservation concerns must be the reason for any certification for a departure from a treaty requirement.[38]

After enactment of the Pelly Amendment, the Secretary of Commerce certified different nations to the President on several occasions, but none of these certifications resulted in the imposition of sanctions by the President.[39] Nevertheless, after each certification the President was able to use the threat of sanctions to get promises that offending nations will comply in the future.[40] For example, in December 1978, the Secretary of Commerce certified Chile, Peru, and the Republic of Korea for exceeding Commission quotas, though none of these nations were members of the Commission or signatories of the Convention. Within sixty days after certification, all three had either joined the Commission or committed to do so by the next scheduled annual meeting. And in 1979, the threatened certification of Spain led that country to agree to adhere to the Commission's fin whale quota for that year, despite having filed a formal objection.[41]

Despite these actions, Congress decided in 1979 that the Pelly Amendment was not effective at persuading commercial whaling nations to comply with the quotas established by the Commission.[42] Accordingly,

---

35. *Id.* § 1978(c).

36. 22 U.S.C. § 1978(a)(3).

37. *See* Florsheim Shoe Co. v. United States, 19 C.I.T. 295, 297 (1995) (approving Pelly-based Presidential proclamation prohibiting importation of all wildlife products from Taiwan, including elk skin shoes, even though the treaty violation involved endangered tigers and rhinos).

38. Japan Whaling Ass'n, 478 U.S. at 233 (suggesting that the Secretary may not refuse to certify a violation for a "reason not connected with the aims and conservation goals" of the treaty; *see also* Greenpeace, U.S.A. v. Mosbacher, 719 F. Supp. 21, 24 (D.D.C. 1989) (noting that "a decision based on factors other than conservation constitutes an abuse of discretion").

39. Japan Whaling Ass'n, 478 U.S. at 225.

40. *Id.*

41. American Cetacean Soc'y, 604 F. Supp. at 1402.

42. *Id.*

Congress passed the Packwood Amendment to the Magnuson-Stevens Fishery Conservation and Management Act, which mandates the President to impose certain sanctions upon certification that are separate from those under the Pelly Amendment.[43] In particular, if the Secretary of Commerce certifies that "nationals of a foreign country, directly or indirectly, are conducting fishing operations or engaging in trade or taking which diminishes the effectiveness of the International Convention for the Regulation of Whaling," the Secretary of State must reduce all of the offending nation's fishery allocations within the United States' exclusive economic zone by at least 50 percent.[44] In other words, the Packwood Amendment automatically triggers the imposition of sanctions once a country is certified, but it does not alter the decision to certify a country in the first instance.

While any noncompliance with the terms of the Convention, and the harvest quota in particular, could in theory "diminish the effectiveness" of the Convention and thus mandate certification, the Supreme Court in *Japanese Whaling Association v. American Cetacean Society* held that neither the Pelly Amendment nor the Packwood Amendment requires the Secretary to certify a country's "departure" from the Convention.[45] Rather, the Secretary "is empowered to exercise . . . judgment in determining whether 'the trade or taking [is] serious enough to warrant the finding that the effectiveness of the international program in question has been diminished.'"[46]

In so holding, the Supreme Court reversed the opinions of the lower courts, which had found that any violation of the Commission quota would require certification.[47] At least one commentator has surmised that while the Court claims to have based its decision on statutory interpretation, in essence the five-to-four decision was a major policy choice, with the Court recognizing the Secretary of Commerce's fundamental conflict

---

43. 16 U.S.C. §§ 1801, *et seq.*

44. 16 U. S. C. § 1821(e)(2)(A)(i), (B). The Magnuson Act, discussed further later, regulates commercial fishing within the United States' 200-mile fishery conservation zone, and allows the Secretary of State to grant foreign nations annual allocations of allowable levels of fishing within the 200-mile zone. *Id.* § 1821.

45. Japan Whaling Ass'n, 478 U.S. at 238–39.

46. *Id.* at 239 (quoting H.R. Rep. No. 95-1029).

47. American Cetacean Soc'y, 604 F. Supp. at 1402; 768 F.2d 426 (D.C.C. 1985).

of interest between the statutory mandate to protect whales from whaling and the pressure to ensure the strength of American commerce.[48]

This conflict has played out with respect to countries that are still whaling, particularly Iceland and Japan. For example, in 1984, the United States threatened to certify Japan under the Pelly and Packwood Amendments in response to Japan's objection to the Commission and Japan's continued whaling. Japan agreed to withdraw its objection to the moratorium and halt commercial whaling by 1988 if the United States promised not to make those certifications.[49] While Japan ended commercial whaling, it immediately announced it would continue to kill hundreds of whales using the scientific research exception in the Convention.[50] The exception allows a member-country to issue itself a special permit to kill whales for scientific research.[51] The only require-ments for such permits are that any whales taken under such a permit "be processed" and that the proceeds be dealt with in accordance with the directions by the country that issued the permit.[52] The Convention also requires a country to provide the Commission with the results of its scientific research, including biological data, where practicable.[53] In this way, the scientific research permit is often seen as merely a license to sell whale meat. Accordingly, despite its promise to end commercial whaling, Japan was able to invoke the scientific research exception to kill hundreds of whales (whose meat would then be sold on the market) in 1987, by doing little more than asserting that it could better understand popula-tion dynamics of minke whales by killing them.[54]

---

48. Virginia A. Curry, *Japan Whaling Association v. American Cetacean Society*: The Great Whales Become Casualties of the Trade Wars, 4 PACE ENVTL. L. REV. 277, 278 (1986).
49. Japan Whaling Ass'n, 478 U.S. at 227–8.
50. Nagtzaam, *supra* note 19 at 429. The Commission's Scientific Review Committee has addi-tional parameters for reviewing scientific research permits and reports, including whether the permit adequately specifies its aims and objectives, whether the permit fulfills a critically important research need, and whether the catches will have an adverse effect on the stock to be taken. *See* The Commission, Scientific Committee Review of Special Permits, https://iwc.int/spw-scientific -review. However, the Committee does not have the power to enforce these parameters, or other-wise stop a country from issuing itself a scientific research permit if it believes the program fails to comply with its parameters.
51. Art. VIII.
52. *Id.*
53. *Id.*
54. *Id.*

Accordingly, the Secretary of Commerce certified Japan under the Pelly and Packwood Amendments in 1988, leading President Reagan to strip Japan of all its fishing rights in U.S. waters under the Packwood Amendment, but this was largely symbolic as the United States had not otherwise allocated Japan a fishing quota; no separate Pelly Amendment sanctions were imposed. [55] The Secretary of Commerce again certified Japan in 2000, following Japan's announcement that it would expand "scientific" whaling to harvest up to 600 whales in the North Pacific. President Clinton told Japan it would not allow Japan to fish in U.S. waters, and instructed the Secretaries of Commerce and State to evaluate potential trade restrictions; in response, Japan agreed to reduce its quota for the season.[56] Since that time, however, the United States has chosen to pursue diplomatic solutions, rather than imposing, or even threatening, sanctions, despite the fact that Japan continues to kill hundreds of whales every year under a "scientific research" program that scientists from other nations have repeatedly deemed inadequate or unjustified.[57]

Similarly, the Secretary of Commerce certified Iceland under the Pelly Amendment in 2014 (the third certification of Iceland related to its continued whaling) for conducting trade in whale meat and products that diminishes the effectiveness of international trade agreements prohibiting the practice.[58] However, President Obama declined to impose sanctions, choosing instead to pursue diplomatic solutions, including directing U.S. officials to raise concerns over Iceland's whaling practices at international meetings and continue to monitor the situation.[59]

Despite the decisions not to impose sanctions against Japan and Iceland, the Pelly and Packwood Amendments (at least in theory) place offending nations in the position of choosing between coming into compliance with the Convention or being prohibited from fishing in U.S.

---

55. Ronald Reagan, Pub. Papers, 704 424–25 (1988); SEAN D. MURPHY, UNITED STATES PRACTICE IN INTERNATIONAL LAW: VOLUME I, 1999–2001, 171 (2003); Steve Charnovitz, *Environmental Trade Sanctions and the GATT: An Analysis of the Pelly Amendment on Foreign Environmental Practices*, 9(3) AM. U. INT'L L. REV. 751–807 (1994).
56. Murphy, *supra* note 55 at 172.
57. *See, e.g.*, Dennis Normille, *Scientists renew objections to Japan's whaling program*, SCI. MAG. (June 19, 2015), *available at* http://news.sciencemag.org/plants-animals/2015/06/scientists-renew-objections-japan-s-whaling-program; *infra* notes 62–69 and accompanying text.
58. Memo from President Barack Obama to the Secretary of State, et al. *re* Pelly Certification and Icelandic Whaling, Apr. 1, 2014
59. *Id.*

waters or importing fish and other products into the United States under the theory that the nation will choose to come into compliance as it is the less damaging economic alternative.[60] According to one former U.S. Representative to the Commission, the threat of automatic sanctions under the Packwood Amendment "is the foundation upon which the present system of international whaling controls has been built."[61] Indeed, some credit the power vested in the United States by the Pelly Amendment as one of the primary reasons the Commission adopted the ban on commercial whaling.[62]

Other Efforts to Protect Whales from Whaling

Other countries have employed different tactics to protect whales from those still involved in whaling, turning to litigation in international courts. Specifically, in 2010 Australia sued Japan in the International Court of Justice, claiming that its program for killing whales in the Antarctic, known as JARPA II, did not constitute scientific research under the Convention.[63] The program allowed Japan to catch nearly 1,000 whales annually, on the basis that the Japanese government needed to ascertain whether there will be enough whales to harvest for profit.[64] Like Japan's other "scientific" whaling program in the North Pacific, the whale meat is considered a byproduct of the scientific research and is sold in food markets and used in pet food.[65] The Japanese Institute for Cetacean Research, the entity that has received scientific research permits to kill whales from Japan, makes $61 million from the sale of whale meat every year.[66]

---

60. *See, e.g.* Japan Whaling Ass'n, 478 U.S. at 239 ("as Senator Packwood put it, '[the Packwood amendment . . . puts] real economic teeth into our whale conservation efforts,' by requiring the Secretary of State to impose severe economic sanctions until the transgression is rectified." (*Quoting* 125 Cong. Rec. 21742 (1979)).
61. American Cetacean Soc'y, 604 F. Supp. at 1403.
62. Nagtzaam, *supra* note 19 at 417.
63. International Court of Justice, Whaling in the Antarctic (Australia v. Japan: New Zealand Intervening), Judgment (Mar. 31, 2014).
64. Joseph Elliott Roeschke, *Eco-Terrorism and Piracy on the High Seas: Japanese Whaling and the Rights of Private Groups to Enforce International Conservation Law in Neutral Waters*, 20 VILL. ENVTL. L. J. 99, 104 (2009).
65. *Id.* at 105.
66. *Id.*

The International Court agreed with Australia, finding no evidence that lethal methods were necessary to the stated scientific objectives of Japan's program, and that the catch limits were not scientifically justified.[67] Moreover, the open-ended time frame of the program, its limited scientific output, and the lack of cooperation with other domestic and international research programs in the Antarctic Ocean also cast doubt as to the characterization of the program as scientific.[68] The Court ordered Japan to revoke any extant permits to take whales in relation to JARPA II, and refrain from granting any further scientific permits in pursuance of that program.[69] While Japan initially indicated it would comply with the Court's order, it subsequently announced that it would resume whaling under the program.[70]

Other nongovernmental groups have taken a more direct approach. In particular, Sea Shepherd Conservation Society uses various methods on the water, including throwing smoke bombs and glass containers of foul-smelling acid at the whaling vessels, dragging metal-reinforced ropes in the water to damage the vessels' propellers and rudders, throwing safety flares with metal hooks at nets hung from the vessels, shining high-powered lasers at the vessels to thwart whaling efforts, and sometimes even ramming its own ships into whaling vessels and sinking them.[71]

After several years of confrontations on the high seas between Sea Shepherd and Japanese whaling vessels, the Institute for Cetacean Research sued Sea Shepherd and its founder, Paul Watson, in federal court in Washington state in 2011. The whalers sued under the Alien Tort Statute, which provides a cause of action for "a tort . . . committed in violation of the law of nations or a treaty of the United States."[72] The Institute claimed that Sea Shepherd's acts constituted piracy and violated international agreements regulating conduct on the high seas. The whal-

67. International Court of Justice, *supra* note 12, at ¶¶ 225–227.
68. *Id.* at ¶ 226.
69. *Id.* at ¶ 245.
70. *See, e.g.*, John Boyd, *Back to the whale hunt for Japan*, AL JAZEERA (Oct. 2, 2014), http://www.aljazeera.com/indepth/features/2014/10/back-whale-hunt-japan-20141011020868460.html
71. Inst. of Cetacean Research, 725 F.3d at 942.
72. *Id.* at 943 (quoting 28 U.S.C. § 1350).

ers sought a preliminary injunction barring the defendants from interfering with their whaling operations.[73]

The District Court dismissed the piracy claims and denied the preliminary injunction, but the Ninth Circuit reversed. The Ninth Circuit held that the whalers stated valid claims for piracy under the United Nations Convention on the Law of the Sea and the High Seas Convention, defined as "illegal acts of violence or detention, or any act of depredation, committed for private ends by the crew or the passengers of a private ship . . . and directed . . . on the high seas, against another ship . . . or against persons or property on board such ship."[74] The Ninth Circuit also held that, contrary to the district court's finding, "private ends" are not limited to those pursued for financial enrichment, but include those pursued on moral, philosophical, or personal grounds, including Sea Shepherd's professed environmental goals of protecting whales.[75] Furthermore, the court held that "violence" extends to malicious acts against inanimate objects, such as whaling vessels. As such, Sea Shepherd's tactics against Japanese whaling vessels constituted piracy, irrespective of how "high-minded [it] believed [its] purpose to be" (and its lack of a peg leg or an eye-patch).[76]

The Ninth Circuit issued an order requiring Sea Shepherd to abide by the terms of a preliminary injunction the court had issued earlier in the litigation, which prohibited Sea Shepherd from attacking Japanese whaling vessels in the Southern Ocean, jeopardizing the safe navigation of such vessels, and from approaching the whalers any closer than 500 yards while on the high seas.[77] In response to the ruling, Paul Watson stepped down from the Board of Directors, transferred all Sea Shepherd's domestic assets to foreign entities controlled by the group, and Sea Shepherd Australia took over the group's annual harassment of Japanese whalers in the Southern Ocean.[78] The following year, the whalers filed

---

73. *Id.* (citations omitted).
74. *Id.* (citations omitted).
75. *Id.* at 944.
76. *Id.* at 942.
77. Inst. of Cetacean Research, 725 F.3d at 947 (referencing order at 702 F.3d 573 (9th Cir. 2012)).
78. Inst. of Cetacean Research v. Sea Shepherd Conservation Soc'y (Cetacean II), 774 F.3d 935, 942–45 (9th Cir. 2014); *cert denied*, 135 S. Ct. 2816 (2015).

a contempt proceeding against Sea Shepherd claiming it was violating the Ninth Circuit's order that it stay 500 yards away from its vessels.[79] The Ninth Circuit agreed, finding that "Sea Shepherd U.S. was liable because it intentionally furnished cash payments, and a vessel and equipment worth millions of dollars, to individuals and entities it knew would likely violate the injunction."[80] The contempt action ultimately settled in 2015, with Sea Shepherd agreeing to pay $2.5 million in exchange for the whalers dropping all of their contempt claims against Sea Shepherd.[81] The piracy claims settled in 2016. The court-ordered settlement prohibits Sea Shepherd "from physically attacking any vessel engaged by [the Institute for Cetacean Research] in the Southern Ocean or from navigating in a manner that is likely to endanger the safe navigation of any such vessel" or providing any other party with money or property in order to so do.[82] The order also prohibits Sea Shepherd from approaching Japanese whaling vessels within 500 yards while on the open seas.[83] Sea Shepherd Australia has vowed to continue fighting Japanese whaling in the Southern Ocean.[84]

As this case highlights, some countries continue to hunt whales for profit, flouting international consensus that such practices should cease. However, the Convention's moratorium on commercial whaling has seen the rebounding of many species of whales, and others that are slowly recovering from near extinction. In this way, the global response to destructive, industrialized whaling is largely a success story, and an example of the change that can occur on a global scale in our oceans when countries work together. At the same time, many whales and other marine mammals are still highly imperiled and remain threatened by other exploitative practices across the globe.

---

79. *Id.* at 940.
80. *Id.* at 952.
81. Sea Shepherd, Press Release, *Sea Shepherd Resolves Contempt Dispute with Japanese Whalers* (June 8, 2015), *available at* http://www.seashepherd.org/news-and-media/2015/06/08/sea-shepherd-resolves-contempt-dispute-with-japanese-whalers-1700.
82. Inst. of Cetacean Research, Order Granting Stipulated Motion for Permanent Injunction, ECF Doc. No. 346, Case No. 2:11-cv-02043-JLR (W.D. Wash. Aug. 25, 2016).
83. *Id.*
84. *See, e.g.,* Nick Perry & Lisa Rathke, *Sea Shepherd Australia Says Will Continue South Ocean Action,* ASSOCIATED PRESS (Aug 25, 2016), http://bigstory.ap.org/article/bb86722d2d2f4647a21cf5cd3eddcb00/us-anti-whaling-group-stop-interfering-japanese.

The Tangled Web of the Commercial Fishing Industry

Each year, more than 650,000 whales, dolphins, porpoises, and other marine mammals are killed or seriously injured in gear used by commercial fisheries targeting a variety of species, including swordfish, tuna, shrimp, and lobster.[85] This "bycatch" threatens the survival of numerous populations of marine mammals across the globe, and is pushing some species to the brink of extinction. This section will discuss the harm to marine mammals from entanglement in commercial fishing gear and the mechanisms available to protect these animals from deadly and painful injuries.

Threats from Entanglements

The U.S. government has recognized bycatch as the "biggest threat to marine mammals worldwide."[86] For example, the baiji (*Lipotes vexillifer*), a freshwater dolphin endemic to the Yangtze River in China has been declared extinct, largely due to bycatch in a variety of fisheries.[87] At its annual meeting in 2007, the Scientific Committee of the International Whaling Commission "expressed its great concern that, despite extensive scientific discourse for more than two decades, little effort was made to implement any real conservation measures for this species."[88] It also noted that "[i]n hindsight, the extinction of this species is not surprising; species cannot be expected to save themselves. The extinction of this species (the first human-caused cetacean extinction) also underscores the risk to other endangered species of small cetaceans and particularly to the vaquita. Such highly endangered species require swift and decisive action before they are lost forever."[89]

85. Andrew J. Read et al., *Bycatch of marine mammals in U.S. and global fisheries*, 20 CONSERV. BIOL. 163–9 (2006).
86. *See, e.g.*, Proposed Rule, Fish and Fish Product Import Provisions of the Marine Mammal Protection Act, 80 Fed. Reg. 48,171, 48,172 (Aug. 22, 2015).
87. Andrew J. Read, *The Looming Crisis: Interactions Between Marine Mammals and Fisheries*, 89 J. MAMMALOGY 541–548 (2008).
88. *Id.* (quoting International Whaling Commission, *Report of the Scientific Committee*, J. CETACEAN RES. & MGMT. 1–80 (2006)).
89. *Id.*

The vaquita is the smallest porpoise in the world at just five feet in length. It has black patches around its eyes and mouth that some have described as black lipstick and heavy mascara that give it a "goth look."[90] The vaquita lives only in an approximately 4,000 km² area within the Upper Gulf of California, the smallest geographical range of any cetacean.[91] The vaquita was identified as a species in the 1950s but even then, it was already likely in decline.[92] From about the 1930s to the 1970s, the primary threat to the vaquita was entanglement in gillnet gear used in the totoaba (the largest member of the drum fish family) fishery.[93] Although Mexico banned its totoaba fishery in 1975 and implemented various conservation measures, vaquita continued to become entangled in legal shrimp and finfish gillnets, as well as in illegal totoaba nets.[94] The species is critically endangered, and its population has plummeted to as few as fifty individuals, declining by more than 40 percent from 2013 to 2014 alone.[95] Scientists predict the vaquita could be extinct by 2018 if vaquita bycatch is not eliminated immediately.[96]

---

90. Darryl Fears, *With Only 100 Left the Small Vaquita Porpoise Is on the Verge of Extinction*, Washington Post (Dec, 7, 2014), https://www.washingtonpost.com/national/health-science/with-only-100-left-the-small-vaquita-porpoise-is-on-the-verge-of-extinction/2014/12/07/08056fe4-7cb9-11e4-b821-503cc7efed9e_story.html.

91. Lorenzo Rojas-Bracho, Randall R. Reeves & Armando Jaramillo-Legorreta, *Conservation of the vaquita* Phocoena sinus. 36 Mammal Rev. 179–216 (2006).

92. *Id.*

93. Jay Barlow et al., *Conservation of the vaquita* (Phocoena sinus) *in the northern Gulf of California, Mexico* in Handbook of Marine Fisheries Conservation and Management (R. Quentin Grafton et al. eds.) 205–14 (2010).

94. CIRVA. 2012. Report of the Fourth Meeting of the International Committee for the Recovery of the Vaquita. Ensenada, Baja California, México, 20–23 February 2012, unpublished report. Illegal totoaba fishing continues still, because the significant demand for this fish's swim bladder in Asia, which is believed to increase fertility and improve skin, has skyrocketed; a single totoaba bladder can now reportedly sell for $14,000. *See, e.g.*, Associated Press & Zoe Szathmary, *'It's aquatic cocaine': Mexican smugglers are now selling FISH BLADDERS for thousands of dollars*, Daily Mail, Aug. 19, 2014.

95. Report of the Scientific Committee of the International Whaling Commission, IWC/66/Rep01 (2015) at 73.

96. International Committee for the Recovery of the Vaquita ("CIRVA"), *Report of the Fifth Meeting of the International Committee for the Recovery of the Vaquita* 2 (2014), http://assets.worldwildlife.org/publications/713/files/original/ 2014_Vaquita_Report_Fifth_Meeting_of_CIRVA.pdf?1408479198. Recognizing the need for urgent action, in April 2015, Mexico announced a two-year ban on most gillnets in the northern Gulf of California and promised to increase enforcement against the growing illegal totoaba fishery. But the remoteness and geography of the Gulf has made enforcement difficult, particularly given the involvement of drug cartels in the illegal totoaba trade. The IWC's 2015 Report noted that the regulations "need to be very strictly enforced if there is to be any hope of averting the extinction of the vaquita." Report of the Scientific Committee, *supra* note 88 at 8.

Other, larger marine mammals such as the North Atlantic right whale—one of the world's most endangered large whale species with fewer than 500 individuals remaining—is threatened by gear used in the lobster fishery and other fisheries from Canada to Florida.[97] Indeed, entanglement in fishing gear is one of the two primary threats to the species' survival and recovery (the second being death from collisions with ocean vessels) and currently the most frequent cause of injury to and death of members of the species.[98]

In addition to the significant conservation impacts, being wrapped in fishing lines, tangled in nets, or snagged on fishing hooks can cause individual animals a great deal of pain and suffering. Gear can wrap around the animal's head, flippers, or tail, preventing them from resurfacing and resulting in drowning. If animals do not immediately drown, the remaining gear can amputate flukes and cut into flesh, which can cause chronic infection, hemorrhaging, and prevent mobility or the ability to feed. And the typical reaction to being burdened in gear—thrashing around to try and shed the gear—only makes these injuries more severe. Large whales have been found severely emaciated and with lacerations deep into their blubber and even into their bones. As these animals are powerful enough to pull the gear with them, the rope continues to tighten and cut into their body over time, often resulting in a slow and painful death. One study found that fatally entangled large whales can take over six months to die.[99]

As the plight of the vaquita demonstrates, entanglements of marine mammals are increasing as the world's human population grows and as fisheries become more industrialized and expand into new waters such as the high seas. However, there are mechanisms in place to reduce this suffering both in U.S. waters and abroad.

---

97. Fisheries Service, *Recovery Plan for the North Atlantic Right Whale* (Eubalaena glacialis) (Aug. 2004) at v.

98. Waring et al., *U.S. Atlantic and Gulf of Mexico Marine Mammal Stock Assessments - 2014* (July 2015) at 12, http://www.nmfs.noaa.gov/pr/sars/pdf/atl2014_final.pdf.

99. Michael J. Moore et al., *Fatally entangled right whales can die extremely slowly*, PROC. MTS/IEEE OCEANS (2006), https://darchive.mblwhoilibrary.org/bitstream/handle/1912/1505/?sequence=1; Michael J. Moore & Julie M. van der Hoop, *The Painful Side of Trap and Fixed Net Fisheries: Chronic Entanglement of Large Whales*, 2012 J. MARINE BIOLOGY 1-4 (2012), *available at* http://www.hindawi.com/journals/jmb/2012/230653/abs/.

U.S. Laws to Protect Marine Mammals from Entanglements in Fishing Gear

Recognizing that "certain species and population stocks of marine mammals are, or may be, in danger of extinction or depletion as a result of man's activities," Congress passed the Marine Mammal Protection Act (MMPA) in 1972.[100] By the time the MMPA was enacted, nearly half a million dolphins were dying every year in the eastern Pacific Ocean as a result of being caught as bycatch by the purse-seine tuna fishery. This extraordinary level of capture and death was due to the fishing method used, known as "setting on dolphins" by which fishers chase and encircle dolphins with a large net that purses at the top, intentionally capturing both tuna and dolphins together. According to the National Marine Fisheries Service, "[t]he number of dolphins killed since the fishery began in the late 1950s is estimated to be over 6 million animals, the highest known for any fishery."[101]

Accordingly, the central purpose of the MMPA is to insure that marine mammals are "protected and encouraged to develop to the greatest extent feasible" and to prevent marine mammal stocks from falling below their "optimum sustainable population" levels, defined as the "number of animals which will result in the maximum productivity of the population or the species, keeping in mind the carrying capacity of the habitat and the health of the ecosystem of which they form a constituent element."[102]

To promote these objectives, the MMPA establishes a general moratorium on the taking of all marine mammals,[103] and expressly prohibits the unauthorized take of a marine mammal by any person.[104] Prohibited "takings" include actions that kill, injure, or capture marine mammals as well as harassment, defined as actions that have the potential to injure

---

100. 16 U.S.C. § 1361(6).

101. Southwest Fisheries Science Center, NOAA Fisheries Service, *The Tuna Dolphin Issue*, http://swfsc.noaa.gov/textblock.aspx?Division=PRD&ParentMenuId=228&id=1408 (updated Dec. 24, 2014).

102. 16 U.S.C. §§ 1361(2), 1362(9).

103. *Id.* § 1371(a).

104. *Id.* § 1372(a).

marine mammals or disrupt natural behavioral patterns, such as migration, breathing, breeding, or feeding.[105]

As one of "man's activities" Congress sought to address was the hundreds of thousands of dolphins drowning in fishing nets each year, numerous provisions of the MMPA are directed at reducing the entanglement of marine mammals.[106] While these provisions are focused on recovering depleted populations rather than protecting individual marine mammals from harm, efforts to reduce entanglements and interactions with other fishing gear are the most effective ways to prevent the pain and suffering that marine mammals endure.

In particular, Section 118 of the MMPA requires the National Marine Fisheries Service (NMFS) to "prevent the depletion" of marine mammals from incidental take by commercial fisheries and requires domestic commercial fisheries to "reduce incidental mortality and serious injury to marine mammals to insignificant levels approaching a zero mortality and serious injury rate," or the "zero mortality rate goal."[107] To implement this requirement, the MMPA requires NMFS to issue a "stock assessment" for each marine mammal population in U.S. waters. The assessment must document the population's abundance and trend, the fisheries each population interacts with, and the numbers of deaths and serious injuries those fisheries cause each year.[108] Based on the stock assessment, NMFS must then determine the "potential biological removal" for each stock, which is the "maximum number of animals . . . that may be removed from a marine mammal stock while allowing that stock to reach or maintain its optimum sustainable population."[109]

NMFS must also classify each commercial fishery according to its rate of fishery-related injury to marine mammals. Specifically, the MMPA requires NMFS to publish each year a list that categorizes each commercial fishery according to the rate of fishery-related injury to marine

---

105. *Id.* § 1362(13), (18).
106. *See, e.g., id.* § 1387(f)(1) (requiring NMFS to "prevent the depletion" of marine mammals from incidental take by commercial fisheries).
107. *Id.* §§ 1387(f)(1), (b)(1).
108. *Id.* § 1386(a).
109. 16 U.S.C. § 1386(a)(6); *id.* § 1362(20).

mammals.[110] The three categories identify fisheries that cause "(i) frequent incidental mortality and serious injury of marine mammals [("Category I" fisheries)]; (ii) occasional incidental mortality and serious injury of marine mammals [("Category II" fisheries)]; or (iii) a remote likelihood of or no known incidental mortality or serious injury of marine mammals [("Category III" fisheries)]."[111] NMFS must develop a "take reduction plan" for all marine mammal stocks in which the level of human-caused mortality exceeds the potential biological removal level, and for any stock listed under the Endangered Species Act (ESA), that interact with Category I and Category II fisheries.[112]

The MMPA sets specific deadlines for when these take reduction plans must be created and when the plans must accomplish their goals. The "immediate goal" of such plans is to reduce, "within 6 months of its implementation," the incidental mortality and serious injury of marine mammals to below the potential biological removal level.[113] The long-term goal of the take reduction plan must be to reduce, within five years, incidental mortality and serious injury "to insignificant levels approaching a zero mortality and serious injury rate."[114] The agency has defined "insignificant levels approaching . . . zero," or the zero mortality rate goal, to mean ten percent of a stock's potential biological removal level.[115]

In enacting the MMPA, Congress expressed its clear intent that Section 118 would require "immediate action to protect . . . marine mammal stocks most affected by interactions with commercial fishing operations."[116] Accordingly, NMFS must amend the take reduction plan as necessary to meet the requirements of the MMPA.[117] All fishermen engaged in a Category I or II fishery must register with NMFS and com-

---

110. *Id.* § 1387(c)(1).

111. *Id.* § 1387(c)(1)(A); 50 C.F.R. § 229.2.

112. 16 U.S.C. §§ 1387(f)(1), 1362(19). The purpose, prohibitions and requirements of the Endangered Species Act are explained further below. *See infra*, notes 119–137 and accompanying text.

113. *Id.* § 1387(f)(2).

114. *Id.*

115. 50 C.F.R. § 229.2.

116. S. REP. NO. 103-220, at 6 (1994) (emphasis added).

117. 16 U.S.C. § 1387(f)(7)(F).

ply with the terms of the take reduction plan, and any amendments, in order to engage in the lawful incidental taking of marine mammals.[118]

Additional protections apply if a marine mammal species or stock is listed as threatened or endangered under the ESA—in which case the take must also be authorized pursuant to Section 101(a)(5)(E) of the MMPA. Specifically, NMFS may authorize a commercial fishery to take listed marine mammals incidental to the operation of that fishery if a recovery plan has been, or is being, developed for the species, and NMFS finds that such take will have a "negligible impact" on the species or stock to be taken and issues take permits to each vessel engaged in that particular fishery.[119] A negligible impact is defined by NMFS as "an impact resulting from the specified activity that cannot be reasonably expected to, and is not reasonably likely to, adversely affect the species or stock through effects on annual rates of recruitment or survival."[120]

Once issued, NMFS can suspend, modify, or revoke such permits if the permittee is not in compliance with the conditions or limitations of its permit and can modify permits as necessary if, during the course of the commercial fishing season, NMFS finds that the level of incidental mortality or serious injury from the fishery "has or is likely to have more than a negligible impact."[121] As NMFS itself has previously recognized, "the congressional choice of imposing an additional regulatory process before authorizing the incidental taking of listed marine mammals reflected a concern for the need for more safeguards."[122]

In addition to the MMPA, the ESA also contains many measures to protect listed marine mammals (and any other listed species) from entanglements in fishing gear. In enacting the ESA, Congress recognized that certain species "have been so depleted in numbers that they are in danger of or threatened with extinction."[123] Accordingly, a primary purpose of the ESA is "to provide a means whereby the ecosystems upon which

118. *Id.* § 1387(c)(3).
119. *Id.* § 1371(a)(5)(E).
120. 50 C.F.R. § 18.27.
121. 16 U.S.C. § 1371(a)(5)(E).
122. 54 Fed. Reg. 40,338, 40,341 (Sept. 29, 1989).
123. 16 U.S.C. § 1531(a)(2).

endangered species and threatened species depend may be conserved, [and] to provide a program for the conservation of such . . . species."[124]

To reach these goals, Section 9 of the ESA prohibits any person from "taking" any endangered species without proper authorization through a valid incidental take permit.[125] The statutory term "take" is defined broadly and includes any "act that actually kills or injures wildlife. Such act may include significant habitat modification or degradation where it actually kills or injures wildlife by significantly impairing essential behavioral patterns, including breeding, feeding or sheltering."[126] The prohibitions cover direct actors as well as third parties that "bring about the acts exacting a taking," including government agencies that authorize the taking of an endangered species.[127]

Moreover, Section 7(a) of the ESA requires that all federal agencies carry out programs to conserve listed species,[128] and "conserve" means to undertake actions necessary to recover listed species to the point that they can be taken off the endangered/threatened species lists.[129] In addition, Section 4(f) specifically requires that NMFS "develop and implement" a recovery plan for each threatened or endangered species that contains specific management measures to conserve the species.[130]

In order to prevent harm to listed species, Section 7(a)(2) of the ESA further requires all federal agencies to ensure that any action "authorized, funded, or carried out" by the agency is not likely to jeopardize the continued existence of any listed species, or adversely modify or destroy

---

124. *Id.* § 1531(b).

125. 16 U.S.C. § 1538(a)(1)(B). Under the ESA, the U.S. Fish and Wildlife Service has jurisdiction over terrestrial and freshwater species, while NMFS has jurisdiction over marine species. Memorandum of Understanding between United States Fish and Wildlife Service and National Marine Fisheries Service Regarding Jurisdictional Responsibilities and Listing Procedures Under the Endangered Species Act of 1973 (Aug. 1974); *see also* 50 C.F.R. § 17.31(a) (extending the "take" prohibition to threatened species managed by the U.S. Fish and Wildlife Service).

126. 50 C.F.R. § 17.3; *see also* Babbitt v. Sweet Home Ch. Of Communities for a Great Oregon, 515 U.S. 687 (1995) (upholding regulatory definition of harm).

127. Strahan v. Coxe, 127 F.3d 155, 163 (1st Cir. 1997).

128. *Id.* § 1536(a)(1); *see also id.* § 1531(c)(1) (it is the "policy of Congress that all Federal . . . agencies shall seek to conserve endangered species and threatened species and shall utilize their authorities in furtherance of the purposes" of the ESA).

129. *Id.* § 1532(3).

130. 16 U.S.C. §§ 1533(f), (f)(1)(B)(i).

their habitat.[131] To comply with this substantive obligation, an "agency shall . . . request" from the appropriate Service (either the U.S. Fish and Wildlife Service, NMFS, or both) information regarding whether any listed species "may be present" in a proposed action area, and if so, the "agency shall conduct a biological assessment" to identify species likely to be affected.[132] The agency must then initiate formal consultation with the Service if a proposed action "may affect" any of those listed species.[133]

After formal consultation, the Service issues a biological opinion to determine whether the agency action is likely to "jeopardize" any species' existence. If so, the opinion may specify reasonable and prudent alternatives that avoid jeopardy.[134] If the Services conclude that the action or the reasonable and prudent alternatives will not cause jeopardy, the Services will issue an incidental take statement that specifies "the impact, i.e., the amount or extent, of . . . incidental taking" that may occur.[135] When those listed species are marine mammals, the take must first be authorized pursuant to the MMPA, and the incidental take statement must include any additional measures necessary to comply with the take authorization under the MMPA.[136] The take of a listed species in compliance with the terms of a valid incidental take statement is not prohibited under Section 9 of the ESA.[137]

Consistent with these statutory requirements, NMFS has implemented several measures to reduce marine mammal bycatch in numerous domestic fisheries. For example, NMFS has banned the use of drift gillnets—which are often a mile or more in length and entangle virtually everything that comes in their path—in most U.S. swordfish fisheries. Specifically, the Atlantic Highly Migratory Species Fishery Management Plan, which governs fishing for swordfish, tuna, and sharks off the East Coast of the United States, prohibits the use of gillnets to fish for

---

131. *Id.* § 1536(a)(2).
132. 16 U.S.C. § 1536(c).
133. 50 C.F.R. § 402.14(a); 51 Fed. Reg. 19,926 (June 3, 1986) ("may affect" broadly includes "[a]ny possible effect, whether beneficial, benign, adverse or of an undetermined character").
134. 16 U.S.C. § 1536(b); 50 C.F.R. § 402.14(h)(3).
135. 50 C.F.R. § 402.14(h)(3).
136. *Id.*
137. 16 U.S.C. §§ 1536(b)(4), (o)(2); 50 C.F.R. § 402.14(i)(5).

swordfish and prohibits a vessel that has a gillnet on board from possessing swordfish.[138] Fishing with drift gillnets is similarly prohibited in the western Pacific Fishery Management Area surrounding Hawaii, except when authorized under an experimental fishery permit.[139] While drift gillnet fishing is not yet banned off the West Coast, it is significantly limited by a complex set of regulations.[140] These regulations require, *inter alia*, the use of pingers (devices that transmit short, high pitched sounds when immersed in water to deter marine mammals) on all drift gillnets; a minimum depth of six fathoms below the surface for drift gillnets; and a prohibition on gillnet fishing in certain areas at certain times of year.[141]

NMFS has also banned or restricted longline fishing for pelagic fish—species that live in the water column, rather than near the shore or the bottom of the ocean. Longline fishing can kill and seriously injure marine mammals that are attracted to the baited hooks and either become hooked themselves or entangled in the line. A single longline set can trail for up to sixty miles, dangling thousands of lines and hooks in its wake and forming a nearly invisible, deadly obstacle for animals in the open water. For example, the West Coast Highly Migratory Species Fishery Management Plan, which governs the swordfish fishery off the U.S. West Coast, prohibits the use of pelagic longline gear in the West Coast exclusive economic zone.[142] The use of longline gear by U.S. vessels to target swordfish is also prohibited outside the U.S.'s exclusive economic zone north of the equator.[143]

Additionally, NMFS adopted the Atlantic Large Whale Take Reduction Plan under Section 118 in 1997 to reduce the impacts of the commercial lobster and other fisheries on critically endangered North Atlantic

---

138. 50 C.F.R. §§ 635.21(e)(4), 635.71(a)(17).

139. *Id.* § 665.30.

140. Pacific Fishery Management Council, West Coast Highly Migratory Species Fishery Management Plan (June 2011) at 67.

141. *Id.* at 67–68. While the time-area closures were implemented to protect threatened and endangered sea turtles, they also protect whales, as whales and marine mammals are entangled in drift gillnet gear on the West Coast. *See* Fisheries Service California/Oregon Drift Gillnet Observer Program Observed Catch - 2013/2014, Fishing Season May 1, 2013, through January 31, 2014, http://www.westcoast.fisheries.noaa.gov/publications/fishery_management/swr_observer_program/drift_gillnet_catch_summaries/observeddgn2013-2014.pdf.

142. West Coast Highly Migratory Species Fishery Management Plan, *supra* note 140 at 70.

143. *Id.*

right whales, and endangered humpback and fin whales.[144] The Atlantic Large Whale Take Reduction Plan, amended in 2007 and again in 2014 in the face of continued entanglements, implements seasonal closures in areas where whales congregate to feed and breed, requires all trap/pot fisheries to use sinking groundline (lines that do not float at any point in the water column), and requires reduced amount of line in the water column to reduce the risk of entanglements.[145] The rules, however, contain a dangerous number of exemptions, so that the numbers of critically endangered North Atlantic right whales killed or seriously injured by commercial fisheries every year is more than triple that which the agency says the population can sustain, and far from a zero mortality rate.[146] However, as imperfect as the rules and NMFS's management of these fisheries are, they are miles ahead of other countries.

U.S. Laws to Protect Marine Mammals from Entanglements around the Globe

Similar to the motivation behind the Pelly Amendment, in enacting the MMPA, Congress recognized that, if the United States' efforts to protect marine mammals from fisheries bycatch were to be successful, it would have to exert pressure on fisheries of other nations to adopt similarly protective measures. Specifically, Section 101(a)(2) of the MMPA requires that the Secretary of the Treasury "ban the importation of commercial fish or products from fish which have been caught with commercial fishing technology which results in the incidental kill or incidental serious injury of ocean mammals in excess of United States standards."[147]

To implement this provision, the Secretary of Commerce must obtain and approve a country's demonstration of the effects of its fishing techniques on marine mammals before allowing that country's fish products

---

144. *See* 16 U.S.C. § 1387(c)(3)(A)(iv); 50 C.F.R. § 229.32. In addition to the Atlantic Large Whale Take Reduction Plan, NMFS also has implemented take reduction plans for harbor porpoise, bottlenose dolphin, Atlantic pelagic longline (to address serious injury and mortality of long and short finned pilot whales and Risso's dolphins), and false killer whales. *See* 50 C.F.R. §§ 229.33–.37.
145. 50 C.F.R. § 229.32.
146. Waring, *supra* note 98 at 11–12.
147. 16 U.S.C. § 1371(a)(2).

to enter the United States.[148] Section 102 also prohibits the import of fish caught in a way that would be illegal for fishers who are under U.S. jurisdiction.[149]

Unfortunately, these provisions have been largely forgotten, and the United States has been slow to implement measures to reduce entanglements abroad. But as of 2016, that situation seemed about to change. In 2014, environmental organizations filed suit against the Secretaries of Commerce, Homeland Security, and Treasury in the U.S. Court of International Trade claiming that the agencies unlawfully failed to respond to a 2008 rulemaking petition requesting that they carry out their non-discretionary duties under Section 101(a)(2) with respect to swordfish fisheries around the world.[150] The lawsuit also alleged that the United States failed to promulgate regulations to implement Section 101(a)(2) for other fisheries and failed to ban other fish imports that kill or seriously injure marine mammals in excess of U.S. standards, in violation of the MMPA.[151]

Pursuant to the terms of a settlement agreement, NMFS issued a final rule to implement Section 101(a)(2) in August 2016.[152] The rule establishes procedures that a harvesting nation must follow to import certain fish to the United States.[153] As Section 102 intended, foreign fisheries will have to comply with essentially the same requirements for the protection of marine mammals as U.S. fisheries. Specifically, the rule establishes a system pursuant to which NMFS will classify and list foreign fisheries based on the likelihood of causing serious injury or mortality to marine mammals.[154]

NMFS would require a harvesting nation to apply for and receive a comparability finding for its fisheries as a condition precedent to import-

---

148. *Id.* § 1371(a)(2)(A).
149. *Id.* § 1372(c)(3).
150. Complaint (Doc. 6) at 17, Ctr. for Biological Diversity, et al. v. Pritzker, No. 14-00157 (Dist. Ct. Intl. Trade, June 2, 2014).
151. *Id.* at 18.
152. 81 Fed. Reg. 54,389 (Aug. 15, 2016).
153. 81 Fed. Reg. at 54,389.
154. *Id.* at 54,391.

ing fish and fish products to the United States.[155] This comparability finding would have two steps. First, it would require the harvesting nation to demonstrate that it prohibits the intentional killing or serious injuring of marine mammals in the course of commercial fishing activities or ensures U.S. exports are not the result of an intentional killing or serious injury of a marine mammal.[156] Second, for fisheries that have more than a remote chance of causing serious injury or mortality to marine mammals, a harvesting nation must also demonstrate that it maintains a regulatory program that is comparable in effectiveness to the U.S. regulatory program in reducing bycatch of marine mammals.[157] Countries will have until 2022 to come into compliance.[158]

In contrast to provisions of the MMPA that specifically seek to prohibit inhumane practices, such as the prohibition on importing marine mammals who were nursing at the time they were captured from the wild,[159] neither this rule nor the other MMPA provisions that seek to promote the recovery of marine mammal populations by reducing entanglements in commercial fishing gear directly focus on animal welfare. However, measures aimed at reducing entanglements will still reduce the drowning, amputations, infection, hemorrhaging, and starvation suffered by marine mammals. By establishing take reduction permits that require strong, comprehensive measures to reduce entanglements in U.S. fisheries, and rules implementing the largely overlooked, forty-year-old provision regarding the import of fish caught in foreign waters, the MMPA can begin to live up to its original intent that the interests of marine mammals come first under the statutory scheme,[160] and its reputation as "an unusual statute . . . motivated by considerations of humaneness towards animals."[161]

155. *Id.*
156. *Id.*
157. *Id.*
158. *Id.*
159. 16 U.S.C. § 1372(b).
160. Kokechik Fishermen's Ass'n v. Sec'y of Commerce, 839 F.2d 795, 802 (D.C.C. 1988).
161. Animal Welfare Inst. v. Kreps, 561 F.2d 1002, 1007 (D.C.C. 1977).

U.S. Laws to Protect Other Species from
Entanglements around the Globe

Similar provisions in other statutes can force comparable protections for other species incidentally caught in foreign fisheries, such as sea turtles. For example, Section 610(a)(1) of the Moratorium Protection Act, enacted in 2006, seeks to reduce bycatch of protected living marine resources— "non-target fish, sea turtles, or marine mammals" protected under U.S. law or international agreement.[162] Under this provision, the Secretary of Commerce must "identify" a nation for bycatch activities if (1) fishing vessels of the nation cause catch of "a protected living marine resource shared by the United States," (2) no international organization has implemented measures to end or reduce the bycatch, and (3) the foreign nation has not implemented a satisfactory program to reduce the bycatch. [163]

Identification of a nation triggers a process that can result in a denial of the nation's fishing vessels' access to U.S. ports, as well as trade restrictions and certification under the Pelly Amendment.[164]

In 2013, NMFS "identified" a nation—Mexico—for the first time under the protected living marine resources provision. The excessive bycatch was identified when 438 endangered North Pacific loggerhead sea turtles washed up dead along the coast of Baja California Sur during the summer of 2012.[165] The strandings were likely caused by gillnet fishery bycatch, especially given scientific studies indicating that gillnet and longline fisheries in Mexico may be killing as many as 2,000 sea turtles per year.[166]

---

162. 16 U.S.C. § 1826k(e)(1).

163. *Id.* § 1826k(a)(1).

164. *Id.* §§ 1826h, 1826k(b); 50 C.F.R. § 300.203(c)(1). *See also id.* § 1826k(c)(1). "[I]n the case of pelagic longline fishing," the foreign regulatory program must "include[ ] mandatory use of circle hooks, careful handling and release equipment, and training and observer programs." *See also id.* §§ 1826a(a)(2)(B), 1826a(a)(2)(A), and 1826a(b)(3).

165. U.S. Department of Commerce, Improving International Fisheries Management, Report to Congress Pursuant to Section 403(a) of the Magnuson-Stevens Fishery Conservation and Management Reauthorization Act of 2006 (Jan. 2013) at 27.

166. S. Hoyt Peckham et al. *High Mortality of Loggerhead Turtles due to Bycatch, Human Consumption and Strandings at Baja California Sur, Mexico, 2003 to 2007.* ENDANGERED SPECIES RES. (2008). published online Oct. 13, 2008.

In 2015, NMFS issued a negative certification, finding that Mexico failed to adequately address loggerhead sea turtle bycatch.[167] The President must now decide what fish or fish products to embargo, while NMFS will continue to work with Mexico to address the issue.[168]

The United States consumes roughly five billion pounds of seafood each year, more than 90 percent of which is imported and about half of which is wild-caught, and is second only to China in the amount of seafood it imports.[169] As such, import restrictions could have a profound impact on fishing practices across the globe. The new MMPA import rules and actions pursuant to the Moratorium Protection Act could save hundreds of thousands of marine animals around the world by requiring foreign fisheries to meet the same protection standards required of U.S. fishermen in order to import their fish into the country.

The Depletion of Ocean Biodiversity by Commercial Fishing

Entanglements of marine mammals are not the only serious threat to the ocean caused by fishing—overfishing of target species is also a huge problem, both in U.S. waters and on the high seas. For example, scientists have found that populations of certain large predatory fish, such as Pacific bluefin tuna and Atlantic cod, have declined by more than 90 percent, and that one in four species of sharks, rays, and skates is now threatened with extinction due to overfishing.[170] Overfishing also has significant

---

167. U.S. Dep't of Commerce, Certification Determination for Mexico's 2013 Identification for Bycatch of North Pacific Loggerhead Sea Turtles (Aug. 2015).

168. *Id.* at 5; 16 U.S.C. § 1826a(b)(3).

169. *NOAA to Work with 10 Nations to Address Illegal, Unreported, and Unregulated Fishing and Stem the Bycatch of Protected Species* (June 22, 2013), http://www.nmfs.noaa.gov/ia/slider_stories/2013/01/msra_2013_report.html.

170. *See, e.g.,* International Scientific Committee for Tuna and Tuna-Like Species in the North Pacific Ocean, *Stock Assessment of Pacific Bluefin Tuna 2014*, http://www.biologicaldiversity.org/species/fish/Atlantic_bluefin_tuna/pdfs/PBF_2014_Exec_Summary_4_04-17.pdf; Northeast Fisheries Science Center, An overview of the 2014 update of the Gulf of Maine cod stock assessment. Presentation to NEFMC, Hyannis, MA, Oct. 1, 2014, http://s3.amazonaws.com/nefmc .org/2014_GoM_cod_update_NEFSC_v2.pdf; Ransom A. Myers & Boris Worm. *Rapid Worldwide Depletion of Predatory Fish Communities*. 423 Nature 280–3(2003). doi:10.1038/nature01610; World Wildlife Fund and Zoological Society of London, *Living Blue Planet Report, 2015.*

impacts for humans; studies estimate that nearly three billion people rely on fish as a major food source and that fishery operations provide livelihoods for more than 10 percent of the world's population.[171] This section will focus on measures implemented in the United States to reduce overfishing both domestically and abroad.

The Magnuson-Stevens Fishery Conservation and Management Act

Historically, fish and fishing activities were regulated by an assortment of both federal regulations regarding trade and vessel licensing and state regulations.[172] However, the state regulations focused primarily on gear restrictions, and only extended to three miles from shore—the territorial limit of a state's jurisdiction.[173] Accordingly, fish were significantly exploited, particularly beyond the state's jurisdiction where there were few regulations protecting fish, and fishers raced to catch more fish than their competitors.[174]

In response, recognizing that fish stocks were dropping "to the point where their survival is threatened" caused by increased fishing pressure and inadequate fishery resource conservation and management, Congress enacted what is now known as the Magnuson-Stevens Fishery Conservation and Management Act (Magnuson-Stevens Act) in 1976.[175] But in contrast to other statutes such as the MMPA and ESA that seek to conserve and recover imperiled species by prohibiting acts that kill or harm such species, the Magnuson-Stevens Act seeks to protect both fish stocks and the fisheries that take such fish to "achieve and maintain . . . the optimal yield from each fishery."[176] In other words, the Magnuson-Stevens Act "balances the twin goals of conserving our nation's aquatic resources

---

171. *Id.*.
172. Josh Eagle *et al.*, *Taking Stock of the Regional Fishery Management Councils*, ISLAND PRESS PUBLICATION SERVICE 8 (2003), http://www.apo-observers.org/docs/pew_science_taking_stock .pdf.
173. *Id.*
174. *Id.*
175. 16 U.S.C. § 1801(a).
176. *Id.* § 1801(b).

and allowing U.S. fisheries to thrive."[177] But the Magnuson-Stevens Act is clear that of these two purposes, "conservation is paramount."[178]

To that end, the Magnuson-Stevens Act establishes a complex regulatory scheme under which the Secretary of Commerce and eight regional Fishery Management Councils oversee the harvest of fish from the nation's oceans.[179] The Councils prepare fishery management plans for each fishery within their respective jurisdictions that "requires conservation and management."[180] Fishery management plans must include measures that prevent overfishing and rebuild overfished stocks, while protecting, restoring, and promoting the long-term health and stability of the fishery.[181]

Specifically, a fishery management plan must, *inter alia*, describe and identify essential fish habitat and, to the extent practicable, minimize adverse effects on such habitat from the fishery.[182] Fishery management plans must also be consistent with the Magnuson-Stevens Act's ten National Standards which, *inter alia*, require: (1) "prevent[ion of] overfishing while achieving . . . optimum yield . . . ;"[183] (2) reliance on "the best scientific information available"; (3) efficient and cooperative management of fisheries; (4) "fair and equitable" allocation of fishing privileges; (5) minimizing bycatch;[184] and (6) promotion of "the safety of human life at sea."[185]

---

177. Oceana, 26 F. Supp. 3d at 36.

178. Chinatown Neighborhood Ass'n v. Harris, 794 F.3d 1136, 1143 (9th Cir. 2015, *cert. denied*; Nat. Res. Def. Council, Inc. v. Nat'l Marine Fisheries Serv., 421 F.3d 872, 879 (9th Cir. 2005) ("[t]he purpose of the Act is clearly to give conservation of fisheries priority over short-term economic interests").

179. 16 U.S.C. §§ 1801(b); 1852; Oceana, Inc. v. Pritzker, 26 F. Supp. 3d 33, 36 (D.D.C. 2014); The Magnuson-Stevens Act also contains a savings provision pursuant to which states retain the authority to manage fishing within the state's jurisdictional waters. 16 U.S.C. § 1856(a).

180. *Id.* § 1853(a)(1)(A).

181. *Id.*; Flaherty v. Bryson, 850 F. Supp. 2d 38, 43 (D.D.C. 2012).

182. 16 U.S.C. § 1853(a)(7).

183. "Overfished" is defined as "a rate or level of fishing mortality that jeopardizes the capacity of a fishery to produce the maximum sustainable yield on a continuing basis." *Id.* § 1802(34).

184. Bycatch is defined in the Magnuson-Stevens Act as "fish which are harvested in a fishery, but which are not sold or kept for personal use and includes economic discards and regulatory discards." 16 U.S.C. § 1802(2). "In simple terms, bycatch kills fish that would otherwise contribute toward the well-being of the fishery or the nation's seafood consumption needs." Conservation Law Found. v. Evans, 209 F. Supp. 2d 1, 14 (D.D.C. 2001).

185. 16 U.S.C. § 1851(a).

If a fishery management plan is approved by NMFS, a finalized plan is subject to public notice and comment.[186] Once approved, fishery management plans are kept current through formal changes, with prevention of overfishing as the primary focus.[187]

Despite these requirements, by the 1990s, many important fish populations were still significantly depleted, including New England cod, Gulf of Mexico red snapper, and swordfish. The Sustainable Fisheries Act of 1996 attempted to address continued overfishing by requiring Councils to establish an objective definition of overfishing in each fishery management plan, and to develop a standardized reporting system for bycatch and determining the mortality of fish caught by catch-and-release.[188] But the Councils often failed to act, and even when they did, overfishing still occurred because, in large part, fishery management plans were required "to adher[e] to scientifically established mortality limits from one year to the next,"[189] and those limits proved inadequate to protect these populations.

To address these issues, and establish "a firm deadline for ending overfishing in America," Congress amended the Magnuson-Stevens Act in 2006.[190] The amendments require the Councils to set Annual Catch Limits—the amount of fish to be caught—which cannot exceed the fishing level recommendations of a Council's scientific and statistical committee.[191] The Councils must also establish accountability measures for ensuring compliance with the Annual Catch Limits.[192] Accountability measures can include closing a fishery when a quota is projected to be reached, lowering catch limits to account for uncertainty in calculating total harvest during the year, or reducing the total harvest for the following year if catch limits are exceeded.[193]

---

186. *Id.* § 1854(b).

187. Natural Resources Defense Council, Inc. v. Daley, 209 F.3d 747, 754 (D.D.C. 2000).

188. Sustainable Fisheries Act, Public Law 104-297 (1996).

189. Coastal Conservation Ass'n v. Locke, No. 2:09-cv-641-FtM-29SPC, 2011 U.S. Dist. LEXIS 111814, at *8 (M.D. Fl. Aug. 16, 2011) (quoting S. Rep. No. 109-229, at 21 (2006).

190. Flaherty, 850 F. Supp. 2d at 43.

191. Magnuson-Stevens Fishery Conservation and Management Reauthorization Act of 2006, Pub. L. No. 109–479, 120 Stat. 3575, 3581, 3584 (2007), codified at 16 U.S.C. §§ 1852(h)(1) (6); 1853(a)(15).

192. *Id.*

193. *See, e.g.,* 50 C.F.R. §§ 600.310(g)(2); (g)(3).

The establishment of Annual Catch Limits and associated regulation of overfished fisheries is one of the primary ways that the sustainable fishery management and conservation goals of the Magnuson-Stevens Act are achieved.[194] If the Secretary determines a fishery has reached overfished levels, a series of actions is triggered to address the issue, requiring adequate response from the appropriate Council.

Despite these requirements, fish continue to be added to the overfished list, and some are struggling for survival. For example, in 2014, Gulf of Maine cod reached their lowest level ever recorded, with a fishing mortality rate near all-time highs.[195] From 1982 to 2014, the stock suffered a massive 90 percent population decline, 77 percent of which occurred from 2009 to 2014.[196] NMFS estimates are that the stock is at a mere 3 to 4 percent of its target abundance.[197] As at least one federal court has recognized, implementation of the Magnuson-Stevens Act "illustrates the difficult balance that environmental regulators often must strike between species conservation and economic priorities."[198] Fishing in this country is big business—in 2013, U.S. fishers landed 9.9 billion pounds of fish and shellfish worth $5.5 billion.[199] The fact the Magnuson-Stevens Act vests much of the authority for developing management measures with those with a financial interest in fishing can frustrate the goal of conserving fish species. Nevertheless, the Magnuson-Stevens Act has been largely effective at ending overfishing and rebuilding depleted fish

194. 16 U.S.C. § 1854(e); Flaherty, 850 F. Supp. 2d at 52–53 (Annual Catch Limits and accountability measures "are so central to effective fishery management and avoidance of overfishing").
195. National Marine Fisheries Service, *Gulf of Maine Atlantic Cod 2014 Assessment Updated Report* (August 22, 2014), http://www.nefsc.noaa.gov/saw/cod/pdfs/GoM_cod_2014_update_20140822.pdf.
196. Northeast Fisheries Science Center, An overview of the 2014 update of the Gulf of Maine cod stock assessment. Presentation to NEFMC, Hyannis, MA, Oct. 1, 2014, http://s3.amazonaws.com/nefmc.org/2014_GoM_cod_update_NEFSC_v2.pdf.
197. National Marine Fisheries Service, *supra* note 195.
198. Conservation Law Found. v. Pritzker, 37 F. Supp. 3d 234 (D.D.C. 2014).
199. NMFS, Request for Comments on Presidential Task Force on Combating Illegal Unreported and Unregulated (IUU) Fishing and Seafood Fraud Action Plan, 80 Fed. Reg. 24,246 (Apr. 30, 2015). A significant portion of this catch is exported overseas for processing, and then reimported into the United States. NMFS, *Fisheries of the United States, 2013: A Statistical Snapshot of 2013 Fish Landings*, http://www.st.nmfs.noaa.gov/Assets/commercial/fus/fus13/materials/FUS2013_FactSheet_FINAL.pdf.

populations.[200] Today, the primary fishing threat comes from practices of other countries, and fishing on the high seas.

Addressing Overfishing and Unsustainable Fishing Abroad

The "high seas"—the waters that fall beyond a coastal nation's territorial waters—make up more than 60 percent of the world's oceans. As such, the majority of the oceans are outside the jurisdiction of any particular government. Highly migratory species such as bluefin tuna face enormous fishing pressure as they travel in and out of the jurisdictions of many different countries. The problems for these species, and others, are often compounded by unsustainable fishing practices employed by many fisheries around the world. For example, bottom trawling, which accounts for most of the deep-sea fishing on the high seas, involves dragging heavy nets across the seafloor, which can destroy deep-water corals and sponges and results in a significant amount of bycatch. Overfishing and unsustainable fishing practices on the high seas can have profound impacts on the ocean environment; it is estimated that nearly half of the biological productivity of the oceans occurs on the high seas.

The 2006 amendments to the Magnuson-Stevens Act also attempt to address international overfishing and unsustainable fishing practices.[201] The Secretary is expressly authorized to investigate and take appropriate action to try to address identified problems.[202] The amendments also specifically require NMFS to address illegal, unreported, and unregulated fishing, also known as "pirate fishing."[203] As NMFS has stated, pirate fishing can devastate fish populations and their habitats and "undermines international efforts to sustainably manage and rebuild fisheries and creates unfair market competition for fishermen who adhere to strict conservation measures," including U.S. fishermen.[204] Pirate fishing represents

---

200. 80 Fed. Reg. at 24,246.
201. Pub. L. No. 109-479, 120 Stat. 3575 (addressing overfishing "due to excessive international fishing pressure.").
202. 16 U.S.C. § 1854(i).
203. *Id.* § 1826j(e).
204. NOAA Fisheries, Press Release, *NOAA to work with 10 nations to address illegal, unreported, and unregulated fishing and stem the bycatch of protected species* (Jan. 11, 2013), http://www .noaanews.noaa.gov/stories2013/20130111_protectedspecies.html.

as much as 40 percent of the total catch in some fisheries.[205] The pirate fishing provisions are similar to the protected living marine resources provision used to address bycatch in foreign fisheries discussed earlier in this chapter.[206]

The United States has used these provisions to identify multiple nations whose vessels are engaged in pirate fishing.[207] The response to U.S. intervention has been positive and seemingly successful: Of ten nations identified in 2013, all had either adopted or amended laws and regulations, sanctioned the offended vessels, and/or improved monitoring and enforcement.[208] The United States also seeks to combat pirate fishing through its participation in Regional Fishery Management Organizations, the primary means by which fisheries in international waters are managed.[209] These measures include development and sharing of lists of pirate fishing vessels, enhanced monitoring programs, adoption of port State inspection schemes, and better regulation of transshipments at sea.[210]

However, the fact that many of the same countries are repeatedly identified for pirate fishing by the United States reflects the scope of the problem, and the lack of meaningful international agreements to address pirate fishing. In 2009, the U.N. Food and Agriculture Organization adopted the Agreement on Port State Measures to Prevent, Deter and Eliminate Illegal, Unreported and Unregulated Fishing—the first binding international agreement focused specifically on combating pirate fishing.[211] The Agreement contains many of the measures that have already been adopted by the United States, including restricting port entry of vessels that have been engaged in pirate fishing or vessels supporting these

---

205. Fisheries Service, Fact Sheet, *Illegal Fishing: Not in Our Ports Port State Measures Agreement and Implementing Legislation,* http://www.nmfs.noaa.gov/ia/iuu/portstate_factsheet.pdf.

206. *See supra* notes 162–168 and accompanying text; 16 U.S.C. §§ 1826j, 1826j(d).

207. NMFS, *Summary of 2015 Biennial Report to Congress* (Feb. 2015), http://www.fisheries.noaa .gov/ia/iuu/msra_page/noaa_iuu_report_final_web.pdf (identifying 10 nations).

208. *Id.* Six more nations were identified in 2015—Colombia, Ecuador, Mexico, Nigeria, Nicaragua, and Portugal.

209. NOAA, *Leveling the Playing Field: NOAA's Priorities to Combat IUU Fishing in 2013,* http:// www.nmfs.noaa.gov/ia/iuu/ltpf.pdf.

210. *Id.*

211. Agreement on Port State Measures to Prevent, Deter and Eliminate Illegal, Unreported and Unregulated Fishing, Art. 2.

activities, particularly those on the pirate fishing vessel list of a regional fishery management organization; requiring vessel inspections at ports; and requiring countries to share information, when evidence of pirate fishing is found during the course of an inspection.[212] The treaty entered into force in 2016 after at least twenty-five nations signed it.[213] Global Ocean Commission has called on the global community to declare the high seas a regeneration zone, where commercial fishing would be prohibited if sufficient action is not taken to turn the tide of fishery declines on the high seas.[214]

In 2015, after nearly a decade of discussions, the United Nations finally recognized the need to regulate fishing on the high seas to prevent overfishing and rebuild depleted stocks. While a specific agreement has yet to be finalized, reports indicate that the United Nations is poised to craft a new international agreement that would declare marine protected areas, where fishing would be restricted or prohibited, in 10 percent of the high seas by 2020, eventually increasing that figure to 30 percent.[215] Such action is necessary to protect and improve the biodiversity of our ocean and the life that depends upon its health.

Ocean Health Threatened by Land-Based Sources of Pollution

In addition to extractive practices in the oceans that kill or injure, marine life is also threatened by pollution, most of which comes from land-based sources. This pollution includes oil spills from oil and gas extraction and transportation; noise pollution from ships, military training, and oil and gas exploration activities; agricultural and stormwater runoff; and the

212. *Id.* at Art. 3, 5, 7, 9, 11.
213. Food and Agriculture Organization of the United Nations, *World's First Illegal Fishing Treaty Now in Force* (June 2016), http://www.fao.org/news/story/en/item/417286/icode.
214. *Id.*
215. Robynne Boyd, *World Closes in on Consensus to Regulate Fishing on the High Seas*, Sci. Am. (Feb. 23, 2015), *available at* http://www.scientificamerican.com/article/world-closes-in-on-consensus-to-regulate-fishing-on-the-high-seas/.

intentional dumping of wastes at sea. This section focuses on some of the most ubiquitous pollution problems—plastic pollution and ocean acidification—that affect nearly all life in the oceans, from mollusks and oysters to sea lions and blue whales, and ways to save the ocean from these significant threats.

Plastic Pollution in the Ocean

Plastics are synthetic organic polymers found in a wide variety of products around the world. There are two primary categories of plastic—user plastic and preproduction plastic. "User plastics" are inexpensive, lightweight, and resistant to corrosion, and are used pervasively as a result. User plastics are present in numerous everyday commercial goods, such as plastic bags, bottle caps, fishing gear, and clothing.[216] Preproduction plastics consist mainly of plastic resin pellets, or "nurdles," and are raw materials transported to manufacturing sites where the nurdles are melted and molded into user plastics.[217]

"[E]xcept for the small amount that's been incinerated . . . every bit of plastic ever made still exists,"[218] and more plastic is being produced every day. Global production of plastic has increased from 1.5 million tons in 1950 to 288 million tons in 2012, with a 620 percent increase since 1975.[219] Between 2000 and 2010, there was more plastic produced than in the entire previous century.[220]

---

216. David K. A. Barnes et al., *Accumulation and Fragmentation of Plastic Debris in Global Environments*, 364 PHIL. TRANS. R. SOC. B. 1985 (2009), http://nora.nerc.ac.uk/10804/1987.

217. Yukie Mato et al., *Plastic Resin Pellets as a Transport Medium for Toxic Chemicals in the Marine Environment*, 35 ENVIRON. SCI. TECH. 318–324 (2001), *available at* http://www.ncbi.nlm.nih.gov/pubmed/11347604.

218. Susan Casey & Gregg Segal, *Our Oceans Are Turning into Plastic . . . Are We?* BEST LIFE MAG. 1 (2007), *available at* http://www.enviroplumbing.com/pdf/Plastic_Oceans_.pdf.

219. Hisashi Hirai et al. *Organic Micropollutants in Marine Plastics Debris from the Open Ocean and Remote and Urban Beaches*, 62 MARINE POLLUTION BULL. 1683–92 (2011), doi: 10.1016/j.marpolbul.2011.06.004; Jenna Jambeck et al., *Plastic Waste Inputs from Land into the Ocean*. 347 SCI. 768 (2015), doi: 10.1126/science.1260352.

220. Richard C. Thompson, *Plastics, The Environment and Human Health: Current Consensus and Future Trends*, 364 PHIL. TRANS. R. SOC. B. 2153–66 (2009).

Much of this plastic ends up in the ocean. It floats on the surface, litters the seafloor, washes up on beaches, and permeates the water column. It varies in size from large plastic bags to microplastics less than five millimeters in diameter.[221] Plastics are now one of the most common and persistent pollutants in ocean waters and beaches worldwide, making up 50 to 80 percent of beach litter, floating marine debris, and trash on the ocean floor; in some areas plastics constitute as much as 90–95 percent of marine litter.[222] Studies predict that 80 percent of marine debris comes from land based sources.[223]

Plastic enters the ocean through a variety of pathways including stormwater runoff, combined sewer overflows, poor waste disposal and management practices, industrial and construction activities, beachgoers who leave behind trash, and illegal dumping, with stormwater runoff being the primary source.[224] In the Los Angeles watershed alone, every three days, 2.3 billion plastic fragments, or about thirty metric tons, are washed into the Pacific Ocean.[225] Scientists estimate that in 2010 between 4.8 and 12.7 million metric tons (or roughly 10.5 billion to 28 billion pounds) entered the oceans from 192 coastal countries around the world.[226] Without adequate improvements to waste management programs, that number is expected to increase by an order of magnitude by 2025.[227]

Plastic pollution is especially prevalent in an area commonly known as the Great Pacific Garbage Patch. The Garbage Patch accumulates garbage from the entire North Pacific Ocean, and covers an area roughly

---

221. Skyke Morét-Ferguson et al. The Size, Mass, and Composition of Plastic Debris in the Western North Atlantic Ocean. 60 MARINE POLLUTION BULL. 1873–8 (2010).

222. Barnes, *supra* note 216.

223. Miriam Gordon, *Eliminating Land-Based Discharges of Marine Debris in California: A Plan of Action from The Plastic Debris Project*, CALIFORNIA COASTAL COMMISSION, 1, 3 (2006), http://www.plasticdebris.org/CA_Action_Plan_2006.pdf.

224. *Id.*; Andres Cozar et al. *Plastic Debris in the Oceans.* 11(28) PNAS 10239–44 (June 6, 2014), www.pnas.org/cgi/doi/10.1073/pnas.1314705111.

225. Charles J. Moore et al., *Quantity and Type of Plastic Debris Flowing from Two Urban Rivers to Coastal Waters and Beaches of Southern California.* 11 J. INTEGRATED COASTAL ZONE MGMT. 65–73 (2011).

226. Jambeck, *supra* note 219.

227. *Id.*

twice the size of Texas.[228] In 1999, plastic pollution in the area out-weighed zooplankton six to one, and averaged over 300,000 pieces per square kilometer of water.[229] Estimates place the total amount of garbage at roughly 100 million tons.[230] Plastic pollution is also common along the U.S. East Coast and in the North Atlantic.[231] Surveys from across the globe indicate that plastic pollution is increasing throughout the world's oceans; in the Southern Ocean, plastic debris increased 100 times just during the early 1990s.[232]

Plastic pollution kills and seriously injures a wide variety of marine species, including fish, coral reefs, sea turtles, seabirds, and marine mammals.[233] While the total number of animals that die each year as the result of plastic pollution cannot be determined definitively, estimates are in the millions.[234]

Sea turtles often mistake plastic bags, balloons, and other debris for jellyfish and other prey. Studies on loggerheads, leatherbacks, and green turtles have all documented high levels of plastic debris in the intestinal tracts of these animals.[235] Consuming this plastic can lead to blockage

---

228. Casey, *supra* note 218.

229. Charles J. Moore, Shelly L. Moore & Molly K. Leecaster, *A Comparison of Plastic and Plankton in the North Pacific Central Gyre*, 42 MARINE POLLUTION BULL. 1297–1300 (2001); Christiane Zarfl & Michael Matthies, *Are Marine Plastic Particles Transport Vectors for Organic Pollutants to the Arctic?* 60 MARINE POLLUTION BULL. 1810 (2010), http://www.ncbi.nlm.nih.gov/pubmed/20579675.

230. Susan L. Dautel, *Transoceanic Trash: International and United States Strategies for the Great Pacific Garbage Patch*, 3 GOLDEN GATE U. ENVTL. L. J. 1 (2009).

231. Kara L. Law et al., *Plastic Accumulation in the Atlantic Subtropical Gyre*, 329 SCI. 1185–8 (2010).

232. H. Ogi, Y. Fukumoto, *A Sorting Method for Small Plastic Debris Floating on the Sea Surface and Stranded on Sandy Beaches.* 51 BULL. FACULTY FISHERIES, HOKKAIDO U. 71–93 (2000); Sophia Copello & Flavio Quintana, *Marine Debris Ingestion by Southern Giant Petrels and its Potential Relationships with Fisheries in the Southern Atlantic Ocean.* 46 MARINE POLLUTION BULL. 1504–15 (2003); Richard C. Thompson et al., *Lost at Sea: Where is All the Plastic?* 304 SCI. 838 (2004), doi:10.1126/science.1094559.

233. David W. Laist, *Impacts of Marine Debris: Entanglement of Marine Life in Marine Debris Including a Comprehensive List of Species with Entanglement and Ingestion Records*, SPRINGER SERIES ON ENVTL MAN. (1997); Emma L. Teuten et al., *Transport and Release of Chemicals from Plastics to the Environment and to Wildlife*, 364 PHIL. TRANS. R. SOC. B. 2027–37 (2009).

234. Charles James Moore, *Synthetic Polymers in the Marine Environment: A Rapidly Increasing, Long-term Threat*, 108 ENVTL. RES. 131–9 (2008), doi:10.1016/j.envres.2008.07.025.

235. N. Mrosovsky et al., *Leatherback Turtles: The Menace of Plastic*, 58 MARINE POLLUTION BULL. 287–9 (2009).

in the gut and even death.[236] Sea turtles can also become entangled in
plastic pollution, which can cause drowning, lacerations, infection, stran-
gulation, and starvation.[237]

Seals and sea lions are often attracted to floating objects in the water,
such as packing loops, which can wrap around their heads. In such
instances the loops create a "lethal necklace" which results in strangula-
tion.[238] Ingested plastics can cause catastrophic infections, organ damage,
and starvation.[239]

Over a hundred seabird species are known to ingest plastic or become
entangled in plastic debris.[240] The birds accidentally ingest plastic when
feeding on the surface of the ocean, and adult birds feed their chicks plastic
particles mistaken for fish.[241] Over 90 percent of northern fulmars found
washed up along shores in the Pacific Northwest had plastic in their stomachs, with an average of 36.8 pieces of plastic per bird.[242] Laysan alba-
trosses—a species of bird that lives in the Northern Hawaiian Islands, an
area littered with thousands of pounds of plastic garbage—have ingested a
greater variety and volume of plastic than any other seabird.[243] A build-up
of plastic debris in the stomachs of albatross chicks causes them to die of
starvation by the thousands.[244] And a 2015 study by the Australian government concluded that plastic can be found in the guts of nine out of ten
seabirds worldwide, with computer modeling predicting that 99 percent of
all seabirds will have consumed plastic by 2050.[245]

236. *Id.*
237. Jose G. B. Derraik, *The Pollution of the Marine Environment by Plastic Debris: A Review,* 44
MARINE POLLUTION BULL. 842–5 (2002).
238. Raymond C. Boland & Mary J. Donahue. *Marine Debris Accumulation in the Nearshore
Marine Habitat of the Endangered Hawaiian Monk Seal,* Monachus schauislandi *1999–2001,* 46
MARINE POLLUTION BULL. 1385–94 (2003).
239. Kimberly Raum-Suryan et al., *Entanglement of Steller Sea Lions* (Eumetopias jubatus) *in
Marine Debris: Identifying Causes and Finding Solutions,* 28 MARINE POLLUTION BULL. 1487–95
(2009).
240. Laist, *supra* note 233.
241. Heidi J. Auman et al., *Plastic Ingestion by Laysan Albatross Chicks on Sand Island, Midway
Atoll, in 1994 and 1995,* 42 ALBATROSS BIOL. & CONSERV. 239 (1997).
242. Stephanie Avery-Gomm et al., *Northern Fulmars as Biological Monitors of Plastic Pollution in
the Eastern North Pacific,* 64 MARINE POLLUTION BULL. 1776–81 (2012).
243. *Id.*
244. *Id.*
245. Chris Wilcox et al., *Threat of Plastic Pollution to Seabirds Is Global, Pervasive, and Increasing,*
PROC. NAT'L ACAD. SCI. (2015).

Plastics in the ocean also have significant toxicity implications. Chemical additives used to make plastic more flexible and durable, such as phthalates and bisphenol A, have adverse impacts on reproduction and development, and plastic litter also absorbs other pollutants from the surrounding seawater.[246] Plastic debris in the ocean can also contain high concentrations of persistent organic pollutants, such as polychlorinated biphenyls (PCBs).[247] PCBs and other persistent organic pollutants are considered among the most lasting anthropogenic organic compounds introduced into the environment and can be highly toxic and have a wide range of chronic effects, including endocrine disruption, mutagenicity, and carcinogenicity.[248]

Mollusks and crustaceans appear to be particularly sensitive to these compounds.[249] As invertebrates are a food source for many species, plastics ingested by invertebrates have greater potential to bioaccumulate and transfer toxic substances up the food web.[250] Even baleen whales, amongst the largest animals on earth, are exposed to microlitter ingestion as a result of their filter-feeding activity; and a study of stranded fin whales documented pollutants traced to microplastic pollution.[251] In other words, if PCBs and other contaminants are abundant in lower trophic levels, they will be amplified through the food chain to levels that can adversely affect higher trophic level organisms, including humans.

246. Marvin Heskett et al., *Measurement of Persistent Organic Pollutants (POPs) in Plastic Resin Pellets from Remote Islands: Toward Establishment of Background Concentrations for International Pellet Watch*, 64 MARINE POLLUTION BULL. 445–8 (2012).

247. Lorena M. Rios, Charles Moore, & Patrick R. Jones, *Persistent Organic Pollutants Carried by Synthetic Polymers in the Ocean Environment*, 54 MARINE POLLUTION BULL. 1230 (2007).

248. Lorena Rios *et al.*, *Quantitation of Persistent Organic Pollutants Adsorbed on Plastic Debris from the Northern Pacific Gyre's "Eastern Garbage Patch"*, 12 J. ENVNTL. MONITORING 12 (2010); Lorena Rios et al. 2007, *supra* note 247.

249. Jörg Oehlmann et al., *A Critical Analysis of the Biological Impacts of Plasticizers on Wildlife*, 364 PHIL. TRANS. R. SOC. B. 2047–62 (2009).

250. Emma L. Teuten et al., *Transport and Release of Chemicals from Plastics to the Environment and to Wildlife*, 364 PHIL. TRANS. R. SOC. B. 2027–45 (2009).

251. Maria Cristina Fossi et al., *Preliminary Results on the Potential Assumption of Microplastics by Mediterranean Fin Whale: The Use of Phthalates as a Tracer*, 6th SETAC World Congress 2012, Berlin, Germany, May 20–24, 2012.

Efforts to Protect Marine Life from Plastic Pollution

Given the ubiquitous nature of plastic pollution, environmental organizations have employed a variety of means to tackle the problem to
evaluate the hazards posed by plastic pollution in the area, and begin
the cleanup and remediation process.[252] One legal mechanism is the
Comprehensive Environmental Response, Compensation, and Liability
Act (Superfund Act). The Superfund Act authorizes the Environmental
Protection Agency (EPA) to remove or arrange for the removal of hazardous substances threatening "public health or welfare," and to provide for
remedial action to address the created or threatened danger.[253]

The Superfund Act allows citizens to petition the EPA for a site to
be added to a National Priorities List if they are, or may be, affected by
the release or threatened release of a hazardous substance, pollutant, or
contaminant.[254] The EPA maintains a National Contingency Plan that
includes criteria for "determining priorities among releases or threatened
releases . . . for the purpose of taking remedial action."[255] The identified
criteria take into account, among other factors, the "potential for destruction of sensitive ecosystems," and "damage to natural resources which
may affect the human food chain."[256]

If a petition is granted, there are two types of potential responses:
removal actions and remedial actions. "'[R]emoval' actions are primarily those intended for the short-term abatement of toxic waste hazards,
while 'remedial' actions are typically those intended to restore long term
environmental quality."[257]

Removal actions could include the movement, treatment, disposal,
or incineration of contaminants, as well as the evacuation or removal of

---

252. *See, e.g.,* Petition from Center for Biological Diversity to Environmental Protection Agency,
Re: Preliminary Assessment of Northwest Hawaiian Islands and the Great Pacific Garbage Patch
for Plastic Contamination under Section 105 of the Comprehensive Environmental Response,
Compensation, and Liability Act, 42 U.S.C. §§ 9601 *et seq.,* Dec. 11, 2012 (seeking investigation
of Great Garbage Patch pollution).
253. 42 U.S.C. § 9604(a).
254. 42 U.S.C. § 9605(d).
255. *Id.* at § 9605(a)(8)(A).
256. *Id.* at § 9605(a)(8)(B).
257. City of New York v. Exxon Corp., 633 F. Supp. 609, 614 (S.D.N.Y. 1986) (citing New York
v. Shore Realty Corp., 759 F.2d 1032, 1040 (2d Cir. 1985)).

highly contaminated earth.[258] Remedial actions include the discovery, selection, study, design, and construction of longer-term actions aimed at a permanent remedy, and are developed after an extensive investigation to discover the nature and extent of the problem.[259] In most cases of plastic pollution, both actions are necessary because it is both an immediate and recurring threat.[260]

Placement on the National Priorities List does not designate primary responsibility to any party for the cleanup. However, the Superfund Act grants the EPA the right to pursue an enforcement action for the cleanup against potentially responsible parties.[261] The Act also authorizes the United States to seek a mandatory injunction against responsible parties, and courts have broad authority to fashion relief to abate the release of hazardous substances.[262]

Other legal mechanisms could prevent further plastic pollution in the future. For example, the Resource Conservation and Recovery Act[263] provides for citizen petitions seeking increased regulation and better management practices of waste.[264] In enacting that law, Congress recognized that economic and population growth accompanied by widespread improvements in the standard of living, "ha[d] resulted in a rising tide of scrap, discarded, and waste materials," leading to the "needless[] pollut[ion]" of the environment and endangerment of public health.[265] Accordingly, the Act prohibits open dumping, establishes guidelines for

---

258. 40 C.F.R. § 300.415(e).

259. *Id.* §§ 300.420–440.

260. Petition from Center for Biological Diversity to Environmental Protection Agency, Petition for Rulemaking Pursuant to Section 7004(A) of the Resource Conservation and Recovery Act, 42 U.S.C. § 6974(A), and Section 21 of the Toxic Substance Control Act, 15 U.S.C. § 2620, Concerning the Regulation of Discarded Polyvinyl Chloride and Associated Chemical Additives, July 24, 2014 ("CBD PVC Petition").

261. 42 U.S.C. § 9607(a)(1)–(4).

262. 42 U.S.C. § 9606(a).

263. 42 U.S.C. §§ 6901, *et seq.*

264. *See* CBD PVC petition, *supra* note 260 (requesting that the EPA designate extremely toxic and omnipresent as hazardous waste and prescribe regulations for its treatment, storage and disposal). *See also* Mark A. Browne et al., *Spatial Patterns of Plastic Debris along Estuarine Shores,* 44 ENVTL. SCI. & TECH. 3404, 3406 (2010). The identified plastics were polyvinyl chloride ("PVC"), vinyl chloride and associated dialkyl- and alkylarylesters of 1,2-benzenedicarboxylic acid, commonly known as phthalate plasticizers.

265. 42 U.S.C. § 6901(a), (b).

the proper management of "solid wastes," and seeks to minimize the generation of "hazardous waste" and their improper disposal by establishing a comprehensive "cradle-to-grave" framework to ensure the safe treatment, handling, storage, and disposal of hazardous wastes.[266]

On a local level, advocates have spearheaded ordinances either prohibiting the use of single-use plastic bags or requiring a fee for the use of such bags.[267] Several states have also begun enacting legislation to prohibit or restrict the use of products containing microbeads to prevent microplastics from entering the oceans.[268] Additionally, the U.S. Congress enacted a law in late 2015 that phases out the manufacture and sale of face wash, toothpaste and shampoo containing plastic microbeads.[269]

But efforts in the United States alone will not be enough to solve the massive plastic pollution problem. Countries across the globe contribute to the marine debris problem. A 2015 study of 193 coastal nations listed the United States as the twentieth worst polluter.[270] China topped the list as the world's largest contributor to plastic pollution problem, responsible for 1.32 to 3.53 of the 4.8 to12.7 million metric tons that enter the oceans each year. Indonesia, the Philippines, Vietnam, and Sri Lanka were also in the top five.[271]

Nor are the numerous international agreements that cover ocean pollution adequate to address the plastic problem. For example, the 1972 Convention on the Prevention of Marine Pollution by Dumping of

---

266. *See Id.* §§ 6941-6969a and §§ 6921-6939g.

267. *See, e.g.,* National Conference of State Legislatures, *State Plastic Bag Legislation* (Jan. 1, 2015), http://www.ncsl.org/research/environment-and-natural-resources/plastic-bag-legislation. aspx (describing state legislation regarding plastic bags); Janet Larson, *Plastic Bag Bans are Spreading in the United States,* TREEHUGGER (Apr. 22, 2014), http://www.treehugger.com/sustainable-product-design/plastic-bag-bans-spreading-united-states.html (describing local ordinances).

268. Bills have been enacted in California, Illinois, Maine, New Jersey, Colorado, Indiana and Maryland. *See, e.g.,* Phil Willon, *California Lawmakers Approve Ban on Plastic Microbeads,* L.A. TIMES (Sept. 8, 2015), http://www.latimes.com/local/political/la-me-ln-california-lawmakers-approve-ban-on-plastic-microbeads-20150908-story.html (describing a bill in California that would ban the sale of personal care products containing plastic microbeads starting in 2020); Rachel Abrams, *Fighting Pollution From Microbeads Used in Soaps and Creams,* N.Y. TIMES (May 22, 2015), http://www.nytimes.com/2015/05/23/business/energy-environment/california-takes -step-to-ban-microbeads-used-in-soaps-and-creams.html?_r=0 (describing legislation in other states).

269. Microbead-Free Waters Act, H.R. 1321, 114th Congress, Public Law No: 114-114.

270. Jambeck, *supra* note 219.

271. *Id.*

Wastes and Other Matter, commonly referred to as the London Convention, regulates intentional dumping of waste into the oceans from vessels, aircrafts, and platforms, but it does not cover discharges from shore, such as stormwater outfalls—the primary source of plastic pollution. Similarly, the United Nations Convention on the Law of the Sea, which recognizes that activities on land contribute to the pollution of the oceans, only requests that countries address the issue domestically.[272] These agreements are clearly not enough to stem the tide.

Luckily, awareness of the issue is growing globally. For example, the European Union enacted new rules in 2015 that require its member-nations to reduce the use of lightweight plastic bags by eighty percent from 2010 levels by 2025, by either introducing taxes on the use of plastic bags or banning or restricting their use.[273]

In 2012, the United Nations Conference on Sustainable Development recognized plastic pollution as a significant environmental issue that must be addressed at the global level. The parties to the Conference "note[d] with concern that the health of oceans and marine biodiversity are negatively affected by . . . marine debris, especially plastic, persistent organic pollutants, heavy metals and nitrogen-based compounds, from a number of marine and land-based sources, including shipping and land run-off."[274] Accordingly, the parties called for action to "achieve significant reductions in marine debris to prevent harm to coastal and marine environments" by 2025.[275] What such action will look like remains to be seen, but there are examples of previous international agreements enacted in reaction to pervasive pollution with widespread detrimental impacts, such as the Montreal Protocol which phased out the production of numerous substances that depleted the ozone layer, that can serve as examples for the creation of meaningful international agreements that prevent plastic pollution.

---

272. U.N. Convention on the Law of the Sea, Dec. 10, 1982, 1833 U.N.T.S. 3, 21 I.L.M. 1261.
273. Julie Levy-Abegnoli, *EU Votes to Drastically Reduce Plastic Bag Use*, PARLIAMENT MAG. (Apr. 30, 2015), https://www.theparliamentmagazine.eu/articles/news/eu-votes-drastically -reduce-plastic-bag-use.
274. Final Report of the U.N. Conf. on Sustainable Development, Rio de Janeiro, Brazil, June 20–22, 2012, ¶ 163 (emphasis added).
275. *Id.*

Greenhouse Gas Pollution and an Acidifying Ocean

Another ubiquitous, but invisible, set of pollutants wreaking havoc on our oceans are greenhouse gases. Greenhouse gas emissions have been increasing at an accelerating pace in the face of rapid industrialization and burning of fossil fuels, and the continued failure of the global community to meaningfully address these issues. This massive, unprecedented pollution is causing, and will continue to cause, changes in the Earth's climate, including species extinction, sea level rise, and increased frequency of droughts, flooding, and storms.

Carbon dioxide is the principal greenhouse gas driving climate change. In 2015, the monthly global average concentration of carbon dioxide surpassed 400 parts per million for the first time in recorded history.[276] This level is almost 1.5 times higher than the preindustrial level of 280 parts per million.[277] And the atmospheric concentration of two other potent greenhouse gases, methane and nitrous oxide, are also increasing, reaching levels of 253 percent and 121 percent, respectively, of their preindustrial concentrations.[278]

Climate change is already impacting our oceans through warming waters, loss of sea ice, and ocean acidification, which will fundamentally change the behavior, survival rates, and interactions of marine mammals and other marine life.[279] While scientists have only recently begun to study the impacts of ocean acidification, it is quickly emerging as one of the greatest threats to marine water quality.

The ocean's absorption of carbon dioxide alters the chemistry of the oceans and makes seawater chemically corrosive.[280] This process has already caused the acidity of the oceans to increase by 30 percent since

276. NOAA National Climatic Data Center. 2015. State of the Climate: Global Analysis for March 2015.

277. IPCC, Geneva, Switzerland; Pachauri et al. 2014, NOAA National Climatic Data Center 2015.

278. Tian et al. *Global Methane and Nitrous Oxide Emissions from Terrestrial Ecosystems due to Multiple Environmental Changes.* 1 ECOSYSTEM HEALTH AND SUSTAINABILITY 4 (2015).

279. United States Global Change Research Program, *Ocean and Marine Resources in a Changing Climate.* 2013.

280. Richard A. Feely et al., *Carbon Dioxide and Our Ocean Legacy* (Apr. 2006), http://www.pmel.noaa.gov/pubs/PDF/feel2899/feel2899.pdf.

industrial times—a rate that is likely faster than anything experienced in the past 300 million years.[281] During the closest analogous ocean acidification event fifty-five million years ago, which was magnitudes slower than the current rate of acidification, approximately 95 percent of marine species went extinct.[282] Scientists predict that seawater acidity could increase 150 to 170 percent by the end of the century if greenhouse gas emissions are not significantly curbed.[283]

One major impact of ocean acidification is that it weakens the ability of plants and animals to build protective calcium carbonate shells and skeletons necessary for their survival, because carbonate minerals, calcite and aragonite, become less available.[284] For example, many species of plankton are vulnerable to decreased calcification resulting in thin and weak shells. Ocean acidification also impairs the ability of shellfish, including northern abalone, mussels, and Pacific oysters, from calcifying their shells.[285] In fact, billions of oyster larvae have already died in the Pacific Northwest as the result of ocean acidification.[286] Increased carbon dioxide levels in the ocean can also result in accumulation of carbon dioxide in the tissues and fluids of fish and other marine animals, and increased acidity in body fluids, which can cause a variety of problems, including difficulties with acid-base regulation, growth, respiration, predation response, and metabolism.[287] As many of these species form the bottom of the food chain or are prey for other species, ocean acidification could have ripple effects up the food chain, altering or decreasing biodiversity in the ocean.

---

281. James C. Orr et al., *Anthropogenic Ocean Acidification over the Twenty-First Century and its Impacts on Calcifying Organisms*, 437 NATURE 681–6 (2005).
282. Richard E. Zeebe, *History of Seawater Carbonate Chemistry, Atmospheric CO2, and Ocean Acidification*, 40 ANN. REV.EARTH & PLANETARY SCI. 141–165 (Dec. 2011)..
283. Feely, *supra* note 280.
284. Orr, *supra* note 281.
285. JEAN PIERRE GATTUSO & LINA HANSSON (eds.), OCEAN ACIDIFICATION (2011).
286. Craig Welch, *Seachange: Oysters Dying as Coast is Hit Hard*, SEATTLE TIMES (Sept. 12, 2013), http://apps.seattletimes.com/reports/sea-change/2013/sep/11/oysters-hit-hard/.
287. Hans O. Pörtner et al., *Synergistic Effects of Temperature Extremes, Hypoxia, and Increases in CO2 on Marine Animals: From Earth History to Global Change*, 110 J. GEOPHYSICAL RES. 1978–2001 (2005).

Coral reefs are particularly vulnerable to ocean acidification, and they cannot exist below a certain level of minimal acidity (7.8 pH).[288] Ocean acidification profoundly impacts corals by decreasing important chemicals in the water and thereby impairing growth.[289] The resulting slowed coral growth can also make corals less able to compete for space and weaken coral skeletons, increasing their vulnerability to erosion, storm damage, and predation.[290] Ocean acidification can also impact reproduction of corals—corals can invest greater energy in calcification to maintain skeletal growth and density, which would divert resources from essential activities such as reproduction and potentially reduce the recolonization ability of corals.[291] Ocean acidification may also increase the frequency of coral bleaching events when coupled with warming waters. Indeed, the Great Barrier Reef has lost 50 percent of its coral cover since 1985 as a result of ocean acidification, global warming, coral bleaching, predation by starfish, and storm damage.[292]

Scientists have concluded that if carbon dioxide levels are allowed to reach 450 parts per million (which could be reached by 2030 at current emission rates), coral reefs will suffer extensive damage, reduction in biodiversity, and extinctions.[293] In other words, "reefs are likely to be the first major planetary-scale ecosystem to collapse in the face of climate changes now in progress."[294]

---

288. Katharina E. Fabricius et al., *Losers and Winners in Coral Reefs Acclimatized to Elevated Carbon Dioxide Concentrations*, 1 NATURE CLIMATE CHANGE 165–169 (2011).
289. Richard Dodge & Richard Aronson, *Synopsis of Conclusions of the 11th International Coral Reef Symposium,* in STATUS OF CORAL REEFS OF THE WORLD: 2008 (Clive Wilkinson, ed. 43–4 2008).
290. C. Mark Eakin et al., *Global Climate Change and Coral Reefs: Rising Temperatures, Acidification and the Need for Resilient Reefs*, in STATUS OF CORAL REEFS OF THE WORLD: 2008 (Clive Wilkinson, ed. 29–34 2008).
291. Ove Hoegh-Guldberg et al., *Coral Reefs Under Rapid Climate Change and Ocean Acidification*, 318 SCI. 1737–42 (2007).
292. Glen De'ath et al., *The 27-year Decline of Coral Cover on the Great Barrier Reef and its Causes*, PNAS, 1–5 (2012).
293. J. E. N. Veron et al., *The Coral Reef Crisis: The Critical Importance of <350 ppm CO2.* 58 MARINE POLLUTION BULL. 1428–36 (2009).
294. *Id.*

The loss of coral reefs could have profound effects, because they are associated with and support one-third of the species known to exist in the ocean.[295] We are dependent on coral reefs for biodiversity, fisheries health, shoreline protection, tourism, recreation, cultural practices, and subsistence. Coral reefs are estimated to support the livelihoods of half a billion people.

Scientists also predict that ocean acidification will cause an increase in the frequency of toxic algal blooms, including those known as "red tides." Some strains of phytoplankton in these blooms produce copious amount of a neurotoxin that poisons shellfish.[296] Harmful algal blooms can cause mortality in marine mammals through contamination of food sources. Specifically, exposure can cause seizures, provoke organ failure, and death in several marine mammal species, from small sea otters to large whales.[297]

Adding insult to injury, noise impacts to marine mammals are predicted to increase as the result of ocean acidification, because the more acidic the water, the less sound waves are absorbed. Researchers predict that ocean acidification will reduce the intrinsic ability of surface seawater to absorb sound at frequencies important to marine mammals by 40 percent and that sounds will travel 70 percent farther by 2050 because of increased carbon dioxide acidifying our oceans.[298] A louder ocean will negatively affect cetaceans that rely on sound for feeding, breeding, nursing, communication, navigation, and other behaviors essential to their survival.

295. *Id.*
296. Donald M. Anderson et al., *Understanding Interannual, Decadal Level Variability in Paralytic Shellfish Poisoning Toxicity in the Gulf of Maine: The HAB Index*, 103 DEEP SEA RESEARCH PART II: TOPICAL STUDIES IN OCEANOGRAPHY 264–276 (2014).
297. Elizabeth A. McHuron et al., *Domoic Acid Exposure and Associated Clinical Signs and Histopathology in Pacific Harbor Seals* (Phoca vitulina richardii), 23 HARMFUL ALGAE 28–33 (2013); Kelly S. Kirkley et al., *Domoic Acid-Induced Seizures in California Sea Lions* (Zalophus californianus) *Are Associated with Neuroinflammatory Brain Injury*, 156 AQUATIC TOXICOLOGY 259–268 (2014); Silje-Kristin Jensen et al., *Detection and Effects of Harmful Algal Toxins in Scottish Harbour Seals and Potential Links to Population Decline.* 97 TOXICON 1–14 (2015).
298. Keith C. Hester et al., *Unanticipated Consequences of Ocean Acidification: A Noisier Ocean at Lower pH*, 35 GEOPHYSICAL RES. LETTERS 31 (2008).

Using the Clean Water Act to Protect
Marine Life from Ocean Acidification

Ultimately, the most important solution to ocean acidification and ocean warming is massive cuts in global greenhouse gas emissions. While the United States has begun to address greenhouse gas emissions from power plants and other sources, and the international community has committed to taking steps to reduce global warming, these efforts fall short of what is necessary to avoid the worst impacts of climate change, including the impacts from an increasingly acidifying ocean. Accordingly, in order to address the myriad deleterious impacts from ocean acidification, environmental organizations have turned to other laws that vest states and the U.S. government with separate authority and duties to control pollutants like greenhouse emissions, and to combat local sources of ocean acidification such as nutrient deposits from agricultural runoff and emissions of nitrogen and sulfur dioxide. One such law is the Clean Water Act.

The Clean Water Act seeks to "restore and maintain the chemical, physical, and biological integrity of the Nation's waters," guarantee "water quality which provides for the protection and propagation of fish, shellfish, and wildlife and provides for recreation," and eliminate water pollution.[299] To meet these goals, the Clean Water Act requires the EPA to publish, and thereafter revise, criteria for water quality based on the latest scientific information on the concentration and effects of pollutants on the oceans and related ecosystems.[300] In response to the EPA's criteria, states are then required to adopt the EPA criteria or come up with other scientifically defensible criteria for all waterways within their respective jurisdictions.[301] States must consider all waterways' uses and values, in all pertinent respects, in adopting their criteria.[302]

An additional requirement of the Clean Water Act is that states must conduct biannual assessments of their waterways every two years and establish an "impaired waters list" (also known as a 303(d) list after the

---

299. 33 U.S.C. § 1251(a).
300. *Id.* § 1314(a)(1).
301. 33 U.S.C. § 1313(a)–(c); 40 C.F.R. § 130.3.
302. 40 C.F.R. §§ 131.2; 131.10; 131.11; 33 U.S.C. § 1313(c)(2); 40 C.F.R. § 130.3.

relevant section in the Clean Water Act), which must be reviewed and approved by the EPA.[303] After review, for all waters listed as impaired, the Clean Water Act then requires the establishment of maximum daily loads of pollutants, which are then monitored by the EPA or the states.[304]

EPA has developed a water quality standard for marine pH, which it originally developed in 1976, when little was known about ocean acidification, and is likely underprotective as a result.[305] But even this weak standard is already being exceeded in certain waters, threatening the protection of fish and shellfish rearing and spawning.[306]

Concerns over dangerous pH levels of waters off the coast of Washington—which affected massive failures in shellfish hatcheries—led to federal litigation involving environmentalists, the EPA, and the state of Washington. As a result, in 2010, the EPA issued a memorandum that recognized the "seriousness of aquatic life impacts" from ocean acidification and instructed states to list waters not meeting the water quality standard for marine pH on their 2012 impaired waters lists.[307] The memorandum also recommended that states solicit information on ocean acidification and begin monitoring and assessing ocean acidification with a focus on vulnerable waters, such as those with corals, shellfish, and fisheries, and list waters impaired by ocean acidification.[308]

The EPA subsequently approved Washington and Oregon's impaired waters list. This decision was upheld by a federal court, finding the EPA "reasonably concluded that Washington and Oregon assembled and evaluated all existing and readily available water quality data."[309]

---

303. 33 U.S.C. § 1313(d); 40 C.F.R. § 130.7(d); 40 C.F.R. §§ 130.7(b)(1),(3); (d)(2).

304. 33 U.S.C. §§ 1313(d), (e); 40 C.F.R. §§ 130.6, 130.7(d)(2).

305. EPA, *Quality Criteria for Water*, 342–43 (1976), http://www.epa.gov/waterscience/criteria/library/redbook.pdf.

306. *See, e.g.,* WAC 173-201A-612; WAC. 173-201-210(1)(a)(i); OAR 340-041-0011; OAR 340-041-0031.

307. Memorandum from Denise Keehner, Director, Office of Wetlands, Oceans and Watersheds, Environmental Protection Agency to Water Division Directors, Regions 1-10, Environmental Protection Agency, *Re: Integrated Reporting and Listing Decisions Related to Ocean Acidification*, Nov. 15, 2010.

308. *Id.*

309. *Id.* at *103.

In light of new science indicating that the EPA's current water quality standard is not sufficient to protect seawater quality and marine life from ocean acidification, the Center for Biological Diversity petitioned the agency to revise its standard in 2013. The petition requests that the EPA establish water quality criteria to protect against ocean acidification with respect to specific chemicals.[310] The petition's requests are based on scientific studies regarding factors influencing ocean acidification. The petition presents two parameters, one chemical and one biological, by which states can measure and monitor the threats of ocean acidification.

The petition also requests that the EPA publish information and guidance on addressing ocean acidification, including factors necessary to prevent ocean acidification from having deleterious impacts on marine life, recommended methods for measuring ocean acidification parameters and considering ocean acidification data and recommendations for developing and implementing total maximum daily loads for ocean acidification.[311]

In response to the petition, the EPA indicated that it was beginning an in-depth study on combating ocean acidification and would convene a workgroup to identify water quality parameters related to ocean acidification and later respond to the petition. However, as this book went to press, the agency had yet to fully answer the petition. It remains to be seen what, if any, ultimate action the EPA will take under the Clean Water Act.

Conclusion

Until relatively recently, the oceans were seen as limitless—their vast resources there for the taking by anyone with the technological capacity to do so. This unrestrained exploitation rendered some species extinct, while driving others to the brink. While some of these practices, such as commercial whaling, have been largely curbed and species have slowly

---

310. Petition from the Center for Biological Diversity to Environmental Protection Agency for Additional Water Quality Criteria and Guidance Under Section 304 of the Clean Water Act, 33 U.S.C. § 1314, to Address Ocean Acidification, Apr. 17, 2013.
311. *Id.*

begun to recover, others, such as fishing on the high seas, continue essentially unabated. And land-based activities, such as the pervasive use of plastics and fossil fuels, exacerbate these ocean-based impacts. The situation has gotten so dire that scientists warn that we are on the precipice of causing a massive die-off in the world's oceans. Fortunately, as described throughout this chapter, there are laws already in place that can be used to address these threats. However, the laws need a voice, and they must be enforced in an effective way to combat the tide of extinction and allow our oceans to heal.

4

Evolving Perspectives on Captive Wild Animals

Anna Frostic and Joan Schaffner

~

Animal species can be classified as domesticated or wild. Domestication results when humans intentionally and selectively breed a species over generations and thereby change the genetic makeup from that of the original wild species.[1] Domesticated animals generally live with and are dependent upon humans. If left to themselves, certain individual domesticated animals may become unsocialized to humans and deemed "feral." This frequently occurs with domestic cats if they are abandoned by their owners and left to fend for themselves. However, the lack of socialization of an individual animal does not alter its status as domesticated.

In contrast, wild animals are those who are not domesticated and usually roam freely in the wild. It is the case that some wild animals are

---

1. Melinda A. Zeder, *The Domestication of Animals,* 68(2) J. ANTHROPOL. RES. 161 (2012).

captured by humans and forced to live in captivity;[2] other wild animals are bred in captivity.[3] These animals retain their "wildness" for many generations because, although the number of generations necessary to domesticate a species is uncertain, domestication requires sustained, intentional, and multi-generational captive breeding.[4] Some individual captive or captive-bred wild animals may become socialized to humans and are sometimes deemed habituated. However, the socialization of an individual animal does not alter their status as "wild." The law also may specifically define a species as "domesticated" or "wild" differently, depending upon where the animals live or how they are used.[5] For purposes of this chapter, reference to captive "wild" animals indicates and includes members of all species of animals who have not been intentionally and selectively bred for many generations.

Humans have captured wild animals for a variety of purposes for centuries. For example, the first recorded wild animal exhibition dates back to Ancient Egypt when Queen Hatshepsut opened the first zoo in 1500 BCE.[6] Today we maintain wild animals in captivity for a variety of uses, including for research, exhibition, entertainment, sport, and as exotic pets. The ethical and legal issues that arise in each context are unique and thus this chapter is organized around each use.

The current legal regime governing our treatment of animals, including the use of captive wild animals, is based on a utilitarian paradigm grounded in the maximization of the good. Simplistically, it involves

---

2. 50 C.F.R. § 17.3 (2012) defines "captivity" to mean when "living wildlife is held in a controlled environment that is intensively manipulated by man for the purpose of producing wildlife of the selected species, and that has boundaries designed to prevent animal, eggs or gametes of the selected species from entering or leaving the controlled environment."

3. 50 C.F.R. § 17.3 defines "bred in captivity or captive-bred" as referring "to wildlife, including eggs, born or otherwise produced in captivity from parents that mated or otherwise transferred gametes in captivity, if reproduction is sexual, or from parents that were in captivity when development of the progeny began, if development is asexual."

4. Zeder, *supra* note 1, at 163–64.

5. For example, the Code of Federal Regulations, includes in the definition of "domesticated animals" the following mammals: Cat (domestic)—*Felis domesticus;* Dog (domestic)—*Canis familiaris;* Horse—*Equus caballus;* White lab mice—*Mus musculus*; and White lab rat—*Rattus norvegicus.* 50 C.F.R. § 14.4.

6. Kali S. Grech, *Detailed Discussion of the Law Affecting Zoos,* ANIMAL LEGAL AND HISTORICAL CENTER (2004), https://www.animallaw.info/article/detailed-discussion-laws-affecting-zoos [hereinafter *Law Affecting Zoos*].

weighing the costs and benefits of an action to determine whether the benefits outweigh the costs, and if so, society agrees that it can be pursued. Under such a paradigm there are no "absolutes." This paradigm is distinguished from one that views an act as morally good because of a characteristic of the act itself, independent of its consequences. This view results in the protection of certain interests or rights, even when such protection may not result in the greater good. Thus, for example, in the United States we value the right of humans to speak freely, even if the speech may be harmful. To date, the law has not recognized a "right" of any nonhuman sentient being that may not be trumped in favor of the greater good for humans. Thus, our laws governing animals are determined based on a weighing of the benefits to humans against the cost to the animals, and other humans, of such use.

As this chapter will demonstrate, for most wild animals, i.e., those who are not protected under a specific statute like the Endangered Species Act (ESA) or the Marine Mammal Protection Act (MMPA), the law prohibits only "unnecessary" harm and thus to the extent there is any "legitimate" (a subjective term) benefit to humans for using an animal, such use will be allowed even if the harm to the animal is severe. The utilitarian balancing, of course, is a function of the specific use and the regulations that govern the treatment of the animal during such use. Some uses serve more important functions than others, and relatedly, some uses harm animals more severely than others. Thus, in the context of captive wild animals, the law balances the benefits to humans and the animal, if any, against the costs—the harm to the animal and some humans—to establish when and under what circumstances we may hold captive and/or use (including killing) the wild animal. This chapter will examine, for an identified complement of circumstances, the use of wild animals and the ethical controversies surrounding such use and how the law regulates such use. A key focus will be to determine whether the law properly and effectively protects the interests of wild animals held in captivity.

The plight of captive wild animals has caught the attention of the American public in recent years, bringing to the forefront the ethical and legal issues these cases raise. For Jerom, a chimpanzee, this awakening came too late. Jerom was born, lived, and died in a research laboratory. Taken from his mother prematurely and infected with human immunodeficiency virus (HIV) at the age of two years and eight months, Jerom suffered extreme physical and emotional pain, only to be euthanized in 1996 at the young age of fourteen (captive chimpanzees can live five or more decades) with the research performed on him serving no useful function for human or animal life.[7]

The ethical and moral issues raised by biomedical experimentation on primates are complex and involve analyzing the scientific efficacy of the research involved, considering alternatives available to achieve similar results without the use of animals, and balancing the intended benefits to humans against the harm suffered by the animals tested. Some will argue that the severe pain and suffering inflicted on the monkeys in scientific experiments cannot be outweighed by the possible human benefit derived while others will argue the possible benefit to humans of a vaccine, for example, is worth subjecting nonhumans to such pain and suffering. The federal Animal Welfare Act (AWA)[8] is the primary law that regulates human use of animals in research in the United States. The AWA provides for minimal standards of care for the treatment of the animals used in research laboratories, but those standards do not interfere with the alleged necessary protocols of research studies. Thus, if the research requires that the animal suffer, the standards generally allow the suffering. Is this state of affairs justified in an enlightened society?

The entertainment/exhibition of captive wild animals presents different problems. In 2006, after the death of two female elephants in four years and no live elephant births in over twenty years, the Bronx Zoo vowed to shut down its elephant exhibit upon the death of two or even one of its remaining three elephants—Patty, Maxine, and Happy. The zoo explained that "[e]lephants prefer living in herds at least a half-dozen strong, need a lot of space to roam, are prone to arthritis and foot diseases, and can become distressed when new elephants are introduced into their enclosures."[9] Thus, if one of the three elephants dies the other

---

7. Project R&R, *Stories of Chimpanzees: Jerom*, http://www.releasechimps.org/chimpanzees/their-stories/jerom.

8. *See* 9 C.F.R. §§ 3.112–3.118.

9. Joseph Berger, *Bronx Zoo Plans to End Elephant Exhibit*, N.Y. Times (Feb. 7, 2006), http://www.nytimes.com/2006/02/07/nyregion/07elephants.html.

two may not get along, and if two die it is inhumane to retain only one elephant in isolation given their need for social interaction. However, the zoo was unable to place Happy, subordinate and shy, with Patty and Maxine. The zoo believed it "too risky" for Happy to be housed with them because Patty and Maxine had aggressively charged Happy's longtime companion, Grumpy, several years before, causing her death. Ten years later, in June 2016, Happy remained isolated and alone at the Bronx zoo, inconsistent with Association of Zoos and Aquariums (AZA) standards.[10]

Zoos and aquariums justify exhibiting wild animals in cages and other captive environments by claiming their exhibition promotes public education and conservation.[11] The MMPA allows permits to capture a marine mammal from the wild for purposes of exhibition, and all other wild animals, even animals covered by the ESA in certain circumstances, may be captured for exhibition. Many zoos and aquariums breed wild animals as part of required programs intended to have babies to exhibit as well as to propagate the species, although virtually none of the animals are released to the wild. The capture itself inevitably results in harm to the animals and their wild family. Once in captivity, the AWA and certain private associations such as the AZA and the Alliance of Marine Mammal Parks and Aquariums (Alliance), set minimal standards for the care and housing of their animals. Nevertheless, animals in zoos and aquariums often suffer in a number of ways, especially those species whose natural habitats and social structures cannot be even moderately replicated in captivity, for example, elephants and orca whales. Do the harms to the wild animals from capture and/or from being in captivity itself justify the alleged benefits of public education and conservation

---

10. Tracy Tullis, *The Bronx Zoo's Loneliest Elephant*, N.Y. Times (June 26, 2015), http://www.nytimes.com/2015/06/28/nyregion/the-bronx-zoos-loneliest-elephant.html?_r=0. AZA elephant standards are not binding, thus the Bronx Zoo remains an AZA member despite the violation.
11. Note that the exhibition of animals is also certainly "entertaining" to humans. One important factor that distinguishes the terms "animal exhibition" and "animal entertainment" for purposes of this chapter is that animals who "entertain" are trained to perform in ways that are unnatural and often the training techniques used cause harm to the wild animal.

efforts? How effectively do the standards of care provide for the well-being of the exhibited animals?

After years of litigation and public pressure, the Ringling Bros. and Barnum & Bailey Circus announced it would retire its elephants from traveling performances in 2016 (and in 2017 announced it would shut down altogether).[12] Nevertheless, the elephants may still be forced to perform in Florida, and other circuses continue to force elephants and other animals to perform. For example, the Kelly Miller Circus has been cited by the U.S. Department of Agriculture (USDA), the agency that promulgates AWA regulations and enforces such regulations, numerous times between 1992 and 2015 for violations of the AWA with respect to its treatment of its wild animals (including elephants, chimpanzees, tigers, and bears). Nevertheless, Kelly Miller retains its AWA license and continues to abuse elephants and other animals as was reported in 2013 when an observer reported the circus for beating with a bullhook an elephant that was carrying four children on her back.[13]

Circuses, marine parks, and other facilities maintain captive wild animals for profit and to entertain the public. Some may engage in education and conservation efforts as a secondary purpose, but many do not. As with zoos and aquariums, some of the animals were captured from the wild and these facilities cannot replicate the natural surroundings nor social environments of the animals who perform. In addition, often cruel techniques, such as the use of bullhooks, are used to train the animals to force them to perform unnatural acts for human entertainment. These entities are governed by the AWA but generally are not subject to private accreditation bodies, such as the AZA. Is it justified to hold captive and train wild animals to perform unnatural acts, often using cruel techniques, for our entertainment?

---

12. J. Susan Ager, *Ringling Will Retire Circus Elephants Two Years Earlier Than Planned*, NAT'L GEO. (Jan. 11, 2016), http://news.nationalgeographic.com/2016/01/160111-ringling-ele-phants-retire/; Jason Bittel, *Ringling Brothers to Retire Its Circus Elephants*, NAT'L GEO. (Mar. 5, 2015), http://news.nationalgeographic.com/news/2015/03/150305-ringling-bros-retires-asian-elephants-barnum-bailey; http://www.npr.org/sections/thetwo-way/2017/01/15/509903805/after-146-years-ringling-bros-and-barnum-bailey-circus-to-shut-down.
13. PETA Factsheet, *Kelly Miller Circus*, http://www.mediapeta.com/peta/pdf/Kelly-Miller-pdf.pdf (last visited Aug. 16, 2015).

Private ownership of captive wild animals can have deadly consequences. In February 2009, Travis, a 200-pound pet chimpanzee living
in a home in Connecticut, attacked a friend of Travis' owner.[14] Police
were called and killed Travis but not before he severely injured the friend,
leaving her in critical condition. Two years later, on October 18, 2011,
eighteen tigers, seventeen lions, eight bears, three cougars, two wolves,
one baboon, and one macaque monkey, all owned by Terry Thompson in
Zanesville, Ohio, were killed by law enforcement after they were intentionally released from their cages by Mr. Thompson. Although at the
time Ohio banned the private ownership of pit bull type dogs, the state
allowed individuals to own wild animals as pets, despite the public safety
and animal welfare concerns which were vividly displayed that horrific
evening.[15] These cases are not isolated events and demonstrate the problems associated with the private ownership of wild animals as pets.

Wild animals are unsocialized and present a risk of danger to
humans—from both physical harm and the transmission of a wide variety of zoonotic diseases (diseases that can be transmitted from nonhumans to humans) such as herpes-B, monkey pox, and salmonellosis.[16]
Moreover, wild animals kept as pets often suffer because of the absence
of natural protections and systems to which they have been adapted for
millennia. In captivity, they require special care, housing, diet, and maintenance that most people cannot provide and that in many cases has
never been fully developed. In fact, even with such special care, most wild
animals are forced into a lifestyle that precludes them from engaging in
their normal behaviors. Moreover, often owners find they are unable to
keep their pets after a few years and then either abandon the animals, sell
them to canned hunt ranches or substandard zoos, or kill the animals.

---

14. *Chimpanzee Attacks, Mauls Connecticut Woman Before Being Killed by Police*, FoxNews (Feb.
17, 2009), http://www.foxnews.com/story/2009/02/17/chimpanzee-attacks-mauls-connecticut-
woman-before-being-killed-by-police.html.

15. Chris Heath, *18 Tigers, 17 Lions, 8 Bears, 3 Cougars, 2 Wolves, 1 Baboon, 1 Macaque and 1 Man
Dead in Ohio*, GQ (Feb. 6, 2012), http://www.gq.com/story/terry-thompson-ohio-zoo-massacre
-chris-heath-gq-february-2012.

16. *Three Reasons for Banning the Private Possession of Exotic Animals*, Born Free USA, http://www
.bornfreeusa.org/facts.php?more=1&p=438 (last visited Aug. 16, 2015).

The private ownership of wild animals as pets provides their owners with some limited companionship, but humans may enjoy the companionship of domesticated animals, many of which are homeless and in need of loving homes, without subjecting the public or wild animals to the perils of keeping captive wildlife

The legality of private ownership of wild animals primarily is a function of state law. States may ban all ownership of wild animals, impose partial bans based on species, require a permit to own a wild animal, or allow ownership subject to a variety of conditions.[17] The utilitarian question with respect to private ownership is: Are the public safety and health risks and animal welfare concerns outweighed by an individual's desire to privately possess a wild animal?

Private involvement with wild animals also extends to circumstances in which they are trapped and killed for sport and/or the entertainment value of those activities—whether the animals are used for food or clothing, or simply as "trophies." Wild animals are hunted and trapped in their own habitats, and captive wild animals are killed on "canned hunting" ranches where people pay to kill animals (including endangered species such as the scimitar-horned oryx, extinct in its native Africa but numbering in the thousands on Texas ranches) who are trapped behind fences and sometimes drugged to make them easy targets.[18] There is virtually no "sport" involved in canned hunting ranches. Animals killed on canned hunting ranches may be hand-raised and bottle-fed by humans so they are not afraid and do not flee when the customers of these ranches approach for the kill. No skill or patience is needed and canned hunts are regularly criticized as unsportsmanlike and immoral, because of the contrast between traditional hunting in the wild. Moreover, maintaining large captive populations of animals can threaten the welfare of the free-roaming population through the transmission of diseases and by encouraging and facilitating the illegal trade in these species. But canned

17. *Summary of State Laws Relating to Private Possession of Exotic Animals,* Born Free USA, http://www.bornfreeusa.org/b4a2_exotic_animals_summary.php (last visited Aug. 16, 2015).
18. *Captive Hunts Fact Sheet: The Unfair Chase,* The Humane Society of the United States (Aug. 17, 2012), http://www.humanesociety.org/issues/captive_hunts/facts/captive_hunt_fact_sheet.html; *see also* Christina Bush, *Canned Hunting—An American Atrocity,* http://www.christinabush.com/cannedhunting.html (last visited Aug. 16, 2015).

hunts thrive because of the significant profit for the owners and the value to those who come to shoot a trophy animal without leaving the United States. Supporters also tout canned hunting ranches as homes for wild animals who are abandoned after they have been used in other venues, such as zoos, circuses, and private homes, when they no longer serve their purpose. The over 1,000 canned hunting ranches exploiting a variety of wild animals in the United States contribute to many Americans' passion for trophy hunting. No federal law explicitly bans canned hunting, even if the animal is from an endangered species, and only about half of the states ban and/or regulate such practices under state law.[19] Does the pleasure of killing an animal trapped on a ranch to gain a trophy justify the threats caused by canned hunting ranches to the free-roaming wild animal populations?

This chapter will explore in detail each of these uses of captive wild animals, the moral arguments for and against each use, and the legal framework that regulates each use. In so doing the chapter will help you answer the questions raised by the practices discussed above.

Laboratories and Primate Research

Moral Considerations

The United States is a world leader in scientific research, with the National Institutes of Health (NIH) allocating approximately $30 billion per year to medical research.[20] The NIH conducts its own research and also financially supports laboratories that conduct animal research, including spending millions of dollars annually on seven National Primate Research Centers.[21] Other federal agencies, such as the Department of Defense and the National Aeronautics and Space Administration,[22]

---

19. *Id.*
20. National Institutes of Health, *What We Do: Budget* (2016), http://www.nih.gov/about/budget .htm.
21. National Institutes of Health, *Primate Resources for Researchers* (2016), http://dpcpsi.nih.gov/ orip/cm/primate_resources_researchers.
22. NASA famously used chimpanzees for initial forays into space. *See* http://www.spacechimps .com/theirstory.html.

also fund and conduct biomedical research on primates, as do private foundations and corporations (such as the pharmaceutical industry). Primate laboratories study human pathologies and diseases, vaccines, psychological disorders, toxicology, transplantation, nutrition, drug abuse, and cloning, and many studies involve invasive procedures such as injections, infections, and biopsies.[23]

There are over 100,000 nonhuman primates kept in U.S. laboratories today, primarily macaque monkeys and more than a dozen other species, including some endangered species like chimpanzees, cotton-top tamarins, and sooty mangabeys. Because humans are a species of primates (and thus are similar to other primates in physiology, neuroanatomy, development, and cognition), for the last century biomedical researchers have conducted experiments on nonhuman primates in hopes of finding solutions to promote human health.[24] However, these similarities are precisely what make the use of nonhuman primates in laboratories so controversial.[25] This controversy is not only an ethical debate about causing suffering in other highly cognitive beings for our own gain, but also about the science underlying the reliability of this research. For example, in the 1980s and 1990s researchers believed that chimpanzees could be used to develop a cure for acquired immune deficiency syndrome (AIDS) and U.S. laboratories bred hundreds of chimpanzees for use in such research; but after learning that chimpanzees infected with HIV almost never developed AIDS, researchers transitioned to using macaque monkeys infected with simian immunodeficiency virus (SIV) as a model. The macaque research has received less scientific criticism, but is still the subject of ethical debates, and to date has not been successful in developing an HIV vaccine.[26]

---

23. Invasive biomedical research is distinguishable from the various forms of behavioral and cognitive research in which chimpanzees in accredited zoos and sanctuaries and traditional research institutions continue to voluntarily participate in cognitive studies.

24. See, e.g., Kimberly Phillips et al., Why Primate Models Matter, 76(9) AM. J. OF PRIMATOL. 801–827 (2014).

25. See, e.g., Kathleen Conlee & Andrew Rowan, The Case for Phasing Out Experiments on Primates, 42(6) THE HASTINGS CENTER REP. (2012), http://animalresearch.thehastingscenter.org/report/the-case-for-phasing-out-experiments-on-primates/.

26. See, e.g., Jarrod Bailey, An Assessment of the Role of Chimpanzees in AIDS Vaccine Research, 36 ALTERNATIVES TO LAB. ANIMALS 381–428 (2008), http://www.releasechimps.org/docs/Chimps_AIDS_research_J._Bailey.pdf.

Monkeys are regularly bred by laboratories and commercial breeders for research purposes, but laboratories also import thousands of wild-caught and captive-bred monkeys from their native countries in Africa and Asia. The vigorous debate about the scientific merit and ethics of using nonhuman primates as subjects for human medical research has recently resulted in groundbreaking consensus between scientists, the federal government, and animal protection and conservation organizations that chimpanzees are no longer needed as a model for biomedical research. As a result, in 2016 approximately 700 chimpanzees began the process of being retired from laboratories, with the lucky ones transferred to lifetime sanctuaries. In 2015, the NIH agreed to retire all federally owned chimpanzees to a sanctuary partially funded by the federal government, and in 2016 a new sanctuary—Project Chimps—was established to facilitate retirement of non–federally owned chimpanzees (beginning with 220 individuals housed at the New Iberia Research Center).[27]

Primates are known to suffer tremendously in laboratory environments for a number of reasons. First, primate infants, who are inseparable from their mothers in the wild, and need maternal contact to properly develop, are prematurely separated from their mothers, causing immediate and long-term harm. Second, primates have complex social needs and often suffer from being housed in isolation (which is frequently deemed necessary for research purposes). Third, many primates are tree-dwelling species but are given no room to climb and forced to live cramped in small metal cages. Finally, the lack of mental stimulation—something in great abundance in their wild habitat—causes extreme stress, which is often compensated for by aberrant, self-destructive and compulsive behaviors (including self-mutilation). This section will discuss the primary federal laws that apply to primates used in research, including the AWA and its psychological well-being regulations, the Public Health Service's guide for the care of laboratory animals, the NIH standards for chimpanzees kept in laboratories or retired to sanctuaries, and the ESA's protection of captive chimpanzees and other imperiled primates.

---

27. *See* National Institutes of Health, *NIH Plan to Retire All NIH-Owned and-Supported Chimpanzees*, http://www.sciencemag.org/news/2015/12/nih-end-controversial-monkey-experiments-poolesville-lab (last visited Nov. 4, 2016).

Laws and Guidelines Regulating Primate Research

The Animal Welfare Act—Primate
Psychological Well-Being Regulations

The AWA was originally enacted in 1966 specifically to protect laboratory animals and to prevent the capture and sale of pets for use in invasive research,[28] and was expanded in 1985 to require the USDA to adopt minimum standards for the housing and care of laboratory primates, including standards for "a physical environment adequate to promote the psychological well-being of primates."[29] Legislative history indicates that through these amendments Congress intended that laboratories be required to allow primates to exercise their "natural instincts and habits."[30] Research facilities must register annually with the USDA,[31] receive annual inspections, "ensure that all scientists, research technicians, animal technicians, and other personnel involved in animal care, treatment, and use are qualified to perform their duties," and provide species-specific training for such employees.[32] Researchers must handle primates "as expeditiously and carefully as possible in a manner that does not cause trauma . . . behavioral stress, physical harm, or unnecessary discomfort."[33] Notably, however, the USDA does not have authority to "interrupt the conduct of actual research or experimentation,"[34] meaning that if causing pain or distress is determined by the laboratory's own Institutional Animal Care and Use Committee (IACUC) to be necessary for a particular research protocol, such activity can lawfully proceed.

---

28. *See* Pub. L. No. 89-544; 7 U.S.C. § 2131(1).

29. 7 U.S.C. § 2143(a).

30. H.R. Rep. No. 99-447 (1985) (Conf. Rep.), at 594.

31. While any institution that uses live animals in tests or experiments must register with USDA, some laboratories also are accredited by the Association for Assessment and Accreditation of Laboratory Animal Care (AAALAC), a private organization whose mission is to "enhance the quality of research, teaching, and testing by promoting humane, responsible animal care and use." *See* http://www.aaalac.org/index.cfm. While over 900 facilities have acquired AAALAC accreditation, animal protection organizations have been critical of the value added by such certification, because of AAALAC's supposed bias in favor of research.

32. 9 C.F.R. Part 2, Subpart 3; *id.* at Part 3, Subpart D.

33. 9 C.F.R. § 2.131(b)(1).

34. 7 U.S.C. § 2143 (a)(6)(A).

In the late 1980s, the USDA began drafting regulatory text to guide laboratories on how to provide an appropriate environment for captive primates.[35] The final rules, adopted in 1991 and still applicable today, require research facilities to "develop, document, and follow an appropriate plan for environment enhancement adequate to promote the psychological well-being of primates."[36] Such enrichment plans "must be in accordance with the currently accepted professional standards"; address the social needs of nonhuman primates and environmental enrichment of enclosures to allow expression of species-typical activities; and provide special considerations for infants and young juveniles, great apes, primates showing signs of distress, and any individually-housed primates.[37] However, research facilities may exempt individual primates from the plan for scientific purposes or on the recommendation of the facility's veterinarian (although such exemptions must be regularly reviewed to determine their continued necessity).[38]

These standards have been criticized as being too vague and leaving too much discretion to the regulated community—indeed, at one point the USDA itself even proposed a new policy establishing criteria for social grouping, social needs of infants, structure and substrate, foraging opportunities, and manipulanda, all of which the agency said were "critical" for enrichment plans.[39] But that policy was never finalized, and litigation challenging the regulations was ultimately unsuccessful, with a federal court of appeals holding that the regulations were within the agency's discretion.[40] However, in 2015, the issue was revived when animal protection groups petitioned the USDA under the Administrative Procedure Act[41] to adopt new standards (by regulations and/or guidance documents) for primate well-being.[42]

---

35. 51 Fed. Reg. 7,950 (March 7, 1986); 54 Fed. Reg. 10,897, 10,913 (March 15, 1989).

36. 9 C.F.R. § 3.81; 55 Fed. Reg. 33,448 (Aug. 15, 1990); 56 Fed. Reg. 6,426 (Feb. 15, 1991).

37. 9 C.F.R. § 3.81(a)–(c).

38. Id. § 3.81(e).

39. 64 Fed. Reg. 38145 (July 15, 1999).

40. See Animal Legal Def. Fund ("ALDF") v. Sec'y of Agric., 813 F. Supp. 882 (D.C.C. 1993) (holding that USDA regulations under the AWA "ignore[d] the plain language of the statute"); ALDF v. Glickman, 204 F.3d 229 (D.C.C. 2000) (upholding the regulations while acknowledging that they "may prove difficult to enforce").

41. 5 U.S.C. § 553(e).

42. See 80 Fed. Reg. 43969 (July 24, 2015).

Data from USDA inspection reports, undercover investigations of laboratories by animal protection groups,[43] and scientific studies show that research facilities repeatedly fail to provide an adequate environment to primates, in many instances not even drafting an enrichment plan, let alone implementing a plan sufficient to promote psychological well-being through social housing and enrichment. Additionally, scientific analysis of the enrichment plans that laboratories have on file (which can be obtained through public records requests for laboratories owned by state universities or the federal government) reveals that many of the plans fail to identify desired outcomes or cite relevant scientific literature, thus calling into question their ability to actually improve the lives of laboratory primates.[44]

Public Health Service Policy and the Guide for the Care and Use of Laboratory Animals

When laboratories receive federal funds to conduct research, they are required to make assurances to the NIH that the research will comply with all applicable regulations and guidelines pertaining to laboratory animals, including the AWA and the Public Health Service (PHS) Policy on Humane Care and Use of Laboratory Animals, and the Guide for the Care and Use of Laboratory Animals (the Guide).[45] The Guide contains standards for space and housing of laboratory animals and practices for providing enrichment, exercise, and handling of laboratory animals and specifically endorses social housing as the default for nonhuman

43. *See, e.g.,* The Humane Society of the United States, *Undercover Investigation Reveals Cruelty to Chimps at Research Lab* (March 4, 2009), http://www.humanesociety.org/news/news/2009/03/undercover_investigation_chimpanzee_abuse.html?referrer=https://www.google.com; The Humane Society of the United States, *Undercover Investigation Reveals Dogs Suffering in Dental Experimentation* (Nov. 22, 2013) http://www.humanesociety.org/news/press_releases/2013/11/georgia-regents-university-dogs-112013.html?credit=web_id503688356#.UwwBGoUlt-c; Wayne Pacelle, *Undercover Investigation Reveals Primate Injuries, Death at Texas Biomed* (Sept. 22, 2014), http://blog.humanesociety.org/wayne/2014/09/texas-biomed-investigation.html; People for the Ethical Treatment of Animals, *Psychological Torture Experiments at NIH Must Stop* (2016), http://investigations.peta.org/nih-baby-monkey-experiments/.
44. Wayne Pacelle, *Monkey Business at Labs and Roadside Zoos Must End* (April 20, 2015), http://blog.humanesociety.org/wayne/2015/04/hsus-legal-petition-monkeys.html (anaylsys of enrichment plans from Dr. Debra Durham, attached to petition from The Humane Society of the United States).
45. *See* 48 C.F.R. § 352.270-5; 76 Fed. Reg. 74803 (Dec. 1, 2011). Similarly, the Food and Drug Administration has adopted "Good Laboratory Practice for Nonclinical Laboratory Studies." 21 C.F.R. Part 58.

primates. The NIH Office of Laboratory Animal Welfare (OLAW) has stated that "group housing is the most appropriate method of ensuring that the animals' social needs are met" and furthermore, "[a]n institution's environmental enrichment practices must be species-specific and appropriate for the animals."[46] These standards largely mirror the AWA standards (although, notably, while the AWA does not apply to birds, mice, and rats bred for use in research, the Guide does). Notably, neither the AWA nor the Guide is designed to limit the type of research conducted, instead simply applying minimum standards of care to be observed when housing research animals.

NIH Standards for Chimpanzees Used in Research

Chimpanzees are genetically closer to humans than any other species. Chimpanzees are more closely related to humans than they are even to gorillas; indeed, chimpanzees and humans are remarkably similar in terms of genetics, anatomy, and mental capacity, due to the fact that our lineages diverged only six to thirteen million years ago.[47] Because of this biological correlation, laboratories have long used chimpanzees in invasive research that cannot ethically be done on humans. But in large part because of that close kinship, the use of chimpanzees in biomedical research has been at the center of the controversy surrounding research on primates and other species. For much of the twentieth century, U.S. laboratories acquired wild chimpanzees from their native African range (likely by hiring local poachers to kill adults and capture infants), and some of those wild-caught individuals are still in laboratories today. After the export of wild chimpanzees was prohibited by both international and federal law,[48] U.S. laboratories began breeding chimpanzees to ensure a

---

46. NIH Office of Laboratory Animal Welfare, http://grants.nih.gov/grants/olaw/positionstatement_guide.htm#nonhuman.

47. *See, e.g.,* Animal Diversity Web, *Pan troglodytes* (2014), http://animaldiversity.org/accounts/Pan_troglodytes/; Oliver Venn et al., *Strong Male Bias Drives Germline Mutation in Chimpanzees*, 344(6189) Sci. 1272–75 (2014) (new genetic evidence suggests that chimpanzee and human lineages diverged from a common ancestor thirteen million years ago, while fossil evidence suggests that our common ancestor persisted until six million years ago).

48. The Convention on International Trade in Endangered Species extended protection to chimpanzees in 1977 and the U.S. Endangered Species Act, 16 U.S.C. § 1531 et seq., extended protection to wild chimpanzees in 1976. 41 Fed. Reg. 45990 (Oct. 19, 1976).

steady supply of research subjects. At the peak, there were over 1,000 chimpanzees in U.S. laboratories, approximately half owned by the federal government (through the NIH) and the other half owned by private laboratories and state universities. However, as discussed in this section, the lack of scientific merit in biomedical research on chimpanzees has been exposed, and now laboratories, the federal government, and the animal protection community are in the process of retiring chimpanzees from laboratories to sanctuaries.

The beginning of the end of chimpanzee biomedical research came in 2011. Following pressure from members of Congress concerned by a proposal to resume invasive research on a group of elderly chimpanzees at the Alamogordo Primate Facility (located on the Holloman Air Force Base in New Mexico),[49] the NIH commissioned the National Academies of Sciences, Engineering, and Medicine to assess the needs and justifications for the use of chimpanzees in biomedical and behavioral research. The National Academies' Institute of Medicine (IOM) initially established a review panel that was not "fairly balanced" or free of conflict of interest, as required by the Federal Advisory Committee Act, but after complaints from animal protection attorneys, the panel was reconstituted and its objective scientific review was led by a bioethicist.[50]

In December 2011, the IOM released a report finding that "[t]he present trajectory indicates a decreasing scientific need for chimpanzee studies due to the emergence of non-chimpanzee models and technologies."[51] Indeed, the IOM did not find a single area of biomedical research for which the panel recommended that research should continue. The IOM established three criteria to assess the necessity of chimpanzee research going forward:

---

49. Tom Udall, *N.M. Senators React to National Academies & NIH on Recommendations that Would Significantly Limit the Use of Chimpanzees in Research* (Dec. 15, 2011), http://www.tomudall.senate.gov/?p=press_release&id=990.

50. 5 U.S.C. App. § 15(b)(1); Jon Cohen, *Chimp Committee Shakeup Follows Humane Society Complaints*, SCIENCE (June 14, 2011), http://www.sciencemag.org/news/2011/06/chimp-committee-shakeup-follows-humane-society-complaints. The National Academies also has a permanent body, the Institute for Laboratory Animal Research that "evaluates and encourages the use, development, and validation of non-animal alternatives." http://dels.nas.edu/ilar.

51. Institute of Medicine & National Research Council, The National Academies, *Chimpanzees in Biomedical and Behavioral Research: Assessing the Necessity*, 4-5 (Dec. 2011), http://www.nap.edu/read/13257/chapter/1#ix.

1. The knowledge gained must be necessary to advance the public's health;
2. There must be no other research model by which the knowledge could be obtained, and the research cannot be ethically performed on human subjects; and
3. The animals used in the proposed research must be maintained either in ethologically appropriate physical and social environments or in natural habitats.

The IOM report similarly recommended criteria for analyzing whether chimpanzees should be used in behavioral research. The report did not evaluate research that is not funded by the NIH, but private companies have increasingly rejected the use of chimpanzees in biomedical research because the species is not a good biomedical research model (and, as discussed further in this chapter, as of 2016 there was no pharmaceutical research occurring on chimpanzees).[52]

Immediately following the issuance of the report, NIH Director Dr. Francis Collins issued a statement adopting the IOM recommendations and suspended federal funding of chimpanzee research.[53] The NIH then established a working group (under the supervision of the NIH Council of Councils) to provide advice on how to implement the IOM recommendations. The Working Group developed quantitative recommendations based on its members' expertise (especially those of Dr. Stephen Ross, who manages the Chimpanzee Species Survival Plan for AZA zoos), consultation with experts, published information about the behavior of wild and captive chimpanzees, and visits to chimpanzee laboratories and

---

52. *See* GlaxoSmithKline, *Use of Non-human Primates (NHPs) in the Discovery and Development of Medicines and Vaccines* (2008), http://www.gsk.com/policies/GSK-public-position-on-NHP.pdf; Idenix Pharmaceuticals, Inc., *Use of Non-Human Primates (NHPs) in the Discovery and Development of Medicines* (2011), http://www.idenix.com/hcv/Use%20of%20Chimp%20Policy.pdf; Abbott Laboratories, *Policy on Use of Chimpanzees in Biomedical Research* (2011), http://www.abbott.com/citizenship/priorities/innovate/animal-welfare.htm.
53. *See* NIH, *Statement by NIH Director Dr. Francis Collins on the Institute of Medicine report addressing the scientific need for the use of chimpanzees in research* (Dec. 15, 2011), http://www.nih.gov/news/health/dec2011/od-15.htm; NIH, Notice No. NOT-OD-12-025 (December 21, 2011).

sanctuaries.[54] The Working Group report was critical in defining the IOM criteria for what constitutes "ethologically appropriate physical and social environments" for chimpanzees used in future research (including enclosure size and design and group size and demographics to promote natural behavior). The "ethologically appropriate" standard would only apply to any facility that receives NIH funding for continued research on chimpanzees (whether biomedical or behavioral), but not to privately funded research or to chimpanzees retired to sanctuary.

The NIH adopted all but one of the Working Group's recommendations (but notably decreased the required size of the chimpanzee enclosure from the recommended 1,000 ft² per individual to 250 ft² per individual).[55] Most importantly, the NIH agreed to retire all of the federally owned chimpanzees and work to establish sanctuary space for hundreds of chimpanzees no longer needed for biomedical research.[56] This decision was in accord with NIH's statutory mandate in the Chimpanzee Health Improvement, Maintenance, and Protection Act (CHIMP Act) to retire federally owned chimpanzees who are "not needed" for research. The CHIMP Act also establishes a national chimpanzee sanctuary system and provides standards for funding and management of retired chimpanzees.[57]

Any request for NIH funding for chimpanzee research must now be analyzed by the agency's Chimpanzees Research Use Panel (CRUP) to determine whether the research survives the cost-benefit equation established by IOM and, if so, whether the chimpanzees are housed and man-

---

54. Council of Councils Working Group on the Use of Chimpanzees in NIH-Supported Research, Report (2013), *at* https://dpcpsi.nih.gov/sites/default/files/FNL_Report_WG_Chimpanzees_0.pdf.

55. 78 Fed. Reg. 39,741 (July 2, 2013); 79 Fed. Reg. 19917 (April 10, 2014).

56. NIH initially announced that it would maintain a colony of 50 chimpanzees for research (*id.*), but in 2015 NIH decided to retire all federally owned chimpanzees to sanctuary. *See* NIH, *NIH Will No Longer Support Biomedical Research on Chimpanzees* (Nov. 18, 2015), http://www.nih.gov/about-nih/who-we-are/nih-director/statements/nih-will-no-longer-support-biomedical-research-chimpanzees.

57. 42 U.S.C. § 283m. *See also* 73 Fed. Reg. 60410 (October 10, 2008) (establishing standards of care for chimpanzees in the national sanctuary system). Currently the only sanctuary specifically approved under the CHIMP Act is Chimp Haven in Shreveport, Louisiana, which operates on a contractual basis with the federal government. Chimpanzees not owned by the federal government may be retired to other sanctuaries, such as those accredited by the Global Federation of Animal Sanctuaries.

aged consistent with the Working Group criteria.[58] To date, the NIH has not funded any chimpanzee biomedical research since establishing these rigorous criteria. Indeed, now that the NIH has announced that it does not see any need to continue investing in maintaining a federally owned chimpanzee research colony, it appears that the only instance in which the CRUP would grant money for chimpanzee research would be for noninvasive behavioral studies that were deemed to benefit human health (which is NIH's mission). However, the scientists interested in conducting behavioral research on chimpanzees are not necessarily interested in doing so to find cures to modern human illnesses, but instead to learn about the evolution of our species. Thus, it remains to be seen if or how the CRUP and the ethologically appropriate standards will be implemented going forward.

Endangered Species Act Protection for Primates in Laboratories

The ESA is our nation's cornerstone wildlife law, and the Supreme Court has acknowledged that the goal of the ESA is to "reverse the trend toward extinction, whatever the cost."[59] In the decades since enactment of the ESA, the U.S. Fish and Wildlife Service (USFWS) has struggled with how to apply the ESA to captive animals, and to primates in laboratories in particular, as detailed in the following section.

In response to citizen petitions from parties interested in protecting (or removing protections from) identified species, or on its own volition, the USFWS lists species[60] as either "threatened" or "endangered"

---

58. National Institutes of Health. *Chimpanzees Research Use Panel*, https://dpcpsi.nih.gov/council/crup.

59. Tennessee Valley Authority v. Hill, 437 U.S. 153, 184 (1978). *See also* 16 U.S.C. § 1531(b) (the purpose of the ESA is "to provide a program for the conservation of such endangered species and threatened species . . ."); 16 U.S.C. § 1532(3) (defining the term "conserve" to mean "to use all methods and procedures which are necessary to bring any endangered species or threatened species to the point at which the measures provided pursuant to [the Act] are no longer necessary").

60. 16 U.S.C. § 1532(16) (the term "species" includes "any subspecies of fish or wildlife or plants, and any distinct population segment of any species of vertebrate fish or wildlife which interbreeds when mature"); 61 Fed. Reg. 4722 (February 7, 1996) (policy on identifying distinct population segments).

depending on the level of imperilment.[61] Protections for endangered species are established by the statute; threatened species are subject to the same prohibitions as endangered species, unless the agency chooses to adopt special rules (also known as "4(d) rules"), which must be "necessary and advisable to provide for the conservation of such species").[62] The ESA requires listing determinations to be made "solely on the basis of the best scientific and commercial data available."[63] However, the demand for certain primate species for use in biomedical research has certainly impacted the USFWS' past listing decisions.

On October 19, 1976, the USFWS listed the chimpanzee, *Pan troglodytes*, as threatened, finding that "vast stretches of suitable habitat" for the chimpanzee had been destroyed for commercial logging and that "large scale exportation" of chimpanzees and habitat destruction was "unchecked by legal restraint."[64] The USFWS specifically noted that "chimpanzees are captured and exported for use in research labs" and that the United States "is the chief importer of the chimpanzee."[65] But at the same time, and with no explanation, the USFWS issued a "special rule" for chimpanzees, providing that the prohibition on "take" would not apply to chimpanzees in captivity in the United States. In other words, for captive chimpanzees only, the USFWS determined that the

---

61. 16 U.S.C. § 1532(6) ("The term 'endangered species' means any species which is in danger of extinction throughout all or a significant portion of its range."); 16 U.S.C. § 1532(20) ("The term 'threatened species' means any species which is likely to become an endangered species within the foreseeable future throughout all or a significant portion of its range.").

62. *Compare* 16 U.S.C. § 1538 *with* 16 U.S.C. § 1533(d). *See also* Sierra Club v. Clark, 755 F.2d 608 (8th Cir. 1985); 50 C.F.R. § 17.31 (if USFWS does not create a special rule for a threatened species, then the species receives the same protections as endangered species). USFWS may also establish experimental populations of species, reintroducing animals to range not currently occupied by the species, and such animals receive limited protection under the ESA; 16 U.S.C. § 1539(j).

63. 16 U.S.C. § 1533(b)(1)(A). *See also* New Mexico Cattle Growers v. U.S. Fish & Wildlife Service, 248 F.3d 1277, 1284-85 (10th Cir. 2001) (*quoting* H.R. Rep. No. 97-567, pt. 1 at 29 (1982)) ("'The addition of the word 'solely' is intended to remove from the process of listing or delisting of species any factor not related to the biological status of the species.'"); H.R. Conf. Rep. No. 835, 97th Cong. 2d Sess. 19-20 (1982) (the limitations on the factors the Service may consider in making listing decisions were intended to "ensure that decisions . . . pertaining to listing . . . are based solely upon biological criteria and to prevent nonbiological considerations from affecting such decisions.").

64. 41 Fed. Reg. 45990 (Oct. 19, 1976).

65. *Id.* at 45993.

ESA provided absolutely no protection to chimpanzees—in whatever capacity they were being used (research, entertainment, public exhibition, and private ownership, or breeding and commercial sales).[66]

Chimpanzee populations continued to decline, and in 1987, the Jane Goodall Institute, The Humane Society of the United States, and the World Wildlife Fund submitted a petition to the USFWS to reclassify chimpanzees from threatened to endangered.[67] That petition spurred the USFWS to find that chimpanzees in the wild were in danger of extinction, noting that "chimpanzees are extensively sought by people, both alive for use in research, entertainment, and exhibitions, and dead, for local use as food and in religious rituals," and that "such utilization is contributing substantially to the decline of the species." The USFWS also highlighted the "alarming recent trend towards killing adult females both for local use as meat and in order to secure their live offspring for export," and stressed that, "because entire family groups may have to be eliminated in order to secure one live infant, and since many of these infants perish during the process, it has been estimated that five to ten chimpanzees die for every one that is delivered alive to an overseas buyer."[68]

However, despite acknowledging the dire plight of the species in the wild, the USFWS continued to maintain a threatened listing for captive chimpanzees, stating that the species "is considered to be of much importance in biomedical and other kinds of research."[69] Furthermore, the USFWS continued to apply the special rule to all captive chimpanzees in the United States, allowing invasive research (and use in entertainment and sale by private owners) on these animals to continue without any scrutiny under the ESA. In the decades that followed, the United States became home to more chimpanzees than any other country outside of Africa, with over 1,000 chimpanzees bred and used by laboratories for biomedical research.

In 2010, eight animal protection and conservation groups—again led by the Jane Goodall Institute and The Humane Society of the United

---

66. *See* 40 C.F.R. § 17.40.
67. *See* 53 Fed. Reg. 9460 (March 23, 1988); 53 Fed. Reg. 52452 (December 28, 1988); 54 Fed. Reg. 8152 (February 24, 1989); 55 Fed. Reg. 9129, 9131 (March 12, 1990).
68. 55 Fed. Reg. 9129 (March 12, 1990).
69. *Id.* at 9130.

States—petitioned the USFWS to eliminate the so-called "split-listing" of the species and extend ESA protection to captive chimpanzees, arguing that the differential treatment of captive individuals actually undermined the conservation of the species by facilitating domestic exploitation that fuels poaching and trafficking of wild chimpanzees.[70] After conducting a comprehensive review of the species (including input from all stakeholders and range countries), in 2013 the USFWS issued a proposed regulation that promised to revolutionize the treatment of captive chimpanzees.[71]

After nearly forty years of denying ESA protection to captive chimpanzees, the USFWS admitted that the split listing was illegal, and acknowledged that the ESA "does not allow for captive-held animals to be assigned separate legal status from their wild counterparts on the basis of their captive state," and proposed to list all chimpanzees as endangered.[72] Over objections from the biomedical research community, that rule went into effect on September 14, 2015, and requires that any person who seeks to harm or harass a captive chimpanzee (for example by conducting invasive biomedical research) must first apply for a permit, and such permits can only lawfully be issued for actions that actually promote conservation of the chimpanzee species.[73]

This action, combined with the NIH decisions to discontinue funding chimpanzee research and retire chimpanzees from laboratories (which were announced within a month of each other in summer 2013), has effectively shut down nearly a century of using our closest living relatives for biomedical research.

Other imperiled primate species continue to be used for biomedical research—both cotton-top tamarins and sooty mangabeys are listed as endangered, but have been used for invasive research in recent years. For example, the Yerkes National Primate Research Center has acquired a

---

70. 76 Fed. Reg. 54423 (Sept. 1, 2011).
71. 78 Fed. Reg. 35201 (June 12, 2013).
72. *Id.* at 35204. *See also* 78 Fed. Reg. 33790 (June 5, 2013) (just one week earlier USFWS foreshadowed this finding by denying a petition by the captive hunting industry to similarly deprive endangered antelopes of ESA protection so that they can be used for trophy hunting); 79 Fed. Reg. 4313, 4317 (Jan. 27, 2014) (NMFS also takes the position that the "ESA does not support the exclusion of captive members from a listing based solely on their status as captive.").
73. 80 Fed. Reg. 34499 (June 16, 2015).

permit from the USFWS to maintain a colony of sooty mangabeys for use in simian immunodeficiency virus (SIV) research, in an effort to learn more about its human analog, HIV. Furthermore, several other threatened primate species continue to be subject to the primate 4(d) rule, meaning that captive individuals of these species have absolutely no protection under the ESA, and can be subjected to invasive research that causes whatever level of suffering is inherent in the research.[74]

As discussed in this section, while the use of chimpanzees for biomedical research has been the subject of much scrutiny resulting in increased protection, monkeys continue to be used in large numbers for laboratory experiments despite the well-established impacts of such activity on animal welfare.[75] While humans' interest in self-preservation drives much of the support for biomedical research, the ethics of using animals who share so many behaviors and emotions with us make this debate quite contentious, even more so than the exploitation of wild animals for the other captive uses discussed in this chapter.

Case Study: Maternal Deprivation Studies

Experts agree that promoting normal infant development is critical to ensuring the long-term well-being of captive primates, but laboratories routinely separate infants before the species-typical age of weaning. For example, the species-typical age of weaning for macaque monkeys, which make up 98 percent of all primates in laboratories, is eighteen months, but laboratories regularly remove macaques from their mothers when they

---

74. 50 C.F.R. § 17.40(c).
75. Monkeys predictably suffer from invasive research protocols that include surgeries, implants, biopsies, and intentional exposures to and inoculation with deadly diseases. *See, e.g.,* Taub v. State, 296 Md. 439 (Md. 1983) (holding that researcher did not violate state cruelty code by conducting research with the goal of retraining humans affected by stroke, using a protocol that surgically ablated all sensation in monkeys' limbs); HSUS, *Undercover Investigation Reveals Primate Injuries, Death at Texas Biomed* (Sept. 22, 2014), http://blog.humanesociety.org/wayne/2014/09/texas-biomed-investigation.html. Notably, in 2015 Harvard shut down the New England National Primate Research Center after years of reports surfacing of monkeys dying because of improper care. *See* Carolyn Johnson, *Harvard's Primate Lab's End Puzzles Researchers,* Boston Globe, May 29, 2015, https://www.bostonglobe.com/metro/2015/05/28/closing-harvard-primate-center-leaves-legacy-discovery-controversy/Ax8wW1NfiIeqaFMbPDBYcI/story.html.

are six to eight months old.[76] It is well-established that this deprivation of the maternal relationship causes "enhanced fear and anxiety, increased anhedonia [mood disorders], impaired cognition, abnormal brain neurochemistry and neurobiology, and alterations in baseline activity as well as stress reactivity of the hypothalamic-pituitary-adrenal (HPA) axis" in the brain.[77]

In addition to these long-term impacts on the infants' behavior, premature separation often leads to nutritional deficiencies and compromises the infants' immune systems. For these reasons, the International Primatological Society, the world's preeminent organization of primatologists working in the field and in laboratories, specifically objects to premature mother-infant separation and takes the position that "Hand-rearing should only be carried out if the health of the infant (or mother) is in jeopardy."[78]

Ironically, some of this information was discovered by laboratories that were studying the negative impacts of maternal deprivation in an effort learn more about human psychological trauma. While many of those studies were conducted in the 1950s through the 1970s, in 2014

---

76. Mark Prescott et al., *Laboratory macaques: When to wean?* 37 APPLIED ANIMAL BEHAV. SCI. 194–207 (2012); M. M. Kempes et al., *Social competence is reduced in socially deprived rhesus monkeys* (Macaca mulatta), 122(1) J. COMP. PSYCH., 62–67 (2008) (finding that macaques removed from their mothers at twelve months of age showed more fearful behaviors and more stereotypic behaviors than those raised in naturalistic groups and weaned naturally).

77. Karen Parker & Dario Maestripieri, *Identifying Key Features of Early Stressful Experiences that Produce Stress Vulnerability and Resilience in Primates*, 35 NEUROSCI. & BIOBEHAV. REV. 1466–83 (2011). *See also* Hani D. Freeman & Stephen R. Ross, *The Impact of Atypical Early Histories on Pet or Performer Chimpanzees*, 2 PEER J. e579 (2014); Amanda M. Dettmer et al., *Physiological and Behavioral Adaptation to Relocation Stress in Differentially Reared Rhesus Monkeys: Hair Cortisol as a Biomarker for Anxiety-Related Responses*, 37(2) PSYCHONEUROENDOCRINOL. 191–99 (2012); X. Feng et al., *Maternal separation produces lasting changes in cortisol and behavior in rhesus monkeys*, 108(34) PROC. NAT'L ACAD. OF SCI. UNITED STATES OF AMER. 14312–14317 (2011); Ina Rommeck et al., *The Effects of Four Nursery Rearing Strategies on Infant Behavioral Development in Rhesus Macaques* (Macaca mulatta), 48(4) J. AM. ASS'N LAB. ANIMAL SCI.: JAALAS. 395–401 (2009); G. A. Bradshaw et al., *Developmental Context Effects on Bicultural Post-Trauma Self Repair in Chimpanzees*, 45(5) DEVELOPMENTAL PSYCH. 1376–88 (2009); MOLLIE A. BLOOMSMITH ET AL., *Early Rearing Conditions and Captive Chimpanzee Behavior: Some Surprising Findings*, in NURSERY REARING OF NONHUMAN PRIMATES IN THE 21ST CENTURY 299 (Gene P. Sackett et al. eds., 2006).

78. International Primatological Society, International Guidelines for the Acquisition, Care and Breeding of Nonhuman Primates (2007) at 21, http://www.internationalprimatologicalsociety. org/docs/IPS_International_Guidelines_for_the_Acquisition_Care_and_Breeding_of_Nonhuman_Primates_Second_Edition_2007.pdf.

the University of Wisconsin at Madison began a new study that involved removing 25 infant monkeys from their mothers soon after birth to be raised in social isolation, exposing the monkeys to live snakes to simulate "early adversity," and then euthanizing the monkeys to conduct brain scans and post-mortem exams in hopes of learning information about whether removing newborn humans from their mothers increases the likelihood of anxiety in the child.[79] Similarly, an NIH-owned laboratory in Poolsville, Maryland, recently engaged in research where infant primates are kept in isolation and deliberately distressed, with some being used later to test drugs that are already used on humans suffering from mental illness.[80]

These studies are designed to inflict pain and extreme distress on captive primates, but federal law does not prohibit them, as the AWA cannot interfere with research and allows the researchers to exempt these individuals from the laboratory's enrichment plan. While legal, this research has sparked public outrage and reignited the debate about the ethics of using highly cognitive beings like primates in invasive and harmful protocols.

Zoo and Aquarium Exhibition

Moral Considerations

Since their early days as entertainment facilities exhibiting magnificent beasts from far-off lands, many U.S. zoos and aquariums are evolving (some far faster than others) into institutions striving to promote wildlife conservation and public education. However, debate rages on about whether keeping wild animals in captivity actually contributes to the conservation of wild populations of the species, whether breeding of

---

79. David Wahlberg, *Controversial UW-Madison Monkey Study Won't Remove Newborns from Mothers,* WISC. STATE J., March 13, 2015, http://host.madison.com/wsj/news/local/education/university/controversial-uw-madison-monkey-study-won-t-remove-newborns-from/article_e8a288f4-5d1a-5ab2-ab50-64b24920b2e3.html.

80. PETA, *Psychological Torture Experiments at NIH Must Stop,* http://investigations.peta.org/nih-baby-monkey-experiments/. *But see* David Grimm, *NIH to End Controversial Monkey Experiments at Poolesville Lab,* SCI., Dec. 11, 2015, http://www.sciencemag.org/news/2015/12/nih-end-controversial-monkey-experiments-poolesville-lab.

captive animals is conducted for profit or preservation, and whether the visiting public truly learns meaningful information about conservation efforts, animal behavior, or ecology. While the capture of wild animals solely for the purpose of public display is waning, it is certainly not obsolete, and this raises important conservation and animal welfare concerns. Additionally, when animals are reduced to captivity, it is virtually impossible for zoos and aquariums to mimic the natural habitat of wildlife, especially for those species that require a large home range size, complex social groups, or diets that normally involve hunting or foraging. Zoos and aquariums, particularly those that have not voluntarily accepted rigorous oversight from a private accreditation body, also can raise significant public safety concerns, both for the visiting public and workers who are tasked with interacting with captive wildlife. In a dramatic and tragic reminder of the animal welfare and public safety concerns inherent in keeping wildlife in captivity, in May of 2016 the Cincinnati Zoo's Dangerous Animal Response Team shot and killed a critically endangered gorilla—a seventeen-year-old silverback named Harambe—when a three-year-old boy fell into his exhibit.[81] Certainly not all zoos and aquariums are created equal (and even different departments within one institution can differ dramatically), with significant distinctions in conservation, education, welfare, and safety standards depending on the level of capacity and resources each facility maintains.

These ethical issues are acutely raised by the keeping of large marine mammals, for example beluga and orca whales, in captivity given their size, intelligence, complex social relationships, and vast natural habitats.[82] The primary rationales for keeping these marine mammals in

---

81. Melissa Chan, *A Gorilla at the Cincinnati Zoo Was Shot Dead after a Boy Fell into the Exhibit*, TIME, May 29, 2016, Update June 2, 2016 11:40 AM ET, http://time.com/4351482/gorilla-cincinnati-zoo-shot-boy/?iid=sr-link4.

82. For example, orcas are large, intelligent, social mammals who, in the wild, live in close-knit family pods, forage and dive for food, and swim up to 100 kilometers per day. *See* Thomas I. White, *Review of Whales and Dolphins: Cognition, Culture, Conservation and Human Perceptions*, 3 J. ANIMAL ETHICS 222–24 (2013); L. E. Rendell & H. Whitehead, *Culture in Whales and Dolphins*, 24 BEHAV. & BRAIN SCI. 309–24 (2001). But in captivity, they are housed in a tank that is "less than one ten-thousandth of 1% of the space available to them in their natural environment" with no natural stimulation, separated from their family, and unable to form social bonds. Lauren Tierney, *Detailed Discussion of Law Concerning Orcas in Captivity*, Animal Legal and Historical Center (2010), https://www.animallaw.info/article/detailed-discussion-laws-concerning-orcas-captivity.

zoos, amusement parks, or aquariums for public display are to promote public education, engage in conservation efforts, and/or to conduct scientific research.[83] However, experts have raised questions about whether the minimum standards required of a conservation education program are met by marine mammal displays, including whether the information disseminated about the animals is accurate and whether there is evidence, based on valid outcome measures, that visitors receive an educational benefit.[84] Furthermore, evidence shows that captive orcas do not live as long as wild orcas,[85] that captive orcas suffer from poor dental health from chewing on concrete walls and metal gates out of aggression or boredom (which, in turn, subjects them to medical conditions such as heart disease and pneumonia),[86] and that captive orcas show more aggression toward each other and humans compared to wild orcas.[87] Moreover, several abnormal behaviors, such as swimming in circles, self-mutilation, vomiting, and unresponsiveness, are well documented among captive

---

83. Alliance of Marine Mammal Parks and Aquariums, *About the Alliance*, http://www.AMMPA. org/about.html (last visited Aug. 16, 2015). Accreditation standards require that Alliance members "offer multiple levels of learning opportunities . . . based on the best current scientific knowledge . . . [and] a written education plan that clearly delineates the facility's education goals, mission statement, and an evaluation strategy." Alliance of Marine Mammal Parks and Aquariums, *Standards and Guidelines* at 4–5, http://www.AMMPA.org/_docs/S_GSummary2010_2.pdf (last visited Aug. 16, 2015) [hereinafter *Alliance Standards*].

84. *See, e.g.,* Statement of Lori Marino, PhD, to The House Committee on Natural Resources Subcommittee on Insular Affairs, Oceans and Wildlife regarding educational aspects of public display of marine mammals (Apr. 27, 2010), http://www.kimmela.org/wp-content/uploads/2012/10/Testimony-Congress-Marino-04272010.pdf. Lori Marino, PhD, was a senior lecturer in neuroscience and behavioral biology at Emory University, a faculty member in the Emory Center for Ethics, an adjunct faculty member in the Department of Psychology at Emory University, and a former research associate at The Smithsonian Institution National Museum of Natural History. *See also* L. Marino, S. Lilienfeld, R. Malamud, N. Nobis & R. Broglio, *Do Zoos and Aquariums Promote Attitude Change in Visitors? A Critical Evaluation of the American Zoo and Aquarium Study,* 18 SOCIETY AND ANIMALS, 126–38 (2010).

85. *See, e.g.,* R. J. Small & D.O. DeMaster, *Survival of Five Species of Captive Marine Mammals,* 11 MARINE MAMMAL SCI. 209–226 (1995).

86. *Compare* X. Li et al., *Systemic Diseases Caused by Oral Infection,* 13 CLINICAL MICROBIOL. REVS. 547–58 (2000), *with* J. K. B. Ford et al., *Shark Predation and Tooth Wear in a Population of Northeastern Pacific Killer Whales,* 11 AQUATIC BIOL. 213–24 (2011).

87. Statement of Lori Marino, PhD, *supra* note 84, at 8.In fact, Tilikum, the largest orca to live in captivity, died from bacterial pneumonia at the age of 36 years in January 2017. Assoc. Press, *Tilikum, Orca that Killed SeaWorld Trainer, Died From Bacterial Pneumomia*, NBC News (Feb. 4, 2017), http://www.nbcnews.com/news/us-news/tilikum-orca-killed-seaworld-trainer -died-bacterial-pneumonia-n716911.

orcas, suggesting abnormal psychological and social development in these individuals.[88]

This section summarizes the primary laws that affect the exhibition of animals by zoos and aquariums, including the AWA (which establishes minimum animal care standards and requires an exhibitor's license to be renewed annually); the ESA (which prohibits the harm or harassment of species listed as endangered); the MMPA (which provides limitations for public display permits); and state laws regarding the possession, sale, and breeding of captive wildlife. In addition to these laws, private accreditation bodies establish qualifications for animal care and facility management that govern zoos and aquariums that are their members. Case studies applying these laws to real disputes include the Georgia Aquarium's application to import eighteen wild-caught beluga whales from Russia to the United States; the plight of Lolita, an endangered orca whale who has lived in a small pool at the Miami Seaquarium for over forty-five years; and a comparison of breeding programs for endangered big cats at different exhibition facilities.

Laws and Guidelines Regulating Zoos and Aquariums

Animal Welfare Act

Congress originally enacted the AWA to protect animals in laboratories, but in 1970 the AWA was amended "to insure that animals intended . . . for exhibition purposes . . . are provided humane care and treatment."[89] The term "exhibitor" is defined to include "any person (public or private) exhibiting any animals, which were purchased in commerce or the intended distribution of which affects commerce, or will affect commerce,

---

88. *See* R. H. DEFRAN & K. PRYOR, *The Behavior and Training of Cetaceans in Captivity,* in CETACEAN BEHAVIOR: MECHANISMS AND FUNCTIONS 319–64 (L. Herman, ed., 1980); J. C. SWEENEY, *Marine Mammal Behavioral Diagnostics,* in CRC HANDBOOK OF MARINE MAMMAL MEDICINE: HEALTH, DISEASE, AND REHABILITATION 53–72 (L. A. Dierauf, ed., 1990); J. C. Sweeney, *Specific Pathologic Behavior in Aquatic Mammals: Self-inflicted Trauma,* 13(1) SOUNDINGS: NEWSLETTER OF THE INT'L. MARINE ANIMAL TRAINERS ASSOC. 7 (1988).
89. 7 U.S.C. § 2131(1); Pub. L. No. 91-579.

to the public for compensation."[90] Thus, the AWA is broadly applicable to animals in zoos and aquariums, but only provides minimal coverage, as the drafters clearly expected that state laws would provide additional protections for captive wildlife.[91]

The AWA outlines the activities for which the USDA must adopt regulations; in particular, Congress has directed that the USDA establish standards "to govern the humane handling . . . of animals by . . . exhibitors" and that such standards must include minimum requirements "for handling, housing, feeding, water, sanitation, ventilation, shelter from extremes of weather and temperatures, adequate veterinary care, and separation by species where the Secretary finds necessary for humane handling, care, or treatment of animals . . ."[92] The Secretary also can promulgate any other regulations deemed necessary to promote animal welfare.[93] Pursuant to this authority, the USDA's Animal and Plant Health Inspection Service (APHIS) has adopted regulations specific to nonhuman primates and marine mammals; however, other exotic wildlife (from big cats to bears to elephants to giraffes) are subject to generic requirements for humane treatment.[94]

The AWA requires all exhibitors, including zoos and aquariums (whether operated for profit or not), to obtain a license (renewed annually) from the Secretary of Agriculture, and provides that "no such license shall be issued until the dealer or exhibitor shall have demonstrated that his facilities comply with the standards promulgated by the Secretary."[95] Prior to licensing in the first instance, APHIS conducts an inspection of the facility. Periodic inspections continue once a facility is licensed.

---

90. 7 U.S.C. § 2132(h). *See also* 907 Whitehead St., Inc. v. Sec'y of U.S. Dep't of Agric., 701 F.3d 1345, 1350 (11th Cir. 2012) (upholding the USDA's decision to require the Ernest Hemingway Home and Museum to obtain an exhibitor license, because the facility displays famous polydactyl cats and charges an admission fee).
91. *See* 7 U.S.C. § 2145(b) (authorizing the Secretary of Agriculture to cooperate with state and local officials to carry out the purpose of state laws protecting animals).
92. 7 U.S.C. § 2143(a)(1), (2).
93. 7 U.S.C. § 2151.
94. 9 C.F.R. Part 3.
95. 7 U.S.C. § 2133; 9 C.F.R. § 2.1(a)(1).

AWA violations identified by APHIS inspectors are included in inspection reports.[96]

An exhibitor ("Class C") license is valid for one year, but the renewal process is far less stringent than the initial licensing process. Renewal applicants are required to certify "to the best of the applicant's knowledge and belief, he or she is in compliance with the regulations and standards and agrees to continue to comply with the regulations and standards."[97] However, APHIS routinely renews licenses for facilities with a long history of noncompliance with the AWA. Animal protection organizations have filed multiple lawsuits challenging the issuance of license renewals to substandard facilities, but a recent opinion from the U.S. Court of Appeals for the Eleventh Circuit affirmed APHIS' position that AWA noncompliance is irrelevant to the agency's decision of whether to renew a license.

In the Eleventh Circuit case, the plaintiffs asserted that it was arbitrary and capricious for the agency to renew the exhibitor license for the Miami Seaquarium despite copious evidence that the aquarium keeps an orca whale named Lolita in social isolation in a tank that fails to comply with the minimum requirements under the AWA (both because it is too small and because it does not contain adequate shade from the sun; notably, the aquarium applied a sunblock protectant to Lolita's skin).[98] The court found that the AWA is silent regarding the procedure for license renewal and that "while the USDA deserves no plaudits for its regulatory draftsmanship," the agency is entitled to deference on its position that license renewal is "purely administrative" and "compliance with AWA standards is not a condition precedent for renewal."[99] The court held that if the AWA

> mandated the revocation of a license whenever USDA thinks the exhibitor has failed to demonstrate compliance on an anniversary date, the due process protections afforded to licensees in § 2149 would be mere surplusage. . . . To revoke a license, USDA would

---

96. *See* Animal Care Information System Search Tool, https://acis.aphis.edc.usda.gov/ords/f?p=116:1:0. From 2011 to 2017, these inspection reports were routinely posted online in a public database, but in February 2017 the Trump Administration removed public access to the database.
97. 9 C.F.R. §§ 2.2(b), 2.3(b).
98. *See* ALDF v. U.S. Department of Agriculture, 789 F.3d 1206 (11th Cir. 2015); 9 C.F.R. Part 3, Subpart E (providing standards specific to marine mammals).
99. *Id.* at 1223-24.

not need to bring an enforcement proceeding against a licensee; the agency could patiently bide its time until the license anniversary rolled around, then immediately revoke the license for failure to demonstrate compliance.[100]

Other cases raising the same issues have been filed in other circuits and it remains to be seen whether these courts will follow the Eleventh Circuit's line of reasoning.[101]

As noted previously, APHIS inspections may lead to citations for AWA violations. In addition to such citations, the agency also issues official warnings and enters into stipulations (where exhibitors pay a fine to settle the claim of noncompliance). The agency also conducts investigations through its Investigative and Enforcement Services (IES) branch, which may lead to the filing of an enforcement complaint, which triggers a hearing before an administrative law judge to determine whether the exhibitor's license should be temporarily suspended or permanently revoked. However, there is a significant backlog with such enforcement actions and it usually takes years from the date of the infractions until a remedy is obtained. For example, since 2010 The Humane Society of the United States has filed multiple complaints with APHIS following undercover investigations at substandard zoos (including Collins Zoo in Mississippi, the Greater Wynnewood Exotic Animal Park in Oklahoma, Natural Bridge Zoo in Virginia, and Tiger Safari in Oklahoma), but it takes years for APHIS to revoke a license to exhibit animals.[102] The investigation into the GreaterWynnewood Exotic Animal Park continued for several years and, at the time this book was published, there was no resolution in sight.

---

100. *Id.* at 1217.

101. *See, e.g.,* ALDF v. Vilsack, 169 F. Supp.3d 6, 2016 WL 1048761 (D.D.C. 2016) (district court adopting the Eleventh Circuit's rationale, on appeal to the D.C. Circuit); PETA v. USDA, Case No. 5:15-cv-429 (E.D.N.C. 2016) (district court upholding USDA's policy and practice of relicensing noncompliant facilities, on appeal at the Fourth Circuit). *See also* Ray v. Vilsack, 2014 WL 3721357 (E.D.N.C. 2014) (dismissing a challenge to USDA's relicensing of Jambbas Ranch Tours, Inc. as moot after USDA took enforcement action against the facility); PETA v. USDA, Case No. 1:15-cv-00920 (D. Colo. 2015) (district court upholding relicensing on factual grounds).

102. *See In re:* Gus White, a/k/a Gustave L. White, III, d/b/a Collins Exotic Animal Orphanage, AWA Docket No. 12-0277 (May 13, 2014) (revoking the exhibitor license for Collins Zoo five years after undercover investigation began).

The Endangered Species Act

The ESA was enacted in 1973. Congress found that "species of fish, wild-life, and plants [threatened with extinction] are of esthetic, ecological, edu-cational, historical, recreational, and scientific value to the Nation and its people"[103] and must be protected through conservation efforts.[104] A spe-cies is listed as "endangered" when it is presently in danger of extinction throughout all or a significant portion of its range and "threatened" if it is likely to become endangered in the foreseeable future.[105] The ESA regulates the export, import, sale or purchase in interstate commerce, and "take" (i.e., harass, harm, pursue, hunt, shoot, wound, kill, trap, capture, or collect, or to attempt to engage in any such conduct) of listed animals.[106] Section 9 of the ESA prohibits the take of an endangered species without a permit.[107] Permits may be issued for the take of an endangered species for "scientific purposes or to enhance the propagation or survival of the affected species, including, but not limited to, acts necessary for the estab-lishment and maintenance of experimental populations."[108] A take includes "harassment," defined as "an intentional or negligent act or omission which creates the likelihood of injury to wildlife by annoying it to such an extent as to significantly disrupt normal behavioral patterns, which include, but are not limited to, breeding, feeding, or sheltering."[109] However, for animals in captivity, the regulations exempt from harassment generally accepted practices including: "(1) animal husbandry practices that meet or exceed the minimum standards for facilities and care under the Animal Welfare Act, (2) breeding procedures, or (3) provisions of veterinary care."[110] The ESA does not prohibit the mere possession or display of endangered spe-cies in zoos and aquariums, but, as discussed later, certain mistreatment of captive animals may constitute harassment.

---

103. 16 U.S.C. § 1531(a)(3).
104. *Id.* § 1531(b).
105. *Id.* § 1532(6), (2).
106. *Id.* § 1538.
107. *Id.* § 1538(a)(1)(B). This does not apply extraterritorially.
108. *Id.* § 1539 (a)(1)(A).
109. 50 C.F.R. § 17.3.
110. *Id.*

The Marine Mammal Protection Act

The MMPA,[111] enacted in 1972, acknowledged that

> man's impact upon marine mammals has ranged from . . . malign
> neglect to virtual genocide. These animals, including whales, por-
> poises, seals, sea otters, polar bears, manatees, and others, have
> only rarely benefitted [sic] from our interest; they have been shot,
> blown up, clubbed to death, run down by boats, poisoned, and
> exposed to a multitude of indignities, all in the interests of profit
> or recreation, with little or no consideration of the potential
> impact of these activities on the animal populations involved.[112]

The MMPA prohibits the "take" of a marine mammal without a permit.[113] Permits may issue for "scientific research, public display, or enhancing the survival or recovery of a marine mammal species of stock."[114] No
permit may issue to import a marine mammal for public display if the
marine mammal was "(1) pregnant at the time of taking; (2) nursing at
the time of taking, or less than eight months old, whichever occurs later;
(3) taken from a species or population stock which the Secretary has, by
regulation, designated as depleted; or (4) taken in a manner deemed inhumane by the Secretary."[115] Moreover, the applicant must be licensed under
the AWA to exhibit the animal, offer public educational and conservation
programs, and be open to the public on a regular basis.[116] The National
Marine Fisheries Service (NMFS), under the National Oceanic and Atmospheric Administration (NOAA), enforces the MMPA for cetaceans and

---

111. Although the primary focus of the MMPA is to protect marine mammals in the wild, it
regulates the take of marine mammals from the wild to be held in captivity and thus is important
to this discussion of captive wild animals.

112. H.R. Rep. 92-707 at 4144 (1972).

113. 16 U.S.C. § 1362. Similarly to the ESA, under the MMPA, "take" is defined as to "harass,
hunt, capture, or kill, or attempt to harass, hunt, capture, or kill."

114. *Id.* § 1371(a)(1); 1374(c).

115. *Id.* §1372 (b). These limitations apply only to public display. Moreover, the Secretary may
allow a take for public display when factors (1) or (2) are present, if it can be established that the
take is necessary for the protection or welfare of the animal.

116. *Id.* § 1374(c).

pinnipeds, while the Secretary of the Interior and the Fish and Wildlife Service enforce the MMPA for all other marine mammals.[117]

While the primary focus of the MMPA is to conserve marine mammals in the wild, the limitations on obtaining a permit to import animals for public display contain three provisions that are designed to protect the welfare of individual animals—the sections prohibiting the take of pregnant or nursing animals, and requiring that the take be "humane." NMFS, in interpreting the nursing provision, had drawn a distinction between obligatory and convenience nursing. The federal Court of Appeals for the D.C. Circuit, reviewing the legislative history of the provision, stated that the "nursing seems to have been used as a measure of infancy, of vulnerability and helplessness" and thus there was no justification to distinguish between obligatory and convenience nursing as in either case the young calf is vulnerable and reliant on his or her mother. [118] This interpretation provides for greater protection for young calves such that they are not taken while they are dependent on their mothers.

Regarding the nature of the take, the MMPA defines "[h]umane in the context of taking a marine mammal [as] that method of taking which involves the least possible degree of pain and suffering practicable to the mammal involved."[119] The House Report stated that the term "humane"

> is not a simple concept and involves factors such as minimizing trauma to groups of highly intelligent, social animals such as whales and porpoises where the taking of any member may be distressing to the group. In many cases, *where an animal may not be taken humanely* the bill will prevent that animal from being taken at all."[120]

---

117. NMFS has stated that its authority ends once the marine mammal is taken and in captivity. *See* Michael P. Payne, Report on the Application for a Public Display Permit (File No. 17324): Recommendation for Denial, Memorandum to Donna S. Weiting, Director, Office of Protected Resources, NMFS, at 7 (Aug. 5, 2013), http://www.nmfs.noaa.gov/pr/permits/sci_res_pdfs/17324_denial_letter_final.pdf [hereinafter Denial Report].
118. AWI v. Kreps, 561 F.2d 1002, 1012 (D.C. Cir. 1977).
119. 16 U.S.C. § 1362(4).
120. H.R. Rep. 92-707 at *4155 (Dec 4, 1971) (emphasis added).

The language italicized above suggests that "humane" would be defined by reference to objective, scientific criteria based on the psychological and physical impact of the take on the individual animal. Such a definition was not codified in the statute. Instead, "humane" is defined in the statute by reference to the available technology to "take" the animal. If the technique used will involve the least degree of pain and suffering practicable, i.e., as compared to other available techniques, the take is "humane," regardless of the actual pain and suffering involved. Under such a definition it is highly unlikely that any take will ever be prohibited as "inhumane."

State Laws

While the AWA sets the minimum standards for the care of exhibited animals nationwide, it expressly allows for states to provide greater protection for exhibited animals under state law.[121] Every state has a criminal anti-cruelty statute that is designed to protect certain animals from abuse and neglect.[122] The majority of states either expressly or impliedly include exhibited animals. For example, Pennsylvania expressly protects zoo animals by making the willful and malicious killing, maiming, disfiguring, or poisoning of a zoo animal in captivity a third-degree felony.[123] Louisiana prohibits the sport killing of any zoo or circus animal, and proscribes the sale by zoos and circuses of their animals to canned hunting ranches.[124] On the other hand, a few states expressly exempt otherwise unlawful conduct involving exhibited animals, if it meets the federal standards under the AWA.[125] A very few, such as Michigan, exempt "the operation of a zoological park or aquarium" from coverage under the anti-cruelty

---

121. See 7 U.S.C. § 2145(b).

122. State anti-cruelty statutes are described in greater detail *infra* section on exotic pet ownership.

123. Penn. Code § 5511(a)(2).

124. La. Rev. Stat. § 14:102.20; *see infra* section on captive hunting ranches.

125. See, e.g., Ga. Code § 16-12-4(e) ("The provisions of this Code section shall not be construed as prohibiting conduct which is otherwise permitted under the laws of this state or of the United States, including, but not limited to, . . . , zoological, exhibition . . . ."); Idaho Code § 25-3514 ("No part of this chapter shall be construed as interfering with or allowing interference with: . . . (9) Any other exhibitions, competitions, activities, practices or procedures normally or commonly considered acceptable.")

laws, independent of whether it meets AWA standards.[126] As a practical matter, because many state anti-cruelty laws prohibit "unnecessary" harming of animals (whether intentional, malicious, or by omission), most exhibition of animals, especially that done in compliance with the AWA, may not violate state cruelty statutes.

In recent years there has been significant movement to eliminate the use of certain captive wild animals for display and/or entertainment. These changes have occurred both through state government action and through corporate reform—for example, in March 2016, SeaWorld announced that it would immediately discontinue breeding of orcas and end its "theatrical performances" with the whales, shifting focus to provide safe haven for stranded wild marine mammals.[127] The decision followed immense public pressure as well as legal action from the California Coastal Commission, which in 2015 conditioned its approval of an expansion of SeaWorld's San Diego facility on a requirement to discontinue breeding orcas. SeaWorld initially filed a lawsuit challenging that decision, but decided instead to adopt such a policy for all of its parks in the United States and abroad. In 2016 California became the first state to pass a law prohibiting breeding of orca whales or using orcas in theatrical performances.[128]

Private Accreditation Entities

In addition to the legal requirements under state and federal law for zoos and aquariums, there are private industry accreditation organizations that provide additional standards for the treatment of captive wildlife. These voluntary standards pertain to animal welfare (such as enclosure size and social grouping), conservation (including research and propaga-

---

126. MICH. CODE § 750.50 (11)(d).

127. See SeaWorld Cares, https://seaworldcares.com/Future?utm_source=Google&utm_medium=Search_Ad&utm_term=Future&utm_content=Future&utm_campaign=Search_US&gclid=CjwKEAjw8bO3BRDp0bP_vL-7_lASJACL_d6wilkrWtN3k-RxvmaX2Ub2LjSjvA6U_50zaollS-RHBBoCztHw_wcB. This dramatic change in policy also includes promises to participate in advocacy campaigns to promote the conservation of wild marine mammals and to ensure that food acquired for the parks' animals and visitors is humanely and sustainably raised.

128. Calif. S.B. 839 § 8.

tion), public safety (such as emergency protocols and contingency planning), and institutional organization (to professionalize the field and ensure financial stability).

For example, the Association of Zoos and Aquariums (AZA) is the only domestic organization that manages endangered species through Species Survival Plans (SSP), which benefit from the expertise of scientists aiming to manage captive populations to maintain genetic integrity as a hedge against extinction.[129] The AZA's Population Management Center (PMC), which consists of a team of population biologists, is responsible for conducting the genetic and demographic analyses needed to develop population management recommendations.[130] The PMC promotes structured decision making in conservation planning to avoid inbreeding of captive populations. Inbreeding leads to reduced longevity, inanition, metabolic diseases, morphological deformities, abnormal birth weights and growth, organ malfunctions, impaired reproductive tracts, immune diseases, and increased susceptibility to stress.[131]

The AZA's SSP programs work in conjunction with the International Union for Conservation of Nature's Conservation Breeding Specialist Group (IUCN CBSG), which promotes "integrated species conservation planning through the joint development of management strategies and conservation actions by all responsible parties to produce one comprehensive conservation plan for the species."[132] Thus, experts agree that for

---

129. See AZA, *Species Survival Plan Programs*, http://www.aza.org/species-survival-plan-program ("There are currently more than 500 SSP Programs, each managed by their corresponding Taxon Advisory Groups (TAGs), within AZA. Each is responsible for developing a comprehensive population Studbook and a Breeding and Transfer Plan which identifies population management goals and recommendations to ensure the sustainability of a healthy, genetically diverse, and demographically varied AZA population").

130. See AZA Population Management Center, https://www.aza.org/population-management-center/; Lincoln Park Zoo Population Management Center, http://www.lpzoo.org/conservation-science/science-centers/population-management-center.

131. See AZA PMC, *Population Management Guidelines*, https://www.aza.org/uploadedFiles/Animal_Care_and_Management/Animal_Management/Population_Management_Centers/PopulationManagementGuidelines.pdf (outlining the importance of, and scientific mechanisms for, demographic and genetic management); see also JONATHAN D. BALLOU ET AL., *Demographic and Genetic Management of Captive Populations,* in WILD MAMMALS IN CAPTIVITY: PRINCIPLES AND TECHNIQUES FOR ZOO MANAGEMENT 219–252 (Devra G. Kleiman et al. eds., 2010).

132. Onnie Byers et al., *The One Plan Approach: The Philosophy and Implementation of CBSG's Approach to Integrated Species Conservation Planning*, 14 WORLD ASSOC. ZOOS & AQUARIUMS MAG. 2-5 (2013), http://www.cbsg.org/sites/cbsg.org/files/WAZA_Magazine_2013.pdf.

captive propagation to serve a conservation purpose, it is essential that breeding be carefully managed to maintain and enhance genetic diversity and integrity. In contrast, the Zoological Association of America (ZAA) also accredits zoos and provides some standards regarding enclosures and husbandry, but has not organized breeding amongst its member facilities through a formalized scientific process.[133] Similarly, unaccredited facilities, roadside zoos, and other private menageries do not participate in any such programs, and, thus, they have a greatly reduced chance of promoting conservation through captive breeding.

The Alliance of Marine Mammal Parks and Aquariums (Alliance) is an international association representing aquariums, zoos, and other facilities housing marine mammals.[134] The Alliance's accreditation standards establish guidelines for acquisition, disposition, housing, care, and training of marine mammals; public educational programming; scientific research; and conservation.[135] Although the Alliance prioritizes acquisition of animals through managed breeding programs at other parks,[136] it supports the "responsible take" of wild marine mammals to support genetically diverse breeding programs and the propagation of marine mammals in captivity. Unlike the AZA, the Alliance provides very little information publicly on their website concerning specific accreditation standards or enforcement.[137]

While domestic accrediting bodies set standards for permanent facilities, the International Air Transport Association (IATA) regulations, adopted in the Convention on International Trade in Endangered Species (CITES) resolution on the transport of live specimens,[138] governs the air transport of live animals and plants[139] and establishes guidelines for the

133. *See* ZAA, *Animal Care & Enclosure Standards and Related Policies* (2016), http://www.zaa .org/images/pages/misc/ZAA_Accreditation_Standards.pdf.
134. *About the Alliance, supra* note 83.
135. *Alliance Standards, supra* note 83.
136. *Id.* at 2.
137. Alliance of Marine Mammal Parks & Aquariums, *Our Members*, http://www.ammpa.org/ ourmembers.html.
138. CITES, Resolution Conf. 10.21 (Rev. CoP16), https://www.cites.org/eng/res/10/10-21R16 .php.
139. IATA, *Live Animals Regulations* (LAR), http://www.iata.org/publications/pages/live-animals .aspx.

non-air transport of animals and plants. In addition, the AWA[140] provides standards for the transport of covered animals.

Case Studies

This section has presented a number of federal and state laws as well as private guidelines designed to provide protection for wild animals put on public display in zoos, aquariums, and public entertainment facilities. The MMPA, and the ESA if the species is endangered, define when and under what circumstances a marine mammal may be taken from the wild and held in captivity for research or public display. CITES and the AWA provide requirements for transport of marine mammals and the AWA regulations provide minimal standards governing the animals' housing, care, and treatment while in captivity.[141] Private accreditation standards may apply and be enforced by private associations such as the AZA and the Alliance for their members. In very rare cases, state anti-cruelty laws may provide protection against the most extreme abuse and neglect. The effectiveness of these rules and standards next will be examined through the use of three case studies.

Wild-Caught Russian Beluga Whales and the Georgia Aquarium

Although maintaining cetaceans in captivity has been controversial for many years, the 2010 killing of an orca trainer by Tilikum, the largest orca ever to live in captivity, and the subsequent release of the movie *Blackfish*, detailing the tragic story, intensified the public debate. On a separate track, in June 2012, the Georgia Aquarium in Atlanta, Georgia, filed an application for a permit to import eighteen wild-caught beluga whales from

---

140. *See* Terrestrial Animal Health Standards Commission, September 2010 Report, Ch. 7.3, Transport of Animals By Land, http://www.aphis.usda.gov/import_export/animals/oie/downloads/tahc_sep10/tahc_transport_animals_land_79_sep10.pdf; Terrestrial Animal Health Standards Commission, September 2009 Report, Ch. 7.4, Transport of Animals by Air, http://www.aphis.usda.gov/import_export/animals/oie/downloads/tahc_sep09/tahc_transport_air_78_sep09.pdf.
141. NMFS has indicated that the welfare of marine mammals in captivity is beyond their jurisdiction. *See* Denial Report, *supra* note 117, at 17.

Russia to the U.S. for public display pursuant to the MMPA.[142] The eighteen beluga whales were captured from the Sakhalin-Amur River region of the Russia Sea of Okhotsk by a company that then transported them over 4,000 miles. They were captured between 2006 and 2011, and they remained in captivity as of June 2016[143] after the controversy surrounding their import to the United States was resolved, with the federal government and the federal court rejecting the Aquarium's efforts.[144]

Beluga whales have been called the canaries of the sea because of their extensive sound repertoire composed of a variety of whistles and pulsed sounds.[145] They range from thirteen to twenty feet in length and weigh from 2,000 to 3,000 pounds.[146] Belugas are highly social creatures who live in pods that may be as large as several dozen. The mother exhibits an intense maternal investment in each calf, giving birth to only one at a time. The calf remains partially reliant on his or her mother for milk until the age of two years.[147] The mother-calf bond is a central feature of beluga social relations, with calves remaining with their mothers for at least four or five years. The average life span of a beluga whale is from thirty-five to fifty years.[148] Although the IUCN[149] lists them as "near threatened," three populations of belugas are critically endangered due to a variety of human activities.

The Georgia Aquarium permit request stated the import of the belugas would "enhance the North American beluga breeding cooperative

---

142. Georgia Aquarium, Inc., Application for Permit to Import Certain Marine Mammals for Public Display Under the Marine Mammal Protection Act (2012), http://www.nmfs.noaa.gov/pr/permits/sci_res_pdfs/17324_final_application.pdf [hereinafter Georgia Aquarium Application].

143. Mark Davis & Bo Emerson, *Georgia Aquarium: No More Whales, Dolphins Taken from Wild*, ATL. JOURNAL-CONSTITUTION, Jun. 22, 2016, at http://www.myajc.com/news/news/georgia-aquarium-no-more-whales-dolphins-taken-fro/nrk2C/ (the Aquarium, as of June 2016, was working to find homes for the beluga whales somewhere in the world).

144. The captive fate of these eighteen belugas is permanent—the only question this case resolved was whether they would live in America under the import permit at issue.

145. Alliance of Marine Mammal Parks and Aquariums, *Beluga Fact Sheet*, http://www.ammpa.org/doc_beluga_factsheet.html.

146. NAT'L GEO., *Beluga Whale*, http://animals.nationalgeographic.com/animals/mammals/beluga-whale/.

147. *See* NOAA Fisheries, *Beluga Whale*, http://www.fisheries.noaa.gov/pr/species/mammals/whales/beluga-whale.html.

148. *Id.*

149. The IUCN Red List of Threatened Species, *Delphinapterus leucas*, http://www.iucnredlist.org/details/6335/0.

by increasing the population base of captive belugas to a self-sustaining level and to promote conservation and education."[150] The plan was to transport the eighteen belugas on simultaneous flights of approximately thirty hours in duration from Russia, through Liege, Belgium, to Atlanta, Georgia. Three of the whales would remain in Georgia and the remaining individuals would be transferred to partner facilities throughout the United States, including SeaWorld[151] in Miami and in San Diego. In August 2013, after conducting extensive analysis and receiving over 9,000 public comments, largely against the permit, recounting concerns over the capture, transport, and holding of the belugas in captivity for public display, NMFS denied the permit.[152] NMFS found that the removal and import of the whales would likely have a significant adverse effect on the wild beluga population and contribute to the demand to capture wild belugas for public display worldwide, and thus was contrary to the purpose of the MMPA.[153] Furthermore, NMFS determined that five of the belugas were likely nursing at the time of capture in violation of the MMPA.[154] The Georgia Aquarium filed suit challenging the denial of the permit as arbitrary and capricious.[155] On September 28, 2015, Judge Amy Totenberg of the U.S District Court for the Northern District of Georgia granted summary judgment to NMFS and the intervenors[156] and dismissed Georgia Aquarium's case.[157] The Georgia Aquarium did not appeal the ruling and in June 2016 announced that it would no longer capture wild whales or dolphins for public display.[158]

---

150. Georgia Aquarium Application, *supra* note 142, at 1.

151. In September 2015 Sea World announced it would not participate in the import of the beluga whales from Russia. Sandra Pedicine, *SeaWorld Says It Won't Take Belugas Whales Captured in Russia*, ORLANDO SENTINEL, Sept. 3, 2015, http://www.orlandosentinel.com/business/os-seaworld-georgia-aquarium-belugas-20150903-story.html.

152. Letter from Donna Weiting to Bill Hurley, Georgia Aquarium (Aug. 5, 2013), http://www.nmfs.noaa.gov/pr/permits/sci_res_pdfs/17324_denial_letter_final.pdf [hereinafter Denial Letter].

153. *Id.* at 1-2.

154. *Id.* at 2.

155. Georgia Aquarium v. Penny Pritzker et al., Civil Action No 1:13-cv-03241-AT (N.D. Ga., Sept. 30, 2013).

156. Intervenors included Animal Welfare Institute, Whale and Dolphin Conservation, Inc., Cetacean Society International, and Earth Island Institute.

157. Georgia Aquarium v. Penny Pritzker et al., 2015 WL 5730661 (N.D. Ga. 2015).

158. Davis & Emerson, *supra* note 143.

NMFS' primary basis for denying the permit was the negative effect that removal of the eighteen belugas would have on the wild population, an issue not directly relevant to this chapter on captive wildlife. However, also raised by this permit request were issues concerning the capture of nursing calves, the manner of capture, the transport of the belugas to the United States, and the care and housing of the belugas at the aquarium and parks where they would reside for public display. These issues are relevant to captive wildlife because they involve the treatment of animals during their capture, a necessary prerequisite to their captivity, as well as their treatment while in captivity. NMFS addressed each issue when it denied the application for an import permit.

First, NMFS denied the permit of five of the belugas, in part, because they found the five youngest whales, estimated at 1.5 years of age, were likely nursing at the time of capture, in violation of the MMPA.[159] NMFS interpreted the nursing provision consistent with the case of *Animal Welfare Institute v. Kreps*[160] to restrict importation to calves that are completely independent of their mothers. The court agreed and held that since the intent of the nursing provision was to protect vulnerable calves from cruel treatment, importation must be restricted to calves fully independent of their mothers.[161] Although no mother-calf pairs were captured, nursing beluga calves easily could have been separated from their mothers during the capture, especially since Georgia Aquarium admitted that calves of nursing age were approached and collected.[162] Because it is well established that belugas nurse for two years and remain with their mothers long after that time, NMFS' determination that the 1.5-year-old belugas were still nursing was not arbitrary and capricious.[163]

Second, the MMPA requires that a permit for public display be denied if the animal was "taken in a manner deemed inhumane by the Secretary."[164] Several commenters argued that the take of the animals was inhumane based on a prior 1999 video involving captures of belugas in

---

159. Denial Report, *supra* note 117, at 10–14.
160. 561 F.2d 1002 (D.C. Cir. 1977).
161. Georgia Aquarium, 2015 WL 5730661, at *44.
162. *Id.* at *45.
163. *Id.* at *46.
164. 16 U.S.C. § 1372 (b)(4).

the same location by the same entity.[165] NMFS noted in reviewing the application that although Georgia Aquarium claimed observers were sent to witness the captures to insure they were humane, no video was made available. Thus they relied solely on the description of the capture as provided in the application. Nevertheless, NMFS stated that the description was similar to that of recent captures in Alaska for a scientific research permit that had been approved.[166] Thus NMFS determined the manner of capture met the statutory requirements and was not inhumane.[167] It is notable that NMFS relied on a comparison to the Alaska capture for scientific research, a take that did not need to meet the humane capture requirement (that provision solely governs takes for public display).[168]

Third, federal regulations require that "the proposed activity is humane and does not present any unnecessary risks to the health and welfare of marine mammals."[169] Here, NMFS evaluated the options presented to transport the belugas from Russia to the United States. Although in every case the belugas would be transported over land and via air for lengthy periods, NMFS stated that the option that was slightly shorter, involved the least number of stops, and no container changes in Belgium met the statutory requirement.[170] It was "humane" because it involved the least degree of pain and suffering practicable to the animal, and any risk to the animals' health was "necessary" because the transport was necessary.

Finally, NMFS summarily dismissed the concerns raised by commenters that maintaining the belugas in captivity for public display is inhumane given "their size, large home ranges, and complex social structure."[171] NMFS stated that the MMPA provides for permits for public display but does not address the requirements for public display of the belugas, those issues are addressed by the AWA. Thus concerns regarding keeping the belugas in captivity are beyond NMFS' scope as it falls under the AWA, which is enforced by the USDA, not NOAA.[172]

---

165. Denial Report, *supra* note 117, at 12.
166. *Id.*
167. *Id.*
168. 16 U.S.C. § 1372(b).
169. Denial Report, *supra* note 117, at 7 (citing 50 CFR 216.34(a)(1)).
170. *Id.*
171. *Id.* at 17.
172. *Id.*

Ironically, Georgia Aquarium claimed the import would enhance the beluga breeding program by introducing new members of the species to the gene pool even though the breeding of belugas in captivity has largely failed. From 1972 through 2013, 56 beluga whales died in captivity, with nineteen dying shortly after birth.[173] During the litigation, a twenty-six-day-old beluga calf born at the Georgia Aquarium failed to thrive, became lethargic and died—the second baby born to the same parents to die in three years.[174]

The baby's heritage may shed some light on her demise. Her mother, Maris, was born at the New York Aquarium, from a wild-caught beluga who was captured as a youngster. Thus Maris did not have the opportunity to learn beluga culture and how to care for her own calf.[175]

> For Maris there is no autonomy, no continuity, and no opportunity to develop within a natural social and physical environment. She and her two infants were all born into an entirely unnatural world, one to which they are not adapted. . . . Studies of welfare in captive belugas support the assertion that belugas cannot live, let alone thrive, in a setting in which they never evolved. In captivity their lives are shorter and mortality rates are higher. They often die of stress-related diseases which break down their immune system function. They fail to thrive.[176]

As a final postscript, on October 22, 2015, Maris died suddenly—a tragic and premature ending to her captive life.[177]

---

173. Animal Welfare Institute Comment on GAI Petition, att. 1 (Oct. 29, 2012), https://awionline .org/sites/default/files/uploads/documents/ML-AWI-BelugaComments10-29-1-2.pdf.

174. James Cave, *Georgia Aquarium's Celebrated Baby Beluga Dies Less Than a Month after Birth*, HUFFINGTON POST, June 9, 2015 (updated). The first baby died only one week after her birth. Although the Georgia Aquarium claims her death is a "mystery," others say the baby succumbed to failure to thrive syndrome, a disease that kills human and nonhuman infants generally as a result of disease or environmental conditions. Lori Marino, *Infant Beluga Death is No Mystery* (June 8, 2015), http://www.kimmela.org/2015/06/08/infant-beluga-death-is-no-mystery/.

175. *Id.*

176. *Id.*

177. Faith Karimi, *Maris the Beluga Whale Dies Suddenly at Georgia Aquarium*, CNN (Oct. 23, 2015), http://www.cnn.com/2015/10/23/us/georgia-maris-beluga-whale-dies/.

The Alliance, discussed in the prior section of this chapter, fully supported the Georgia Aquarium's efforts to import the belugas. In a 2013 press release the Alliance stated that the MMPA "encourages the practice of caring for these animals at aquariums and zoos in order to advance scientific study and research and encourage conservation action by U.S. citizens by raising public awareness."[178] But rather than "encourage" imports, the MMPA actually imposes a moratorium on the take of marine mammals from the wild; the statute allows capture and imports only under limited circumstances to promote the well-being of the wild marine mammal populations, arguably through the mandated programs for education or conservation that meet professionally recognized standards.[179]

Lolita: Forty-Five Years in Captivity at Miami Seaquarium

On August 8, 1970, in Penn Cove off the coast of Washington state, Lolita, a member of the "L" pod of the Southern Resident Killer Whale (SRKW) community[180] was surrounded by nets, physically separated from her family, and taken from the company of her mother. Five orcas, including four baby calves, drowned in that capture.[181] Lolita, believed to be between four and six years of age, was delivered to Miami Seaquarium.[182] She lived and performed with Hugo, who had been captured from the same whale

---

178. Alliance for Marine Mammal Parks and Aquariums, *Statement on Georgia Aquarium's Complaint Seeking to Overturn Permit Denial for Beluga Whale Import,* http://www.ammpa.org/doc_131001BelugaWhaleImport.html.

179. 16 U.S.C. § 1371.

180. The Orca Project, *Lolita the Orca; Facts, Legal Issues and How to Get Her Home,* https://theorcaproject.wordpress.com/2010/09/01/lolita-the-orca-her-life-her-legal-issues-and-her-way-home/ [hereinafter *Lolita Facts*].

181. Orca Network, *Lolita's Capture,* http://www.orcanetwork.org/captivity/lolitacapture.html. The MMPA did not govern Lolita's capture, as it had not yet been enacted.

182. Lolita performs and thus "entertains" her audience while also being "exhibited," and the Seaquarium claims that her exhibition serves the approved MMPA goals of public education and conservation efforts. Her case study plainly straddles the exhibition and entertainment categories and thus could be placed under either. Given the legal issues surrounding her treatment do not focus on her training and performance, per se, but rather on her captivity generally, her case study is included in this section on exhibition.

community in 1968, for nine years until his death.[183] Since then she has had no contact with members of her own species and lives a solitary life save for a few dolphins and her human trainers.[184] In 2005, the group from which Lolita was taken was listed as endangered under the ESA,[185] but on the grounds that Lolita was in captivity at the time of listing, she was exempted from the listing. Ten years later, in February 2015, the exclusion from endangered status for captive orcas was removed, and Lolita was included in the SRKW listing as endangered.[186] While that event would seem to have guaranteed her freedom and return to her family, it was not the case.

As of December 2016, Lolita, measuring twenty feet in length and weighing about 7,000 pounds,[187] continues to reside in the oldest and smallest orca tank in the United States[188] in violation of AWA standards, as discussed previously.[189] For years advocates have unsuccessfully attempted to have Lolita returned to her native waters.[190] On July 20, 2015, a lawsuit seeking Lolita's retirement to a sea pen in her native waters[191] was filed against Miami Seaquarium, alleging a violation of the ESA.[192] The complaint stated that Seaquarium does not have the proper permit under the ESA required to keep Lolita in her current condition.

---

183. In 1980, Hugo repeatedly bashed his head against his tank wall until his death. The Orca Project, *Miami Seaquarium*, https://theorcaproject.wordpress.com/killer-whale-orca-marine-parks/miami-seaquarium/. *See also Necropsy—Killer Whale Hugo*, http://www.scribd.com/doc/85184008/Necropsy-Killer-Whale-Hugo (Dr. Jesse R. White, DVM determined Hugo died from "rupture of saccular aneurysm of one or more cerebral arteries" and based on "additional information" stated that it had "been commonly reported that Hugo would regularly and intentionally smash his head against the sides of the pool. In the early 1970s this resulted in a serious injury.")
184. *Lolita Facts, supra* note 180.
185. 50 C.F.R. § 224.101; 70 Fed. Reg. 69903 (Nov. 18, 2005).
186. 80 Fed. Reg. 7380 (Feb. 10, 2015). *See generally* NOAA Fisheries, Southern Resident Killer Whale—Lolita—Included in Endangered Listing, http://www.westcoast.fisheries.noaa.gov/protected_species/marine_mammals/killer_whale/lolita_petition.html [hereinafter NOAA Fisheries—Lolita].
187. ALDF v. USDA, 2015 WL 3653162 at *2 (11th Cir. June 15, 2015).
188. Orca Network, *Lolita's Life Today*, http://www.orcanetwork.org/captivity/lolitatoday.html.
189. Seaquarium is not a member of the AZA but is a member of the Alliance. The authors are aware of no action taken by or filed with the Alliance on behalf of Lolita.
190. *See* The Orca Project, *Justice for Lolita. Taking her Fight with APHIS to the Next Level*, https://theorcaproject.wordpress.com/2011/06/07/APHIS-fails-killer-whale-lolita-at-miami-seaquarium/.
191. Orca Network, *Lolita*, http://www.orcanetwork.org/Main/index.php?categories_file=Lolita.
192. *Id.*

The plaintiffs argued that "Seaquarium's ongoing practice of keeping Lolita in a small, barren, and unprotected tank, deprived of interaction with a member of her own species, and with incompatible animals violates the" ESA's prohibition on "taking" or "harassing" endangered species.[193] On June 1, 2016, the trial judge granted summary judgment for Miami Seaquarium. After finding that the plaintiffs had standing, a jurisdictional hurdle many animal law cases struggle to get over, the judge held that although Lolita suffers from a variety of ailments caused by her inadequate enclosure, her ailments do not "gravely threaten" her existence and thus do not qualify as a "take" under the ESA.[194] The decision, which appears inconsistent with Supreme Court precedent,[195] was appealed to the Eleventh Circuit to challenge this narrow interpretation of "take" for endangered wildlife held in captivity.

Lolita has captured the hearts of thousands, depicted by the demonstrations outside the Seaquarium[196] and comments sent to NMFS in support of her release.[197] She still makes her family calls—orcas have complex cultures and communicate with distinctive calls and whistles unique to each pod[198]—and four living females old enough to be her mother remain in the pod from where she was captured, so that she could live the rest of her life reunited with her family, even if protected in a sea pen. Lolita's story presents a real-life example of the applications of the laws designed to protect this species.

Miami Seaquarium is a licensed exhibitor under the AWA, the law enacted by Congress to ensure that animals on public display are "provided

193. Complaint for Declaratory and Injunctive Relief, Animal Legal Defense Fund v. USDA, CV 12-4407 at para. 74 (N.D. Cal. Aug. 21, 2012) [hereinafter Lolita Complaint].
194. *See generally* PETA v. Miami Seaquarium, Order, Case No. 1:15-cv-22692-UU (S.D. Fl. June 1, 2016).
195. *See* Babbitt v. Sweet Home Chapter of Communities for a Great Oregon, 515 U.S. 687 (1995) (upholding USFWS' broad interpretation of "harm" in the definition of "take", citing legislative history making clear that Congress' intent was to define "take" "in the broadest possible manner to include every conceivable way in which a person can 'take' or attempt to 'take' any fish or wildlife") (internal citations omitted).
196. Laura Rodriguez and Cherine Akbari, *Protesters March to Free Orca Lolita from Miami Seaquarium*, NBC6 SOUTH FLORIDA, Jan. 18, 2015, http://www.nbcmiami.com/news/local/Protesters-March-to-Free-Orca-Lolita-from-Miami-Seaquarium-288921671.html.
197. NOAA Fisheries—Lolita, *supra* note 186.
198. Lisa Stiffler, *Understanding Orca Culture*, SMITHSONIAN MAG., August 2011, http://www.smithsonianmag.com/science-nature/understanding-orca-culture-12494696/?no-ist.

humane care and treatment."[199] Congress directed the Secretary of Agriculture to promulgate standards for the "humane handling, care, treatment,
and transportation of animals by . . . exhibitors"[200] including "minimum
requirements for handling, housing, feeding, watering, sanitation, ventilation, shelter from extremes of weather and temperatures, [and] adequate
veterinary care."[201] The size of the pool is an essential requirement for an
orca. The regulations state that "marine mammals must be housed in primary enclosures . . . constructed and maintained so that the animals . . .
are provided sufficient space, both horizontally and vertically, to be able
to make normal postural and social adjustments with adequate freedom
of movement, in or out of the water."[202] Minimum space requirements
for cetaceans are defined by four factors: minimum horizontal dimension
(MHD), depth, volume and surface area.[203] The orca pool must have an
MHD of at least forty-eight feet and a depth of at least twelve feet. If
these requirements are met, the volume and surface area requirements are
also met.[204] Outdoor enclosures must provide shelter to protect the animal
"from the weather or from direct sunlight."[205] Moreover, because orcas are
highly social mammals, they "must be housed in their primary enclosure
with at least one compatible animal of the same or biologically related species," unless the facility's veterinarian determines social housing is not in
the animal's best interest.[206]

   Lolita's living conditions arguably do not comply with the AWA
requirements. Lolita lives in a concrete tank with an unobstructed MHD

---

199. 7 U.S.C. § 2131(1).

200. 7 U.S.C. § 2143(a)(1).

201. 7 U.S.C. § 2143(a)(2)(A); see 9 C.F.R. §§ 3.100—3.118.

202. 9 C.F.R. § 3.104(a). Notably, in 2016 USDA proposed to amend the AWA standards for
marine mammals, but declined to increase the required minimum tank size. 81 Fed. Reg. 12832
(March 11, 2016).

203. Id. § 3.104(b).

204. Tierney, supra note 82. Notably, the USDA Animal and Plant Health Inspection Service
admits that the minimum depth requirement for orcas should be updated. The minimum depth
requirement has been under review since 1996, with no amendment. Animal Welfare Institute
Comment on 79 FR 4313, Letter from Naomi Rose to Lynne Barre, Branch Chief, 4 (Mar.
27, 2014), https://awionline.org/sites/default/files/uploads/documents/AWI-LolitaESAListing
Comments-03272014.pdf [hereinafter AWI Letter].

205. 9 C.F.R. § 3.103(b).

206. Id. § 3.109.

of thirty-five feet,[207] compared with the minimum MHD of forty-eight feet. APHIS approved the tank in the 1990s with no waiver under the theory that the platform in the pool that intersects the required minimum does not violate the standard. However, the agency has recently indicated that the required minimum dimension must be unobstructed.[208] Furthermore, her tank leaves her exposed to direct sunlight, in violation of the shelter provision.[209] And finally, since Hugo's death in 1980, Lolita has had no orca companionship but instead shares her pool with white-sided dolphins who some argue are not sufficiently related to her to provide proper companionship, arguably violating the social compatibility provision of the AWA.[210] APHIS, "widely regarded as being a more permissive, less effective agency, with a reputation for being more 'industry friendly,'"[211] continues to renew the Seaquarium's license despite the noncompliance. Additionally, the USDA has the sole authority to initiate enforcement proceedings but has not done so.

Lolita's fate remains uncertain as of the publication of this book, more than forty-five years after her capture. And although NMFS suggested, and the trial court has held, that maintaining Lolita in captivity does not constitute harassment in violation of the ESA, NMFS further claimed that releasing Lolita to the wild might constitute harassment. NMFS has stated that

> issues surrounding any release of Lolita to the wild are numerous and complex and are not ripe for analysis in this listing rule. Such issues would be better evaluated in the context of a specific section

---

207. Lolita Complaint, *supra* note 193, at paras. 64–67; *see also* Orca Project, *Lolita the Orca: Facts, Legal Issues and How To Get Her Home,* https://theorcaproject.wordpress.com/2010/09/01/lolita-the-orca-her-life-her-legal-issues-and-her-way-home/ (detailing with pictures, diagrams and measurements, the Miami Seaquarium pool).

208. Jonathan Kendall, *Lolita's Miami Seaquarium Tank Doesn't Meet Federal Standards, Activists Argue UPDATED,* MIAMI NEW TIMES, Mar. 21, 2016 at 8:30 AM.

209. Lolita Complaint, *supra* note 193, at paras. 69–75; *see also Lolita the Orca: Facts, Legal Issues and How To Get Her Home,* https://theorcaproject.wordpress.com/2010/09/01/lolita-the-orca-her-life-her-legal-issues-and-her-way-home/.

210. Lolita Complaint, *supra* note 193, at paras. 76–81.

211. Tierney, *supra* note 82 (quoting http://endcap.eu/wp-content/uploads/2014/12/dying-to-entertain-you.pdf).

10 permit application. Any such process would include rigorous review by the scientific community, the Marine Mammal Commission, and the public, and be subject to an associated NEPA analysis, prior to action being taken.[212]

Captive Breeding of Endangered Animals

The breeding of endangered species, such as tigers, cheetahs, elephants, chimpanzees, and lemurs provides a useful case study for the application of the ESA to captive wildlife. The USFWS regulations provide that breeding practices that are not "generally accepted" constitute harassment (although the regulations do not define "generally accepted").[213] Additionally, the USFWS has recognized that there is a danger of "captive-bred animals . . . [being] used for purposes that do not contribute to conservation, such as for pets . . . or for entertainment"[214] and that "uses of captive wildlife can be detrimental to wild populations."[215] Therefore, it is imperative that captive breeding of endangered species be carefully planned and humanely implemented; however, not all captive breeding achieves these goals.

For example, compare the breeding of big cat species at AZA and ZAA facilities. It is well established that breeding cheetahs in captivity is fraught with difficulties—the species has "more challenges [than other big cats], ranging from poor genetic variability and gamete malformation to behavior nuances."[216] Additionally, cheetahs may have "a prolonged

212. 80 Fed. Reg. 7380, 7398 (Feb 10, 2015), http://www.gpo.gov/fdsys/pkg/FR-2015-02-10/html/2015-02604.htm.
213. 50 C.F.R. § 17.3 (definition of "harass").
214. 57 Fed. Reg. 548, 550.
215. 44 Fed. Reg. 30044, 30045 (May 23, 1979). *See also* 77 Fed. Reg. 431, 434 (Jan. 5, 2012) ("While the Service does believe that captive breeding can provide a significant benefit to endangered species, such benefits can only be realized when the breeding program is scientifically based and conducted in a manner that contributes to the continued survival of the species. . . . However, breeding just to breed, without adequate attention to genetic composition and demographics of the breeding population, may not provide a clear conservation benefit to an endangered species.")
216. Jennifer Frank & Craig Saffoe, *Breeding Management Strategy for Cheetahs* (Acinonyx jubatus) *at the Smithsonian's National Zoological Park*, 7/8 Animal Keeper's F. 393–397 (2005).

stress response when moved between facilities" that "may exacerbate infertility and disease."[217]

The ZAA has developed a "Cheetah Management Plan," but it is simply a memorandum of participation signed by ZAA members and not a scientific analysis of the ZAA cheetah colony's demographics or genetics, nor does it establish clear management goals and strategies or identify breeding recommendations.[218] This document pales in comparison to the rigorous, science-based plans established according to conservation principles by the AZA Felid Taxon Advisory Group Species Survival Plans. Furthermore, the ZAA has, to date, not produced any other population management plans (science-based or otherwise) for other endangered species it is breeding.

Compare, for example, the AZA Amur Tiger SSP 2013–2014 plan, which includes ample data revealing how the AZA Amur Tiger SSP conducts its captive propagation activities. This AZA SSP works in a coordinated manner with the World Association of Zoos and Aquariums (WAZA) Global Species Management Plan (GSMP), which recognizes that "[t]o fulfill the full suite of conservation roles required of animals in zoos and aquariums, they must be demographically robust and genetically representative of wild counterparts. Many species will be able to sustain these characteristics for the foreseeable future only when cooperatively managed at a global level." The AZA Amur Tiger SSP "strive[s] to maintain at least 90 percent gene diversity . . . for the next 100 years" and the "population has a 100 percent traceable pedigree from which all kinships (genetic relationships between tigers) can be calculated." The AZA Amur Tiger SSP consists of a team of reputable scientists who are developing ways to predict the likelihood of successful breeding and

217. Amy Wells, D.V.M. et al., The Stress Response to Environmental Change in Captive Cheetahs (Acinonyx jubatus), 35(1) J. Zoo & Wildlife Med. 8–14 (2004); see also Ros Clubb & Georgia Mason, *Captivity Effects on Wide-Ranging Carnivores*, 425 Nature 473–4 (2003).

218. In correspondence between the U.S. Fish and Wildlife Service and a ZAA-accredited facility (Wildlife World Zoo and Aquarium) regarding an application for a permit to import cheetahs from South Africa (PRT-20003B), USFWS concluded that "The ZAA Cheetah Management Plan is not adequate documentation to demonstrate that a binding agreement between ZAA members will actively advance the captive propagation and care of this species in captivity." *See* 79 Fed. Reg. 14528 (March 14, 2014).

studying the effects of contraception in order to better manage the SSP population given space restrictions.

The USFWS has allowed multiple ZAA facilities to import cheetahs from breeding facilities in South Africa to private menageries in the United States, with the claimed goal of conservation.[219] In order to obtain these permits, ZAA facilities have attempted to offset these commercial imports with a donation to organizations such as the Cheetah Conservation Fund (even though the cost of purchasing the cheetahs from a South African breeder is exponentially higher than such donations).[220] While the ESA appears to require a direct link between the authorized action and the required effect (enhancement or conservation science),[221] the USFWS has nonetheless approved of these unsupported promises to pledge money in the future, and allowed import of cheetahs for what are primarily entertainment and profit reasons.[222]

Even if such donations were permissible to justify otherwise prohibited activities, there is no indication that the relatively minor sum of money that ZAA applicants propose to donate would affect a meaningful change in the species' chances for survival in the wild. Successful

---

219. For example, in 2012 USFWS issued a permit to Metro Richmond Zoo to import six female cheetahs from South Africa (PRT-57466A); over the next eighteen months, the zoo produced twenty cheetah cubs, but at least three died for unknown reasons. *See* WTVR, *Cheetah Cub Dies at Metro Richmond Zoo Days after Check-Up* (May 31, 2015), http://wtvr.com/2015/05/31/cheetah-cub-dies-at-metro-richmond-zoo/; Susan Bahorich, *Second Cheetah Cub Dies at Metro Richmond Zoo*, NBC (Oct. 12, 2014).

220. *See, e.g.,* Carson Springs Wildlife Foundation (PRT-86835A, permit issued 5/17/13); Lionshare Farm Zoological LLC (PRT-88756A, permit issued 6/21/13); Metro Richmond Zoo (PRT-57466A, permit issued 5/7/12); Project Survival (PRT-58624A, permit issued 8/20/12); Tanganyika Wildlife Park (PRT-25482A, permit issued 2/18/11); Wild Acres Ranch (PRT-64940A, permit issued 11/29/12); Wild Wonders Zoofari (PRT-88777A, permit issued 9/16/13), and Wildlife World Zoo (PRT-20003B, permit issued 8/7/14).

221. The plain language of the ESA require that the individual authorized action (the take, interstate commerce, import, or export) must itself cause the required effect (e.g., enhancement). 16 U.S.C. § 1539(a)(1)(A) (FWS "may permit . . . *any act otherwise prohibited by Section 9 . . .* to enhance the propagation or survival of the species") (emphasis added). *See also* 58 Fed. Reg. 32,632 (June 11, 1993) (questioning "whether there is a *direct cause and effect relationship* between education through exhibition of living wildlife and enhancement of survival in the wild of the species exhibited") (emphasis added).

222. For example, Project Survival, which obtained an import permit from the USFWS based on an offset donation, takes cheetahs to elementary schools (for a fee of $500) and allows members of the public to go into an enclosure with the big cats. *See* https://cathaven.com/school_story/.

conservation efforts normally cost millions of dollars, not merely a few thousand dollars. Furthermore, the USFWS has not conducted a comprehensive analysis of the cumulative impacts of this new ZAA cheetah import program. This is particularly concerning given recent action by the (CITES) Animals Committee, which recently issued a warning about the impacts of illegal trade of cheetahs, particularly those originating from South Africa.[223]

Captive propagation programs may have conservation value, when necessary to bolster wild populations and conducted pursuant to well-established conservation science principles, but much of the breeding of exotic animals in America does not meet such standards and instead is conducted for personal fancy or financial gain and to the detriment of animal welfare and public safety.

Circuses and Animal Entertainment

Moral Considerations

A public debate has been ongoing for years over the use of wild animals like elephants, tigers, lions, bears, apes, and monkeys in circuses, other live performances, television and films, and interactive experiences. Animal protectionists allege animals used for entertainment purposes are routinely separated from their mothers soon after birth so that they can be reared by human handlers (often through abusive training tactics) in order to force these animals to perform on cue.[224] Although technological advances in computer graphics have obviated the need to use live animals for filming,[225] many producers still use them. Additionally, dozens of

---

223. *See* CITES, AC27 Doc. 18, Appendix C, https://cites.org/sites/default/files/eng/com/ac/27/E-AC27-18.pdf.

224. *See, e.g.,* Association of Zoos and Aquariums, *White Paper: Apes in Media and Commercial Performances,* https://www.aza.org/white-paper-apes-in-media-and-commercial-performances/.

225. For example, the most recent Planet of the Apes movies did not use a single live chimpanzee on film, but instead the filmmakers recorded the sounds of chimpanzees at the national sanctuary for retired laboratory chimpanzees (Chimp Haven) and used computer-generated imagery for the acting scenes.

circuses and other exhibitors continue to travel around the country and provide animal performances and interactive experiences with the public. As discussed in this section, such activity has significant negative impacts on the welfare of the animals (and can also undermine public safety and conservation efforts), and it is subject to a patchwork of federal, state, and local laws.

Laws Regulating Circuses and Animal Entertainment

The use of captive wildlife in commercial media, circuses, and roadside menageries that allow public interactions with exotic animals is governed by local, state, and federal law. The AWA requires a license to exhibit animals to the public and provides minimum standards for humane handling of animals.[226] The ESA prohibits the "take" of captive endangered species (such as tigers, cheetahs, elephants, apes, and lemurs), so that it is unlawful to harm or harass those animals.[227] State and local governments in the United States and abroad have become more active in this area in recent years, using their police power to prohibit or limit the use of animals in circuses and live performances.[228] Additionally, federal legislation has been introduced to restrict the interstate transport, possession, and breeding of exotic animals to reduce the use of these animals in circuses and commercial exhibition.[229]

The Animal Welfare Act—Animal Handling Regulations

Captive wild animals used in performances and interactive experiences are routinely trained from a very young age, with their indoctrination to human contact sometimes beginning within minutes or days after

---

226. 7 U.S.C. §§ 2131 *et seq.*

227. 16 U.S.C. § 1538; 50 C.F.R. § 17.11.

228. *See, e.g.,* Jeremy Pelzer, *Another $500K in Exotic Animal Funding Approved by Ohio Board,* Cleveland.com (Nov. 18, 2015).

229. For example, the Captive Primate Safety Act, the Big Cat Public Safety Act, and the Traveling Exotic Animal Protection Act have been introduced in multiple Congresses, but have yet to be enacted.

birth.[230] In order to mold exotic mammals like big cats, primates, and elephants for use in the circus, commercial media, or interactive experiences with the public, animal handlers frequently remove infants from their mothers in order to hand-rear the animals in an attempt to make the wild animal "tame."[231] It is well established that mammals have extraordinary mother-infant relationships that are essential to the biological and social development of these species. Mammalian mothers fiercely protect their young at least until they are weaned and self-sufficient; thus, it often requires force, deception, or chemical immobilizers to separate these bonded pairs.[232] When trainers or exhibitors prematurely separate (either immediately or after a few days or weeks) animal infants from their mothers, they deprive them of vital development and cause the infants to suffer from behavioral abnormalities, such as mental and reproductive disorders.[233] For this reason, the laws affecting such handling practices are of particular interest.

Pursuant to its authority under the AWA,[234] APHIS has adopted the following standards for exhibitors:[235]

(b)(1) Handling of all animals shall be done as expeditiously and carefully as possible in a manner that does not cause trauma,

230. *See, e.g., infra* note 245; The Humane Society of the United States, *Undercover Investigations Reveal Abuse of Tiger Cubs at Roadside Zoos* (Jan. 22, 2015), http://www.humanesociety.org/news/press_releases/2015/01/ok-va-exotics-investigation-012215.html?referrer=https://www.google.com/.

231. *Id.*

232. *See* M. ELSBETH MCPHEE & KATHY CARLSTEAD, *The Importance of Maintaining Natural Behaviors in Captive Mammals*, in WILD MAMMALS IN CAPTIVITY (Debra Kleiman et al. eds.) 303–313 (2010) ("In most mammals, the mother-infant relationship is critical to the future development of offspring, affecting future defensive responses and reproductive behavior. . . . A disturbed mother-infant relationship may deprive the young animal of specific stimulation essential for the development of normal emotional regulation, social interaction, and complex goal-directed behaviors, in particular, maternal and sexual behaviors."); R. C. Newberry & J. C. Swanson, *Implications of Breaking Mother-Young Social Bonds*, 110 APPLIED ANIMAL BEHAV. SCI. 3–23 (2008) (maternal bonding between mammalian mother and young is mediated by hormones and neurotransmitters that facilitate attachment and maternal behavior).

233. *Id.*
234. 7 U.S.C. § 2143.
235. 9 C.F.R. § 2.131.

overheating, excessive cooling, behavioral stress, physical harm, or unnecessary discomfort.

(2)(i) Physical abuse shall not be used to train, work, or otherwise handle animals. (ii) Deprivation of food or water shall not be used to train, work, or otherwise handle animals; Provided, however, that the short-term withholding of food or water from animals by exhibitors is allowed by these regulations as long as each of the animals affected receives its full dietary and nutrition requirements each day.

(c)(1) During public exhibition, any animal must be handled so there is minimal risk of harm to the animal and to the public, with sufficient distance and/or barriers between the animal and the general viewing public so as to assure the safety of animals and the public.

(2) Performing animals shall be allowed a rest period between performances at least equal to the time for one performance.

(3) Young or immature animals shall not be exposed to rough or excessive public handling or exhibited for periods of time which would be detrimental to their health or well being.

(4) Drugs, such as tranquilizers, shall not be used to facilitate, allow, or provide for public handling of the animals.

(d)(1) Animals shall be exhibited only for periods of time and under conditions consistent with their good health and well being.

(2) A responsible, knowledgeable, and readily identifiable employee or attendant must be present at all times during periods of public contact.

(3) During public exhibition, dangerous animals such as lions, tigers, wolves, bears, or elephants must be under the direct con-

trol and supervision of a knowledgeable and experienced animal handler.

(4) If public feeding of animals is allowed, the food must be provided by the animal facility and shall be appropriate to the type of animal and its nutritional needs and diet.

These requirements provide licensed exhibitors substantial discretion regarding how to comply with the law and therefore they make enforcement difficult. This is particularly true with regard to the use of big cats, bears, and nonhuman primates for direct contact with paying members of the public at roadside menageries, state fairs, shopping malls, and other entertainment settings.

For example, because lions and tigers are explicitly mentioned as examples of dangerous animals in Section 2.131(d)(3), "during public exhibition" such animals must be "under the direct control and supervision of a knowledgeable and experienced animal handler."[236] In addition to being under the "direct control" of the handler, big cats (as with all other animals) "must be handled so there is minimal risk of harm to the animal and to the public, with sufficient distance and/or barriers between the animal and the general viewing public so as to assure the safety of animals and the public."[237] Frequently, licensees and inspectors have different opinions on how to determine if a big cat is indeed under a handler's "direct control" and what constitutes "sufficient distance and/ or barriers" for an individual big cat.[238]

Further, USDA inspectors have inconsistently applied the standards of what constitutes "excessive public handling" of young animals and what constitutes "minimal risk of harm to the animal."[239] Some agency guidance documents previously suggested that APHIS believes there is

236. 9 C.F.R. § 2.131(d)(3).

237. *Id.* at § 2.131(c)(1).

238. *See* Antle v. Johanns, 2007 WL 5209982 (D.S.C. 2007), *aff'd per curiam*, 264 F. App'x 271 (4th Cir. 2008) (upholding USDA decision that found a violation of 9 C.F.R. § 2.131 when persons who are to be photographed with an adult big cat are allowed to stand behind the cat without any barrier between the cat and the persons being photographed).

239. 9 C.F.R. § 2.131(c)(1), (3).

a "risk of harm to the animal" or the public when the public is allowed to handle a big cat species under the age of eight weeks or over the age of twelve weeks.[240] This patchwork of guidance created the impression among certain members of the regulated community that the USDA affirmatively sanctioned public contact with big cats between the ages of eight and twelve weeks; however, no such formal policy exists and the performance standards can nevertheless be violated when exhibiting animals within that age range.

Current regulations regarding primate handling specifically allow public contact with "trained nonhuman primates" if the animals "are under the direct control and supervision of an experienced handler or trainer at all times during the contact."[241] There is no specific guidance regarding the age of primates who may be used for public contact exhibition and the term "trained nonhuman primate" is not defined. Thus, chimpanzees and other primates who are known to inflict severe injuries to humans on occasion, without warning, are technically permitted to come into direct contact with humans.[242]

In 2012, a coalition of animal protection and conservation groups filed a rulemaking petition with the USDA, requesting amendment to these animal handling regulations to explicitly prohibit public interaction with big cats, bears, and nonhuman primates and to prohibit unnecessary

240. See APHIS, Handling of Dangerous Animals Letter ("direct public contact with juvenile ["over three months of age"] and adult felines (e.g., lions, tigers, jaguars, leopards, cougars) does not conform to the handling regulations, because it cannot reasonably be conducted without a significant risk of harm to the animal or the public"), https://www.aphis.usda.gov/animal_welfare/downloads/Animal%20Care%20Inspection%20Guide.pdf. See also In re Jamie Michelle Palazzo, d/b/a Great Cat Adventures and James Lee Riggs, AWA Docket No. 07-0207 Appeals Decision and Order (May 10, 2010) (confirming that the performance standard may be violated when the public is allowed to come into contact with a big cat over 12 weeks old); USDA, The Big Cat Questions and Answer: Commonly Asked Big Cat Questions ("Although we do not encourage public contact with cubs, it is possible for an exhibitor to exhibit cubs over approximately 8 weeks of age (i.e., when their immune systems have developed sufficiently to protect them from most communicable diseases), to the public, and still comply with all of the regulatory requirements."), http://www.aphis.usda.gov/animal_welfare/downloads/big_cat/big_cat_q&a.pdf; but cf. In re Craig A. Perry (d/b/a/ Perry's Wilderness Ranch & Zoo), AWA Docket No. 05-0026, 2012 WL 1563490 (March 29, 2012) ("Even cubs can harm the public").
241. 9 CFR §§ 3.77(g), 3.78(e), 3.79(d).
242. See, e.g., Andy Newman, Pet Chimp Is Killed after Mauling Woman, N.Y. TIMES, February 17, 2009, at A30.

separation of mothers and infants. In 2016, the USDA took action to address the most egregious public contact practices, issuing a Technical Note regarding the treatment of exotic felids four weeks of age and under, stating that "Licensees who do not house neonatal nondomestic cats in a controlled, sanitary, temperature-controlled environment and do not handle such animals in a manner that does not expose them to any form of public contact, including public feeding and handling, are considered noncompliant with the veterinary care and handling requirements of the Animal Welfare Act regulations."[243] Although the USDA has twice solicited public comment on the petition, the agency has not yet taken formal action to regulate public contact with primates, bears, or exotic cats over four weeks of age.[244]

Endangered Species Act—Take and Trade of Animals in Circuses and Commercial Entertainment

The USFWS regulations exempt "generally accepted" husbandry and breeding practices from the ESA's definition of "take," as noted previously. The USFWS has, however, specifically acknowledged that "maintaining animals in inadequate, unsafe or unsanitary conditions, physical mistreatment, and the like constitute harassment because such conditions might create the likelihood of injury or sickness." So as an overall matter, the USFWS believes that the ESA "continues to afford protection to listed species that are not being treated in a humane manner."[245]

Given the inherent vagueness in the term "generally accepted," there is significant ongoing debate about both the scope and legality of these the USFWS regulations on harassment of captive endangered species. The use of animals like elephants and tigers in circuses and other enter-

---

243. USDA, *Handling and Husbandry of Neonatal Nondomestic Cats* (March 2016), https://www .aphis.usda.gov/publications/animal_welfare/2016/tech-neonatal-nondomestic-cats.pdf. The Technical Note also provides that "Neonates will obtain most immunity from their mother, primarily through suckling antibody-rich colostrum (first milk), and should be housed with their mother for as long as possible after birth to promote good health."

244. *See* 81 Fed. Reg. 41257 (June 24, 2016); 78 Fed. Reg. 47215 (Aug. 5, 2013); http://www .regulations.gov/#!docketDetail;D=APHIS-2012-0107.

245. *Id.* 63 Fed. Reg. 48634, 48638 (September 11, 1998) (emphasis added).

tainment exhibition is on the front lines of this battle. There is a significant difference (in terms of breeding and husbandry) between what is generally accepted by certain exhibitors (such as AZA-accredited zoos) versus what is generally accepted by those in the entertainment trade. For example, the AZA breeds tigers pursuant to a science-based management plan and has made significant effort to allow tigers to be reared by their mothers,[246] while tigers used for commercial entertainment are often bred for aesthetics and reared by humans to be groomed for public contact (frequently resulting in nutritional deficiencies and behavioral abnormalities).[247] Similarly, while the AZA has adopted standards recommending that elephant keepers manage captive elephants without direct contact, circuses continue to use endangered Asian elephants in performances (usually by wielding a bullhook, a fire-poker-like object used to control elephants in their interactions with trainers that can cause injury and distress to the elephants).[248] Animal protection groups have taken the position, for example, that subjecting an endangered tiger cub to excessive handling by paying customers constitutes harassment, and that the use of a bullhook is not a generally accepted husbandry practice (in addition to actually harming the elephant), and thus such activities constitute a take under the ESA.

It also may be the case that enforcement of the ESA as applied to exotic animals in captivity in the United States (note that the "take" prohibition does not apply extraterritorially) is not always a top priority for the USFWS and the U.S. Department of Justice. However, the ESA contains a citizen suit provision through which private parties can assist in enforcement of the law, and there is ongoing litigation challenging

---

246. *See, e.g.,* Angela S. Kelling et al., *Socialization of a Single Hand-Reared Tiger Cub,* J. 16(1) Applied Animal Welfare Sci. 47–63 (2013) (discussing how modern zoos no longer hand-rear animals if it can be avoided).

247. *See supra,* note 245.

248. *See* AZA, Standards for Elephant Management and Care (2012), https://www.aza.org/uploadedFiles/Accreditation/AZA%20Standards%20for%20Elephant%20Management%20and%20Care.pdf; ASPCA v. Ringling Bros., Case No. 1:03-cv-02006 (D.D.C. Complaint filed 2003).

the actions of particular exhibitors as constituting unauthorized takes.[249] Unless or until the USFWS amends its regulations to make clear what constitutes a take by animal entertainment enterprises (as requested in a 2015 rulemaking petition filed by The Humane Society of the United States), the scope of this regulation will be shaped by the judicial branch.

In addition to the prohibition on take, the ESA has implications for the use of performing animals in interstate and foreign commerce. The ESA makes it unlawful to "deliver, receive, carry, transport, or ship in interstate or foreign commerce, by any means whatsoever and in the course of commercial activity" endangered species, or to "sell or offer for sale in interstate or foreign commerce any such species."[250] The term "commercial activity" means "all activities of industry and trade, including, but not limited to, the buying or selling of commodities and activities conducted for the purpose of facilitating such buying and selling . . ."[251] Thus, on its face, the ESA regulates both interstate sale and commercial transport of endangered species. Importantly, the prohibitions on take and interstate commerce apply to all captive listed species, regardless of the date the animal was reduced to (or born into) captivity.[252]

However, the USFWS has adopted a regulatory definition of "industry or trade" (part of the statutory definition of "commercial activity")

249. See, e.g., Kuehl et al., v. Sellner et al., 2016 WL 590468 (N.D. Iowa 2016) (district court holding that private menagerie's confinement of tigers in squalid conditions and lemurs in social isolation violates the ESA, pending on appeal at time of publication); Hill et al., v. Coggins et al., 2016 WL 1251190 (W.D. NC 2016) (holding that plaintiffs failed to demonstrate that keeping grizzly bears in concrete pits violates the ESA, pending on appeal at time of publication); Breaux et al., v. Haynes et al., Case No. 3:2015-cv-00769 (M.D. LA 2015) (alleging that private menagerie keeps chimpanzee in social isolation and gives her cigarettes in violation of the ESA); PETA v. Dade City Wild Things, Inc. et al., Case No. 8:16-cv-02899 (M.D. Fl. 2016) (alleging that roadside zoo that allows members of the public to swim with tiger cubs violates the ESA take prohibition).

250. 16 U.S.C. § 1538(a)(1)(E), (F).

251. 16 U.S.C. § 1532(2) (emphasis added).

252. 16 U.S.C. § 1538(b). See also ASPCA v. Ringling Bros. and Barnum & Bailey Circus, 502 F. Supp. 2d 103 (2007) (holding that Congress intended the take prohibition to apply to "pre-Act" wildlife); Loggerhead Turtle v. County Council of Volusia County, Fla., 896 F. Supp. 1170, 1180 (M.D. Fl. 1995) (the prohibition on take applies to "[a]ny taking and every taking—even of a single individual of the protected species").

to mean "the actual or intended transfer of wildlife or plants from one person to another person in the pursuit of gain or profit."[253] In *Humane Society of the United States v. Babbitt*, the plaintiff argued that USFWS' determination that an Asian elephant used by Hawthorn Corp. for entertainment purposes does not constitute "commercial activity" was in conflict with the ESA. The lower court found that the plain language of the ESA is ambiguous and gave deference to the the USFWS' interpretation of the statute. On appeal, the U.S. Court of Appeals for the District of Columbia Circuit dismissed the case on other grounds and vacated the district court opinion.[254] When this issue subsequently came up in a different case in the context of a motion for preliminary injunction to stop the transport of endangered elephants from one zoo to another, the court found that "if the exhibition of [the elephants] would result in gain or profit for the defendant zoos, then the transportation of the animals (which would facilitate the exhibition) can also be said to be undertaken for gain or profit, and that this would constitute commercial activity within the meaning of the ESA."[255] Therefore, the USFWS regulations arguably do not comply with the ESA, but as of 2016, this issue remains unresolved, and the USFWS' interpretation is still being applied.

Any entity that seeks to engage in the take, import, export, or interstate sale or commercial transport of captive endangered species must first apply for a permit under Section 10 of the ESA. Circuses and other traveling menageries (such as those that take young animals to shopping malls and state fairs to profit from photographic opportunities) regularly move endangered species (such as tigers and elephants) across state lines and even internationally for performances, and thus the USFWS processes numerous permit applications from these exhibitors.

Congress intended to "limit substantially the number of exemptions that may be granted under the act," by requiring that the USFWS make certain that granting the permit "will not operate to the disadvantage" of the species and will be consistent with the conservation purposes of

---

253. 50 C.F.R. § 17.3.
254. HSUS v. Babbitt, 46 F.3d 93 (D.C. Cir. 1995).
255. Elephant Justice Project v. Woodland Park Zoo et al., Case No. 2:15-cv-00451-JCC, at 6 (W.D. Wash. April 7, 2015).

the statute.[256] Section 10 provides the USFWS authority to issue permits for otherwise unlawful activities involving endangered species, but only if such activity is "for scientific purposes or to enhance the propagation or survival of the affected species . . ."[257] The USFWS regulations provide guidance on this requirement, but still leave much room for interpretation. Specifically, the USFWS has defined "enhancement" with a nonexhaustive list of examples specific to captive animals, such that a permit can be issued for a captive endangered species for activities like administering contraception to promote genetic vitality and transferring animals for breeding loans.[258] For all enhancement permits for captive animals, the USFWS must ensure that the activity would not cause a detriment to wild or captive populations of the species.[259] In comments opposing the issuance of circus permit applications, animal protection groups have taken the position that commercial entertainment involving endangered species undermines conservation and thus cannot meet the enhancement standard.

It remains an open question to what extent conservation education qualifies as "enhancement." When it adopted the regulatory definition of enhancement in the 1970s, the USFWS took the position that "exhibition of living wildlife in a manner designed to educate the public about the ecological role and conservation needs of the affected species" constitutes enhancement.[260] But in the 1990s the USFWS began to question the true conservation education value obtained by the exhibition of captive wildlife, especially for foreign species used in performances, finding that "[e]ven with good material and a good faith effort at delivery by the exhibitor, there may be a limit to the amount of educational content a public which came (and paid) to be entertained will absorb."[261] In an effort to forge a middle ground, the USFWS has stated that exhibition might affirmatively benefit wild populations for "(1) Species that provide

---

256. Friends of Animals v. Salazar, 626 F. Supp. 2d 102, 119 (D.D.C. 2009); 16 U.S.C. § 1539(d).
257. 16 U.S.C. § 1539(a)(1)(A).
258. 50 C.F.R. § 17.3 (definition of "enhance the propagation or survival").
259. *Id.*
260. *Id. See also* 41 Fed. Reg. 18618, 18621 (May 5, 1976); 44 Fed. Reg. 54002 (Sept. 17, 1979).
261. 57 Fed. Reg. 548, 551 (Jan. 7, 1992).

popular products such as elephant ivory, to the extent that the public would be dissuaded from purchasing the product, and (2) 'glamor' species for which the public could be moved to donate significant amounts of money, provided the Service could ensure that the funds were spent to benefit the species in its native country."[262] The most definitive statement that the USFWS has made on this subject was to require that to obtain a Captive-Bred Wildlife Registration (CBW)—a type of ESA permit the USFWS created specifically for activities involving animals born in captivity in the United States of species that are not native to the United States—"[p]ublic education activities may not be the sole basis to justify issuance" of a CBW.[263]

Circuses have long asserted that their performances are educational and that such education qualifies as enhancement for purposes of obtaining a permit to export and reimport animals for international performances. However in the 2000s the USFWS began informing circuses that their claims of educational activities were not sufficient to obtain such permits. In response, circuses have begun using financial offsets—contributing money to organizations working on the ground to protect the species at issue—to demonstrate enhancement. Animal protection groups have opposed the issuance of ESA permits based on what has become known as a "pay-to-play" theory, asserting that the statute does not authorize the USFWS to issue permits for activities that do not directly benefit conservation and that the amount of money donated by circuses is insufficient to actually achieve a conservation benefit.[264]

As the use of endangered Asian elephants in U.S.-based circuses wanes (see next section), this debate will largely center on the commercial use of tigers. Pursuant to an exemption in the CBW regulations, circuses and private menageries were (until 2016) long exempt from permitting requirements for the take of or interstate commerce in tigers whose genet-

262. *Id. See also* 58 Fed. Reg. 32632, 32635 (June 11, 1993); 63 Fed. Reg. 48634, 48636 (Sept. 11, 1998).
263. 50 C.F.R. § 17.21(g)(3)(i); 58 Fed. Reg. 68323, 68325 (Dec. 27, 1993).
264. *See, e.g.,* People for the Ethical Treatment of Animals v. U.S. Fish and Wildlife Service, 2015 WL 5474477 (E.D. VA 2015). *See also* Case Study: International Transport of Endangered Circus Animals, *infra.*

ics are not known to be of a particular subspecies (so-called "generic" tigers).[265] But the import and export of tigers has always required a permit under CITES, and the USFWS will continue to receive applications from circuses and private menageries to transport their tigers internationally, unless the USFWS takes regulatory action to discontinue this activity or a court rules that such activity is inconsistent with the conservation purpose of the ESA.

State and Local Laws Prohibiting
Use of Elephants in Circuses

Circuses have often taken the position that they cannot use elephants in live performances without employing bullhooks to control captive elephants. At the same time, animal advocates have urged state and local legislators to prohibit the use of bullhooks in order to address the use of elephants by traveling menageries. In March 2015, in a landmark event in the animal entertainment arena, after nearly 150 years of exhibiting elephants in its circuses, Feld Entertainment (the parent company of Ringling Bros. and Barnum & Bailey Circus) announced that it would phase out the use of elephants in its performances by 2018. In January 2016 the circus announced that it would be phasing out elephants faster than expected, and that all elephants would be out of Ringling Bros. circuses by May 2016. And in January 2017, the circus announced its closing. Feld cited the increase in local ordinances prohibiting the use of bullhooks and the use of animals in circuses generally, as the primary reason for the decision.

Dozens of cities and counties—from Los Angeles to Richmond to Minneapolis to Austin—have passed ordinances prohibiting the use of bullhooks and in 2016 two states—California and Rhode Island—enacted similar bans.[266] Moreover, states and localities are increasingly considering legislation to ban the use of elephants and other exotic ani-

---

265. 50 C.F.R. § 17.21(g)(6) (2015); 81 Fed. Reg. 19923 (April 6, 2016).
266. *See* Nick Cahill, *California Bans Use of Elephant Bullhooks*, Courthouse News Service (Aug. 30, 2016), *at* http://www.courthousenews.com/2016/08/30/california-bans-use-of-elephant-bull-hooks.htm.

mals in traveling acts, regardless of whether a bullhook is used.[267] This trend is gaining momentum on the global scale—thirty countries have explicitly prohibited the use of all or some animals in circus perfor- mances, protecting both elephants and other species used for commercial entertainment.[268]

Case Studies

Yost Chimpanzees and Berosini Orangutans

Social science research reveals that the use of chimpanzees in entertain- ment has negative impacts on efforts to conserve the species in the wild. For example, in one study, people viewing an image of a chimpanzee with a human standing nearby were 35.5 percent more likely to consider wild populations to be stable and healthy compared to those seeing the same image without a human.[269] This misperception of the species' plight undercuts programs to educate the public about the need to take action to eliminate threats to chimpanzee existence. In another study, "when par- ticipants were given the opportunity to donate part of their earnings from the experiment to a conservation charity, donations were least frequent in the group watching commercials with entertainment chimpanzees."[270] Not only does the use of chimpanzees for entertainment undermine conservation efforts by decreasing public awareness about the plight of endangered species and decreasing donations to conservation programs, but there is substantial evidence that chimpanzees and orangutans used

267. For example, New York City and the State of New Jersey both introduced legislation in 2016 that would prohibit the use of elephants in traveling animal acts. *See* John C. Ensslin. *N.J. Could Be the First State to Bar Circuses from Using Elephants*, THE RECORD (Sept. 13, 2016), http://www.north jersey.com/counties/n-j-could-be-first-state-to-bar-circuses-from-using-elephants-1.1659507; Jen- nifer Fermino, *Bill Barring the Circus from Using Exotic Animals for Entertainment Gaining Momen- tum in City Council*, N. Y. DAILY NEWS (Oct. 11, 2016), http://www.nydailynews.com/new-york/ bill-banning-circus-wild-animals-heads-city-council-article-1.2825459.
268. *See* Animal Defenders International, *Circus Bans: An Expanding List of Worldwide Circus Bans and Restrictions*, http://www.stopcircussuffering.com/circus-bans/.
269. Stephen R. Ross et al., *Specific Image Characteristics Influence Attitudes about Chimpanzee Conservation and Use as Pets*, 6(7) PLoS ONE (2011). *See also* Steve R. Ross et al., *Inappropriate Use and Portrayal of Chimpanzees*, 319 SCI. 1487 (2008).
270. Kara Schroepfer *et al.*, *Use of "Entertainment" Chimpanzees in Commercials Distorts Public Perception Regarding Their Conservation Status*, 6(10) PLoS ONE (2011).

in the industry have been brutally abused and otherwise mistreated to perform for human enjoyment.[271] Today the market has shifted away from exploiting our ape cousins for a cheap laugh and as of early 2016 there were very few trainers who still made chimpanzees and orangutans available for entertainment media and performances (e.g., Steve Martin's Working Wildlife and Kevin "Doc" Antle).

Whistleblowers and undercover investigations have revealed that the only way to use captive apes for public performances (television, film, live shows) is through a process of physical and psychological abuse and the use of fear to command performances. For example, a 2005 federal lawsuit against Hollywood chimpanzee trainer Sidney Yost alleged that Mr. Yost violated the Endangered Species Act[272] and the California animal cruelty statute by violently beating five chimpanzees (Apollo, Sable, Cody, Angel, and Tea) with sticks, punching them, and inflicting excessive pain in order to coerce the chimpanzees to perform for movies, commercials, and television shows.[273] Sarah Baeckler, a primatologist who worked undercover as a volunteer for Yost, witnessed such abuse firsthand:

> I saw sickening acts of emotional, psychological, and physical abuse every single day on the job. . . . If the chimpanzees try to run away from a trainer, they are beaten. If they bite someone, they are beaten. If they don't pay attention, they are beaten. . . . The plain truth is this: the only thing that will make them stop behaving like curious, rambunctious chimpanzees, and, instead, routinely perform mundane tasks over and over again on cue is abject fear of physical pain.[274]

---

271. *See, e.g.,* The Chimpanzee Collaboratory, *Serving a Life Sentence for Your Viewing Pleasure* (2003), http://animalsfree.org/uploads/pdf/chimpanzee_collaboratory.pdf.

272. As discussed in a previous subsection, until 2015, USFWS regulations deprived captive chimpanzees of ESA protection, but this lawsuit aimed to challenge that regulation for being inconsistent with the spirit and language of the statute.

273. Animal Legal Defense Fund v. Sidney Jay Yost, Case No. 05-1066 (C.D. Cal. filed Nov. 18, 2005).

274. Eyes on Apes, *Campaign to End the Use of Chimpanzees in Entertainment*, http://www.eyes onapes.org/apes_in_entertainment/trainers/undercover/undercover_at_a_training_facility.pdf.

Fortunately, pursuant to a settlement Mr. Yost agreed to stop working with and to retire the chimpanzees in his possession; the chimpanzees went to sanctuaries in Florida.[275]

In another example of the routine practices of animal trainers, videotapes showed Las Vegas showman Bobby Berosini beating his orangutans (Berosini acquired the orangutans from the Yerkes National Primate Research Center) with a metal rod backstage before live shows for seven nights in a row.[276] The tape was publicly released (and shown on national television), which prompted Berosini to sue two animal protection groups for defamation and invasion of privacy.[277] That lawsuit was ultimately unsuccessful, with the Nevada Supreme Court finding that the videotape was not defamatory because it was "an accurate portrayal of the manner in which Berosini disciplined his animals backstage before performances."[278] Like the Yost chimpanzees, the former Berosini orangutans are now retired.

Although American exhibition facilities have largely moved away from using apes in entertainment performances, Hollywood films and shows seen around the world have created a trend, and wild chimpanzees and orangutans continue to be captured for entertainment use. For example, since 2007, more than 100 wild-caught chimpanzees have been exported from Guinea to China for exhibition and orangutans removed from the wild in Borneo and Sumatra have ended up in mainland Malaysia and Indonesia for entertainment use.[279]

---

275. Animal Legal Defense Fund, *ALDF Files Suit against Hollywood Chimpanzee "Trainer" in Federal Court* (November 18, 2005), http://aldf.org/press-room/press-releases/aldf-files-suit-against-hollywood-chimpanzee-trainer-in-federal-court/.

276. DALE PETERSON & JANE GOODALL, VISIONS OF CALIBAN: ON CHIMPANZEES AND PEOPLE, 157–179 (1980).

277. People for Ethical Treatment of Animals v. Bobby Berosini, Ltd., 895 P.2d 1269 (Nev. 1995).

278. *Id.* at 1272.

279. Great Ape Survival Partnership, *Stolen Apes—The Illicit Trade in Chimpanzees, Gorillas, Bonobos and Orangutans. A Rapid Response Assessment.* United Nations Environment Programme (2013), http://www.un-grasp.org/stolen-apes-report/.

International and Interstate Transport
of Endangered Circus Animals

The use of endangered species in commercial entertainment ventures is a dying trend, as public awareness of the inherent cruelty of using wild animals in circuses and other trained acts continues to rise; but scores of tigers, leopards, elephants, chimpanzees, orangutans, whales, and other animals continue to be confined and transported around the globe for use in live performances for human amusement.

In traveling menageries such as those that allow for public contact, animals are repeatedly exposed to lengthy transport, confined to cramped travel cages, and placed in unfamiliar environments.[280] Several studies demonstrate that even short-term transports have a detrimental impact on the well-being of large carnivores. One study found that cortisol— a hormone that is an indicator of stress levels—increased as much as 482 percent and remained elevated for nearly two weeks following brief transport periods. Other consequences, such as increased respiration rates (indicating stress and other negative physiological responses) and pacing (an aberrant psychological response to increased stress) were also noted.[281]

While the USFWS has acknowledged that using captive animals for entertainment can undermine the conservation of endangered species in the wild,[282] the agency nevertheless authorizes circuses to engage in otherwise prohibited activities under the ESA. For example, the USFWS has routinely issued permits to commercial entertainment companies (such as Feld Entertainment/Ringling Bros. and Barnum & Bailey Circus, Ferdinand and Anton Fercos-Hantig, Hawthorn Corporation, Hollywood Animals Inc., Tarzan Zerbini Circus, and Steve Martin's Working Wildlife)

---

280. *See also* Ros Clubb & Georgia Mason, *Captivity Effects on Wide-Ranging Carnivores*, 425 NATURE 473 (Oct. 2, 2003) ("Among the carnivores, naturally wide-ranging species show the most evidence of stress and/or psychological dysfunction in captivity . . . husbandry of these species in captivity is therefore in need of improvement").

281. *See* D. P. Dembiec et al., *The effects of transport stress on tiger physiology and behavior*, 23 ZOO BIOL. 335–46 (2004).

282. 57 Fed. Reg. 548, 550 (January 7, 1992) (recognizing the danger of "captive-bred animals . . . [being] used for purposes that do not contribute to conservation, such as for pets . . . or for entertainment"); 44 Fed. Reg. 30044, 30045 (May 23, 1979) ("uses of captive wildlife can be detrimental to wild populations").

to transport endangered felids and elephants to locations around the world for live performances. As noted earlier in this section, these entities have long acquired such permits by asserting that the circus and television performances are educational, but the USFWS has recently adopted a practice, whereby circuses can continue to use endangered species by offsetting their actions with a financial "pay to play" contribution to a conservation effort of their choosing to benefit the species in the wild (and thereby allow the USFWS to make the required "enhancement" finding pursuant to Section 10 of the ESA).

Animal protection organizations have challenged this rationale, arguing in comment letters opposing circus permit applications that the use of endangered animals in circus performances undermines the conservation of the species by commercializing wildlife, increasing the demand for exotic pets, and potentially facilitating poaching and trafficking of wild populations, and therefore such activities cannot be lawfully issued under the ESA enhancement standard. Despite these objections, these permits are routinely granted. In addition, as discussed below, the USFWS has determined that certain circus activities are exempt from the ESA permitting scheme.

The ESA provides that endangered species that were kept in captivity on the date that the species was listed can be exported without complying with the standard ESA permitting requirements, provided that such animals are not used in the course of commercial activity.[283] Asian elephants have been protected under the ESA since 1976, but since this species is so long-lived, there are multiple Asian elephants in captivity in the United States (including in circuses) that were reduced to captivity before that date. If a circus' use of Asian elephants was deemed "commercial activity," then it would not qualify for the pre-Act exception and ESA permits would be required for any export, reimport, and interstate commercial transport of the endangered elephants (regardless of their date of birth).[284] However, under the USFWS's definition of commercial activity,[285] the

---

283. 16 U.S.C. § 1538(b).
284. 16 U.S.C. §§ 1538(a), (b), 1532(2).
285. 50 C.F.R. § 17.3 ("industry or trade").

use of endangered elephants and tigers in international circuses has been deemed to not constitute commercial activity.[286]

The Administrative Procedure Act provides a mechanism for challenging such permitting decisions, and there have been multiple lawsuits brought against the USFWS for issuing circus permits in violation of the ESA.[287] In a 2012 lawsuit, People for the Ethical Treatment of Animals (PETA) challenged the USFWS' decision to exempt endangered elephants used by the Ringling Bros. and Barnum & Bailey circus (a multimillion dollar, for profit business) under this "pre-Act" exception.[288] However, that case was dismissed after the district court found that plaintiffs lacked "standing" to bring a lawsuit (a common jurisdictional barrier that animal protection plaintiffs face).[289]

PETA argued that it had standing to challenge the USFSW's decision that Ringling's elephants are not used in the course of a commercial activity because by eliminating the permitting process for that circus export, the agency deprived PETA of information pertaining to these otherwise prohibited activities. Furthermore, PETA argued that this injury would be redressed by a determination from the court that the elephants are subject to the ESA permitting requirements, in which case the circus would almost certainly be required to obtain such permits in order to continue its standard business practices. However, the court

---

286. *But see* U.S. Fish and Wildlife Service, Policy on Giant Panda Permits, 63 Fed. Reg. 45839, 45847 (Aug. 27, 1998) ("Under the ESA, the transfer of a giant panda to another institution across state lines constitutes interstate commerce, and therefore requires an ESA permit, since it is expected that the receiving facility gains financially or otherwise by having that animal at their facility. The Service has a long-standing policy that legitimate non-commercial breeding loans do not need interstate commerce permits because they generally do not involve the transfer of specimens in the pursuit of gain or profit. However, panda loans present exceptional facts that require the recipient of any panda transfer to address all the elements of the panda policy and interstate commerce permits would be required for any interstate transfer since exhibition of giant pandas generate much public interest and monetary gain for the exhibiting institution.").

287. *See, e.g.,* PETA v. FWS et al., 59 F. Supp. 3d 91 (D.D.C. 2014); PETA v. FWS et al., 2015 WL 5474477 (E.D. VA 2015).

288. PETA et al., v. FWS et al., Case No. 2:12-cv-04435 (C.D. Cal. 2012); PETA et al. v. FWS et al., Case No. 14-55471 (9th Cir. 2014) (appeal voluntarily dismissed by appellants after animals at issue returned to the United States).

289. Lujan v. Defenders of Wildlife, 504 U.S. 555, 560–61 (1992). In order to establish standing in federal court, a plaintiff must demonstrate that: (1) "injury in fact, (2) a causal relationship exists between the injury and the challenged conduct, and (3) that there is a likelihood that the injury will be redressed by a favorable decision of the court."

found that although PETA had demonstrated the first two prongs of the standing test, the redressability prong was not met because to redress this injury Feld Entertainment (a third party) would have to submit a permit application to the USFWS, which the "Court's order would not compel and whose occurrence is merely speculative."[290]

The definition of commercial activity is not only relevant to determining whether the export of pre-Act animals requires an ESA permit, but also implicates the USFWS's regulation of interstate transport of endangered species, and in 2015 The Humane Society of the United States filed a rulemaking petition to clarify this regulatory definition.

Exotic Pet Trade

Moral Considerations

America today is facing an epidemic of unqualified individuals possessing dangerous wild animals as pets. This threatens both public safety and animal welfare, and it undermines conservation efforts to protect endangered species.[291] Tens of thousands of big cats, bears, primates, venomous snakes, large constrictor snakes, and other dangerous wild animals currently live in backyards, basements, and other private menageries across the country.[292]

Wild animals have specialized needs that are exceedingly difficult to meet in captivity. These species typically require vast spaces, natural habitats, specialized diets, exercise, and opportunities to express natural behaviors such as foraging, hunting, socializing, climbing, digging, denning, and exploring.[293] Accredited zoos and bona fide wildlife sanctuaries spend considerable resources to provide animals with an enriched

---

290. PETA et al., v. FWS et al., Case No. 2:12-cv-04435 (C.D. Cal. 2012).

291. *See, e.g.,* Rich Schapiro, *All It Takes Is $45,000 and a Phone Call to Get a Pet Chimp*, N.Y. DAILY NEWS, February 22, 2009; Peter Laufer, *Exotic Animals as Pets: An Unregulated Risk*, N.Y. TIMES, Oct. 20, 2011.

292. *See, e.g.,* Keith Thomson, *It's Not Just Chimps: Americans Have 7,000 Pet Tigers*, HUFFINGTON POST, Feb. 18, 2009. (quoting an exotic pet owner as saying "Tigers are the new pit bulls.").

293. *See, e.g.,* WILD MAMMALS IN CAPTIVITY: PRINCIPLES AND TECHNIQUES FOR ZOO MANAGEMENT (Devra G. Kleiman et al. (eds., 2nd ed. 2010).

environment to alleviate profound boredom and psychological distress,[294] but the same cannot be said of unqualified individuals who house their animals in cages, backyards, garages, and basements.

Exotic pets (including many endangered species) are bred irresponsibly and often spend their lives—sometimes half a century—in small, barren cages, living on concrete or hard compacted dirt, and are denied even the basic necessities of adequate food, shelter, veterinary care, and companionship.[295] They develop an array of captivity-induced health problems and neurotic behaviors as a result of living in grossly substandard conditions. For example, scientists have found high stress levels in caged carnivores who in the wild would roam vast territories.[296]

Exotic pet breeders frequently separate infants from their mothers, which causes permanent damage and deprives them of a normal biological and behavioral development. The infants are then hand-reared and groomed for a lifetime of human interaction.[297] Dangerous animals are subjected to painful declawing or defanging procedures in a futile attempt to make them safe for human interaction once they mature.[298]

Exotic pets can also pose a risk to human health and safety. For example, in addition to the obvious bodily threat that large carnivores pose to humans,[299] one study confirms that "an exotic animal may harbor a raft of potentially infective microbes and macroparasites making any animal a possible Trojan Horse of infection and infestation."[300] Popular species

294. *See, e.g.*, Ass'n of Zoos & Aquariums, *Animal Care Manuals*, https://www.aza.org/animal-care-manuals; Global Fed'n of Animal Sanctuaries, *Standards of Excellence*, http://www.sanctuaryfederation.org/gfas/for-sanctuaries/standards/.

295. *See, e.g.*, AZA, *Personal Possession of Non-Human Primates* (July 2015), https://www.aza.org/uploadedFiles/About_Us/Board%20Approved%20Position%20Statement%20and%20White%20Paper%20-%20Personal%20Possession%20of%20Non-Human%20Primates%207.21.2015.pdf.

296. *See* Ros Clubb & Georgia Mason, *Captivity Effects on Wide-Ranging Carnivores*, 425 NATURE 473 (Oct. 2, 2003).

297. *See* Association of Zoos and Aquariums, *White Paper: Apes in Media and Commercial Performances*, *at* http://www.aza.org/white-paper-apes-in-media-and-commercial-performances/.

298. *See, e.g.* The Dodo, *Anonymous Woman Surrenders Tiger Cub at Shelter*, https://www.thedodo.com/anonymous-woman-surrenders-baby-tiger-1338171876.html.

299. For example, in February 2009, Stamford, Connecticut police shot and killed a 14-year-old, 200-pound chimpanzee ("Travis") after he brutally mauled his owner's friend (Charla Nash). *See* Andy Newman, *Pet Chimp Is Killed after Mauling Woman*, N.Y. TIMES, February 17, 2009, at A30.

300. Clifford Warwick et al., *A Review of Captive Exotic Animal-Linked Zoonoses*, 12(1) J. ENVTL. HEALTH RES. (2012).

of exotic pets are known to carry numerous bacterial, viral, fungal, and parasitic pathogens.[301]

In addition to these public safety and animal welfare concerns, the exotic pet trade can undermine conservation efforts, even when the animals are captive-bred and not sourced from wild populations. Many popular exotic pets (such as tigers, lions, leopards, and gibbons) are listed as threatened or endangered under the ESA, and wild populations of these species are imperiled in part because of unsustainable trade in live animals and parts.[302] Conservationists have raised concerns that the exotic pet trade may contribute to the supply of parts for illegal wildlife trade.[303]

Laws Regulating Exotic Pets

While the federal government is limited to regulating activity pursuant to its specific enumerated powers in the U.S. Constitution, state and local governments have broad power to adopt laws that protect residents and promote societal values. Thus, while federal laws (such as the AWA, ESA, and Captive Wildlife Safety Act [CWSA]) address the interstate trade in exotic pets, states and localities use their general police power to establish prohibitions on the mere possession of dangerous wild animals in captivity.

State Laws

Traditionally, state wildlife laws were enacted to preserve native wild animals for human use. Often state codes grant a natural resources agency with broad authority and discretion to manage wild animals within the

---

301. *See* The National Association of State Public Health Veterinarians, *Compendium of Measures to Prevent Disease Associated with Animals in Public Settings*, 60(4) CDC Morbidity and Mortality Weekly Rep. (May 6, 2011); Eunice C. Chen et al., *Cross-Species Transmission of a Novel Adenovirus Associated with a Fulminant Pneumonia Outbreak in a New World Monkey Colony*, 7(7) PLoS Pathology e1002155 (2011).
302. *See* 50 C.F.R. § 17.11.
303. *See* Douglas F. Williamson & Leigh A. Henry, *Paper Tigers: The Role of the U.S. Captive Tiger Population in the Trade in Tiger Parts*, TRAFFIC North America and World Wildlife Fund (2008), http://www.traffic.org/home/2008/7/31/paper-tigers-us-regulations-on-captive-tigers-flawed.html.

state, but questions frequently arise regarding whether and how these laws apply to privately possessed wild animals (especially those species that are not native to the state). For example, a 2015 Indiana Court of Appeals decision held that a statutory declaration that "[a]ll wild animals, except those that are . . . legally owned or being held in captivity . . . are the property of the people of Indiana" means that the state Department of Natural Resources has no authority to regulate captive wildlife, despite a broad statutory directive that "[t]he department shall protect and properly manage the fish and wildlife resources of Indiana."[304] Following that case, which struck down the regulation of canned hunting ranches (discussed in the following section) the state agency informed exotic pet owners that the state would no longer be exercising oversight of such activity.[305]

Many states have adopted legislation specifically to address the burgeoning trend of keeping exotic pets in local communities. Indeed, all but five states (Nevada, Wisconsin, Alabama, North Carolina, and South Carolina) now have regulations pertaining to the private possession of certain species of dangerous wild animals.[306] These laws either simply enact a permitting scheme (operating as a registry but allowing continued acquisition) or actually prohibit private possession of certain species.[307] Often existing exotic pets are grandfathered into these laws, with varying levels of oversight of such animals.

Exotic pets are also routinely protected under state animal welfare and cruelty laws. While cruelty laws often criminalize intentional mistreatment of animals, some states have laws similar to the AWA that impose minimum standards for humane treatment. For example, the Virginia Comprehensive Animal Care Law requires owners of nonhuman primates and other exotic animals to provide their animals with adequate

---

304. IDNR v. Whitetail Bluff, LLC, 25 N.E.3d 218 (Ind. Ct. App. 2015).

305. *See, e.g.,* Niki Kelly, *Ruling De-regulates Some Wild Animal Possession Permits,* J. Gazette (July 1, 2015), http://www.journalgazette.net/news/local/indiana/Ruling-de-regulates-some -wild-animal-possession-permits-7504326.

306. *See* The Humane Society of the United States, *Dangerous Wild Animal Laws* (2015), http:// www.humanesociety.org/assets/pdfs/wildlife/exotics/state-laws-dangerous-wild-animals.pdf.

307. *See, e.g.,* Wash. Rev. Code Chapter 16.30 (prohibiting the private possession of big cats, wolves, bears, hyenas, primates, and venomous snakes, except for qualified institutions); MO Stat. § 578.023 (requiring exotic pet owners to register their animals).

feed, water, space, exercise, shelter, and veterinary care.[308] Furthermore, the law requires captive wildlife to be managed pursuant to a "responsible practice of good animal husbandry, handling, production, management, confinement, feeding, watering, protection, shelter, transportation, treatment, and, when necessary, euthanasia, appropriate for the age, species, condition, size and type of the animal."[309]

While state laws are often necessary to completely prohibit the possession of exotic pets, federal laws also aid in curtailing the exotic pet trade. For example, the ESA prohibits the interstate sale of endangered species, such as chimpanzees and tigers, for use as pets; although, as discussed previously, exotic pet sales may circumvent the USFWS oversight when they are disguised as breeding loans.[310]

Federal Lacey Act

The Lacey Act, originally enacted in 1900, is one of the nation's oldest wildlife laws.[311] Its principal proscription is against the transport in interstate commerce of wildlife taken in violation of state, foreign, or international law. The Lacey Act also includes the CWSA,[312] which restricts interstate trade in big cats (regardless of whether such activity violates another law).

The CWSA addresses concerns about public safety, animal welfare, and wildlife conservation caused by private ownership of "big cats" in the United States. Specifically, the CWSA makes it unlawful "to import, export, transport, sell, receive, acquire, or purchase in interstate or foreign commerce" a big cat, unless one of the exemptions applies.[313] Big cats covered by the CWSA include lions, tigers, leopards, snow leopards, clouded leopards, jaguars, cheetahs, and cougars, and all subspecies and hybrids of these species.[314] Exempt from the law are USDA-licensees,

---

308. *See* Va. Code. Ann. § 3.2-6503(A).
309. *Id.*; Va. Code. Ann. § 3.2-6500 (definition of "adequate care").
310. 16 U.S.C. § 1538(a)(1)(F).
311. 16 U.S.C. § 3372.
312. P.L. No. 108-191.
313. 16 U.S.C. § 3372(a)(2)(C).
314. *Id.* at § 3371(g).

state-licensed wildlife rehabilitators, wildlife sanctuaries, state universities, licensed veterinarians, and temporary transporters.[315]

Congress has introduced legislation to broaden the scope and restrictions of this law. One proposed expansion, the Captive Primate Safety Act, would add primates to the definition of "prohibited wildlife species" protected under the law. The Big Cat Public Safety Act (pending before Congress) would add prohibitions on the possession and breeding of big cats and would also narrow the scope of exemptions under the CWSA. Relevant to circuses and entertainment, the bill would prohibit possession of big cats by exhibitors that allow members of the public to interact directly with the animals.

Another provision of the Lacey Act pertaining to "injurious species" also impacts the exotic pet trade.[316] Since 1960 the Lacey Act has authorized the Secretary of the Interior to prohibit the import of wildlife that is "injurious to human beings, to the interests of agriculture, horticulture, forestry, or to wildlife or the wildlife resources of the United States . . ."[317]

Pursuant to this authority, the USFWS has adopted regulations prohibiting the import of and interstate commerce in eight species of large constrictor snakes.[318] The agency made its decision to prohibit trade in these species of snakes (which can reach lengths exceeding twenty feet and kill their prey by constriction) in reliance on scientific evidence produced by the U.S. Geological Survey of the risks large constrictor snakes pose to native wildlife.[319]

Because some of these species (such as Burmese pythons and reticulated pythons) are popular in the lucrative exotic pet trade, the U.S. Association for Reptile Keepers challenged the regulation, asserting that the Lacey Act does not authorize the federal government to regulate trade

---

315. *Id.* at § 3372(e).

316. 18 U.S.C. § 42(a)(1).

317. *Id.*

318. 80 Fed. Reg. 12702 (March 10, 2015); 77 Fed. Reg. 3330 (Jan. 23, 2012); 50 C.F.R. § 16.15. (Indian pythons (including Burmese pythons), Northern African pythons, Southern African pythons, yellow anacondas, reticulated python, DeSchauensee's anaconda, green anaconda, and Beni anaconda)

319. Robert N. Reed & Gordon H. Rodda, *Giant Constrictors: Biological and Management Profiles and an Establishment Risk Assessment for Nine Large Species of Pythons, Anacondas, and the Boa Constrictor* (2009), http://pubs.usgs.gov/of/2009/1202/pdf/OF09-1202.pdf.

of snakes within the continental United States, but only to prohibit the introduction of species into the continental United States.[320] The USFWS (along with intervenors The Humane Society of the United States and Center for Biological Diversity) has staunchly opposed this interpretation, which turns on the congressional intent behind the law's authorization to regulate "shipment between the continental United States."[321] The case, which could undermine dozens of regulations pertaining to invasive species, was pending at the time of publication.

Case Study: Zanesville, Ohio—Exotic Pet Tragedy

The public safety threat posed by exotic pets played out in the national press in October 2011 when a disturbed Zanesville, Ohio man released nearly fifty big cats, bears, and primates from his backyard menagerie, leading to dozens of animals being killed in order to protect the surrounding community.[322] Because there were no records of how many exotic pets were released, residents were warned to stay in their homes, a sign on the interstate cautioned drivers to stay in their cars, and schools were closed. Dozens of animals who could not be humanely contained were shot, including endangered tigers.

Ohio had long neglected to regulate the hotbed of exotic pet breeding and sales (including open auctions) in the state, but after this incident was persuaded to enact a comprehensive law regulating the private possession, sale, and breeding of dangerous wild animals.[323] The law prohibits future exotic pet ownership and has multiple exemptions, including exotics owned at the time of enactment; use in exhibition, research, rescue, veterinary care, temporary transport and for disabled persons; and even as sports mascots.

---

320. USARK v. Jewell, 2015 WL 2396074 (D.D.C. 2015).

321. 18 U.S.C. § 42(a)(1).

322. *See* Greg Bishop & Timothy Williams, *Police Kill Dozens of Animals Freed on Ohio Reserve*, N.Y. TIMES (Oct. 19, 2011), http://www.nytimes.com/2011/10/20/us/police-kill-dozens-of -animals-freed-from-ohio-preserve.html.

323. OHIO REV. CODE. Chapter 935 (covering hyenas, gray wolves, lions, tigers, jaguars, leopards, cheetahs, lynxes, cougars, caracals, servals, bears, primates, elephants, rhinoceros, hippopotamus, cape buffalo, wild dog, komodo dragons, alligators, crocodiles, caimans, gharials, large constrictor snakes, and venomous snakes).

Several owners of exotic animals brought a constitutional challenge to the law in federal court. The plaintiffs claimed that the law violated their First Amendment rights to freedom of speech and association by forcing them to join a zoological accreditation organization that they disagreed with on policy matters. Plaintiffs further claimed that the law (and in particular its requirement that animals be microchipped) was an unconstitutional taking of private property.

The District Court for the Southern District of Ohio upheld the law, and the Sixth Circuit affirmed, holding that plaintiffs had multiple options to comply with the law:[324] "Mere unwillingness to conform their conduct to the permitting requirements or the other 13 exemptions does not mean that the Act compels appellants to join the AZA or the ZAA. The Act imposes a choice on appellants, even though it is not a choice they welcome. . . . The burden of regulation may, unfortunately, fall heavier on some than on others, but that, without more, is not enough to render this Act unconstitutional . . ."[325]

The appellate court found the Takings Clause claim even weaker, given the states' general police power to enact laws for the "general welfare," and pointing out that even after being microchipped, the animals remained plaintiffs' possessions, as is the case with the "myriad state laws regarding the microchipping of exotic and domesticated animals as well as the ear-tagging of agricultural animals," none of which constitute a Fifth Amendment taking.[326]

The Sixth Circuit opinion, in conjunction with that of *DeHart v. Austin,* [327] represents important precedent confirming that state laws strictly prohibiting the possession of exotic pets are within the state's general police power.

---

324. Wilkins v. Daniels, 913 F. Supp. 2d 517 (S.D. Ohio 2012); Wilkins v. Daniels, 744 F.3d. 409 (6th Cir. 2014).

325. *Id.* at 416.

326. *Id.* at 419.

327. DeHart v. Town of Austin, 39 F.3d 718 (7th Cir. 1994) (holding that municipal ordinance regulating the possession and use of exotic animals is not preempted by the Animal Welfare Act, is not an impermissible attempt to regulate interstate commerce, and does not deprive exotic animal owners of due process rights under the Fourteenth Amendment of the U.S. Constitution).

Captive Hunting Ranches

Moral Considerations

Captive hunting facilities, also known as "canned hunting ranches," confine exotic or native wildlife (often ungulates, but big cats as well) in fenced outdoor enclosures (ranging from cages to large ranches) and offer trophy hunters the guaranteed opportunity to kill animals and obtain the pelt and meat of the killed animals. These operations often allow their herds to breed, but they also acquire animals from animal dealers, auctions, or as cast-offs from substandard exhibition facilities. Captive hunting operations frequently provide food to the animals (as opposed or in addition to providing them grazing land), habituating them to human presence and making them an easier target for hunters. Some hunting organizations (like Boone and Crockett Club, Pope and Young Club, and the Izaak Walton League) oppose captive hunting because it lacks the element of "fair chase." It is estimated that there are well over 1,000 captive hunting facilities in the United States, with approximately 500 ranches in Texas alone.

Native species like white-tailed deer make up a significant percentage of the animals in the captive hunting industry, with deer selectively bred for their large and unusual antlers. Maintaining large captive populations of native deer can threaten the health of wild populations of deer, elk, moose, and livestock through the transmission of disease, such as tuberculosis, brucellosis, and chronic wasting disease (CWD). CWD is of particular concern, as it is a prion disease (transmitted by infectious proteins, similar to bovine spongiform encephalopathy or mad cow disease) and hunters are advised to avoid eating meat from an animal infected with the disease.[328] CWD has now been found in 22 states and there is evidence that the captive hunting industry is responsible for exacerbating the spread of the disease.[329]

---

328. American Veterinary Medical Association, *Disease precautions for hunters* (2016), https://www.avma.org/public/Health/Pages/Disease-Precautions-for-Hunters.aspx#cwd.

329. Ryan Sabalow et al., *Buck Fever*, Indy Star (March 27, 2014), http://www.indystar.com/story/news/investigations/2014/03/27/buck-fever-intro/6865031.

Captive hunting is a lucrative industry, with trophy hunters paying thousands of dollars to kill a single animal. For example, at Laguna Vista Ranch in Texas, customers can shoot a white-tailed deer for $2,500 to $14,000 or an elk for $6,500 to $17,000 (depending on the size of the antlers), or exotic animals like Armenian mouflon ($4,000), gemsbok ($6,500), or zebra ($7,500).[330]

Several states have prohibited the practice of captive hunting, but in other states captive hunting is legal, with few limitations. It has become especially popular for the facilities to stock endangered antelopes and cervids for canned hunts, particularly in those states with warmer climates.[331]

Although captive hunting ranches claim that their colonies are refugia for dwindling wild populations, opponents of recreational hunting of captive endangered species argue that captive hunting of these animals and the subsequent trade of the animals' body parts as trophies can have a negative impact on wild populations of those species, citing studies showing that the existence of legal markets for endangered species can both encourage and facilitate poaching of those species.[332] Global commercialization of wild animals and plants is a multibillion-dollar industry and can result in extreme animal cruelty (such as cutting off a rhinoceros' horn while the animal is alive) and serious population declines. Illegal wildlife trade is second only to the illegal drug trade in terms of profitability and raises serious national security concerns when poaching proceeds are used to fund terrorist groups.[333] Furthermore, because trophy hunters generally prefer wild-sourced animals over farmed ones, the increased demand also increases the poaching incentive, resulting in a negative conservation impact on wild populations.

Supporters of canned hunting, especially of endangered species, often argue that their activities promote conservation because captive hunt-

---

330. Laguna Vista Ranch (2016), http://www.lagunavistaranch.com/.

331. Captive hunting ranches advertise imperiled species including scimitar-horned oryx, addax, dama gazelle, barasingha, Arabian oryx, and Eld's deer, which are native to Asia and Africa.

332. *See, e.g., See* Valerius Geist, *How Markets in Wildlife Meat and Parts, and the Sale of Hunting Privileges, Jeopardize Wildlife Conservation*, 2(1) CONSERVATION BIOL. 16 (Mar. 1988); DAVID M. LAVIGNE ET AL., *Sustainable Utilization: The Lessons of History*, in THE EXPLOITATION OF MAMMAL POPULATIONS 251, 260 (Victoria J. Taylor et al. eds., 1996).

333. The White House, *National Strategy for Combatting Wildlife Trafficking* (Feb. 2014), https://www.whitehouse.gov/sites/default/files/docs/nationalstrategywildlifetrafficking.pdf.

ing ranches are breeding animals for potential introduction into native ecosystems and contributing money to in situ conservation efforts for the species. The federal government and the international community have largely sanctioned this concept, authorizing trade in trophies derived from captive hunting facilities.[334]

Laws Pertaining to Captive Hunting

It is generally within a state legislature's power to prohibit captive hunting or the import of any animals, whether to protect captive animal welfare or the health of native wildlife or livestock. Indeed, 22 states prohibit the import of captive deer and a few states have adopted legislation expressly outlawing hunting of captive animals, while others merely require a license to conduct such activity.[335] Not surprisingly, these laws have come under attack by the captive hunting industry.[336]

For example, in 2005 Indiana's Department of Natural Resources (IDNR) adopted emergency regulations to crack down on the captive hunting industry in an effort to prevent the spread of CWD. As discussed previously, a captive hunting facility challenged these regulations, and the Indiana Court of Appeals held (and the Indiana Supreme Court declined to review) that the broad grant of authority directing IDNR to "protect and properly manage the fish and wildlife resources of Indiana" does not apply to animals held in captivity.[337] In 2016 the Indiana legislature adopted legislation regulating, but not prohibiting, the captive hunting industry.

Similarly, in 2015 the captive hunting industry challenged the Missouri Conservation Commission's regulations limiting the import of deer to the state and requiring minimum enclosure size for canned hunt-

---

334. *See, e.g.,* 50 C.F.R. § 17.21(h) (authorizing captive hunting of three endangered species without even requiring a permit for the lethal take or transport of the trophy across state lines).
335. Ryan Sabalow et al., *Buck Fever,* Indy Star (March 27, 2014), http://www.indystar.com/story/news/investigations/2014/03/27/buck-fever-intro/6865031/.
336. Ryan Sabalow, *Missouri veto resonates through captive deer hunting industry,* Indy Star (July 14, 2014), http://www.indystar.com/story/news/2014/07/14/missouri-veto-resonates -captive-deer-hunting-industry/12548493/; Ryan Sabalow, *Missouri tightens rules on deer farms, hunting preserves,* Indy Star (Oct. 17, 2014http://www.indystar.com/story/news/2014/10/17/missouri-tightens-rules-deer-farms-hunting-preserves/17453883/.
337. IC 14-22-1-1(b); IDNR v. Whitetail Bluff, LLC, 25 N.E.3d 218 (Ind. Ct. App. 2015).

ing facilities, arguing that the regulations exceed the agency's statutory authority because captive animals are not "wildlife," violate the federal dormant commerce clause by discriminating against interstate commerce, and violate the state constitutional right to farm.[338]

Without a unified federal scheme (the USDA currently maintains a voluntary National CWD Herd Certification Program but does not have any binding standards for the industry), states are free to allow breeding and trade of captive cervids (deer, elk, moose, and others of the Cervidae family) regardless of the risk that such activities contribute to the spread of CWD. But members of Congress have recently expressed their desire for the USDA to exercise its existing statutory authority under the Animal Health Protection Act[339] (AHPA): "Considering USDA's limited resources, it would be prudent for the agency to adopt a precautionary approach, consistent with its regulatory authority, and prohibit interstate transport of captive-bred cervids in order to quell the burgeoning threats the inhumane canned-hunting industry poses to the health of livestock, native wildlife and even humans."[340]

While state wildlife agencies and the USDA are directly involved with regulating the use of native species in the captive hunting industry, the use of exotic animals and endangered animals implicates federal and international wildlife law. As discussed in prior sections and detailed in the case study that follows, the ESA requires a permit to conduct otherwise prohibited activities (including the interstate sale of trophies or the lethal take of captive endangered species on U.S. ranches). The USFWS routinely issues permits to captive hunting ranches to sell hunts of foreign species based on a rationale that donations of a percentage of trophy fees to organizations working to protect the species in the wild benefit conservation. Additionally, U.S. hunters routinely engage in captive hunting of imperiled species in foreign countries, such as white rhinoceros and

---

338. Hill et al., v. Missouri Conservation Comm'n et al., Case No. 150S-CC00005-01 (20th J. Cir. MO 2015); MO. CONST. Art. I, § 35. Plaintiffs allege that the "right of . . . ranchers to engage in . . . ranching practices" guaranteed by the Missouri Constitution prohibited the Commission's regulations of captive hunting. The case was still pending at the time of publication.

339. 7 U.S.C. 8301 *et seq.*

340. Rep. James Moran et al., Letter to Secretary of Agriculture (June 6, 2014), https://www.documentcloud.org/documents/1185021-captive-deer-breeding-ltr-to-usda-6-6-14.html.

bontebok in South Africa.[341] The international shipment of trophies is regulated under both the ESA and CITES. CITES is discussed at length in other chapters of this book, but here it is relevant to say that CITES requirements are generally relaxed for species bred in captivity and that there have been concerns that certain countries are not adequately overseeing captive wildlife such that animals removed from the wild (and later stocked in a captive hunting facility, for example) might be unsustainably traded. The Lacey Act also provides a mechanism for federal enforcement against individuals who take wildlife in violation of state, foreign, or international law and then move the trophy in interstate commerce.[342]

Case Studies

The Three Amigos—Endangered Antelopes in Texas

The USFWS has recognized that "uses of captive wildlife can be detrimental to wild populations," specifically noting that "consumptive uses" can "stimulate a demand for products which might further be satisfied by wild populations."[343] Yet contrary to that approach, the USFWS continues to issue permits authorizing the lethal take of endangered species.

The USFWS has issued over 100 CBWs and take permits to facilities that sell captive hunts of listed antelopes and cervids.[344] The USFWS has even issued a step-by-step guide for canned hunting facilities to help them apply for permits to sell hunts.[345]

The so-called "three amigos" are three species—scimitar-horned oryx, addax, and dama gazelle—native to Northern Africa. According to IUCN (an expert scientific body), addax and dama gazelle are criti-

---

341. Notably, while U.S. hunters for years imported hundreds of lions killed in South African captive breeding facilities, in 2016 USFWS decided not to allow the import of captive-bred lion trophies, finding that such hunting does not promote the conservation of the species. 80 Fed. Reg. 79999 (Dec. 23, 2015); Dan Ashe, *A Major Step Forward for Lion Conservation in Africa*, HUFFINGTON POST (Oct. 21, 2016), http://www.huffingtonpost.com/entry/a-major-step -forward-for-lion-conservation-in-africa_us_5808f6ffe4b099c434319294.

342. 16 U.S.C. § 3372(a)(2)(A).

343. *See* 44 Fed. Reg. at 30,045.

344. *See* 78 Fed. Reg. 33790, 33797 (June 5, 2013).

345. *See* USFWS, *African Antelope* (2016), http://www.fws.gov/international/permits/by-species/ three-antelope.html.

cally endangered and scimitar-horned oryx are extinct in the wild.[346] In 2005, the USFWS listed these three species as endangered under the ESA.[347] The USFWS simultaneously issued a regulation exempting U.S. captive-bred individuals of the three species from the ESA's prohibitions on "take" and transport in interstate commerce.[348] Under the rule, any person could kill, export, sell, or commercially transport in interstate commerce, these live endangered animals or "sport-hunted trophies" of these three species without having to obtain a permit or other specific authorization.[349] Animal welfare organizations challenged this rule in federal court, arguing that the blanket exemption for take of endangered species violated the ESA (which requires individualized permitting decisions). The U.S. District Court for the District of Columbia agreed and overturned the hunting rule in 2009.[350] Although the government initially appealed the court's decision, that appeal was later withdrawn.

However, the regulation remained on the books until 2012, when the USFWS rescinded the rule and began requiring (and routinely issuing) ESA permits for captive hunts of these three species.[351] The Exotic Wildlife Association (a trade organization whose members are captive hunting operations) filed a lawsuit against the USFWS, challenging the rescission of the exemption, and Safari Club International (SCI) filed a challenge to the endangered species listing status for these species. These cases were consolidated, and the U.S. District Court for the District of Columbia held that because a judge had previously ruled that the blanket canned hunting rule was inconsistent with the ESA, it was reasonable for the USFWS to revoke that rule and apply the ESA permitting requirements to these species. The court also found that the USFWS's decision to include captive antelopes in the endangered listing (over SCI's objection) was consistent with the purpose of the ESA (and also consistent

---

346. *See* IUCN SSC Antelope Specialist Group, Addax nasomaculatus (2016), http://www.iucnredlist.org/details/512/0; IUCN SSC Antelope Specialist Group, Oryx dammah (2016), http://www.iucnredlist.org/details/15568/0; IUCN SSC Antelope Specialist Group, Nanger dama (2016), http://www.iucnredlist.org/details/8968/0.

347. 70 Fed. Reg. 52319 (Sept. 2, 2005).

348. 70 Fed. Reg. 52,310 (Sept. 2, 2005).

349. 50 C.F.R. § 17.21(h).

350. Friends of Animals v. Salazar, 626 F. Supp. 2d 102 (D.D.C. 2009).

351. 77 Fed. Reg. 431, 434 (Jan. 5, 2012).

with the USFWS's concurrent decision to list all chimpanzees as endangered, recognizing that a "split listing" based solely on an animal's captive state was insupportable under the ESA).[352]

Congress then intervened and directed the USFWS to reinstate the regulation exempting captive hunting from ESA permitting requirements (despite prior court orders holding that this regulation violates the ESA).[353] Friends of Animals then filed an unsuccessful lawsuit challenging the constitutionality of the Congressional appropriations rider.[354]

While no permits are required for captive hunting of the three amigos, lethal take of other endangered ungulates for recreational purposes may be permitted if such activity is offset by a donation to an in situ conservation project. Indeed, the USFWS has provided explicit guidelines for how to acquire a permit to engage in captive hunting operations (far more guidance than the agency has provided for permits for exhibitors, for example). The guidelines inform potential applicants that they need to provide a justification for the "culling" of animals, and how the operation will support in situ conservation efforts.[355]

Pursuant to the agency's direction, dozens of captive hunting operations have obtained ESA permits in exchange for donating a few thousand dollars to organizations of which they may be members, and those permits allow them to carry on their captive hunting business. This "pay-to-play" policy (discussed previously in this chapter) raises ethical and legal concerns. Conservationists have questioned whether it is right to kill an individual animal—usually a male in his prime—in an effort to save the species from extinction (especially when the species is imperiled because of poaching and perpetuating the demand for trophies and wildlife parts contributes to poaching).

There is also debate over whether the USFWS' implementation of the ESA permitting scheme comports with the agency's statutory mandate.

---

352. SCI v. Jewell, 960 F. Supp. 2d 17 (D.D.C. 2013).
353. *See* 50 C.F.R. § 17.21(h); 79 Fed. Reg. 15250 (March 19, 2014).
354. Friends of Animals v. Jewell et al., 82 F. Supp. 3d 265 (D.D.C. 2015), *aff'd* 2016 WL 3125204 (D.C. Cir. 2016).
355. USFWS, *African Antelope* (2016), http://www.fws.gov/international/permits/by-species/three-antelope.html.

Once a permit is granted under the ESA regulations, only the permit-tee or its agent is authorized to take the otherwise unlawful action.[356] Specifically, when a take or commerce permit is granted, only a "person who is under the direct control of the permittee, or who is employed by or under contract to the permittee for purposes authorized by the permit, may carry out the activity authorized by the permit."[357] ESA permits are "not transferable or assignable."[358] However, the captive-hunt facilities apply for an enhancement authorization to hunt, sell, and transport listed animals and their parts, but the facility's hunter clients actually take and transport the animals.

Exotic Meat on the Menu

Not only are captive wild animals stocked for recreational hunts on pri-vate reserves, they are also slaughtered for sale in the exotic meat market. For example, USDA-licensed exhibitor "Woody's Menagerie" in Illinois acquired at least forty-six bears, twenty African lions, four cougars, one leopard, four tigers, and four ligers from eleven facilities in five states between April 2006 and January 2012 (as documented by The Humane Society of the United States through news reports and state public records of certificates of veterinary inspection).[359] This facility appears to be a dumping ground for unwanted exotic animals, including animals that are no longer profitable for public contact programs, because they have become too large and dangerous. The facility's owner has acknowledged to a USDA inspector that he has slaughtered bears and African lions, apparently for their meat and hides.[360]

There are exotic meat processors that have butchered bears and lions for human consumption; for example, an investigation by Born Free USA

---

356. 50 C.F.R. § 13.25(a).

357. *Id.* § 13.25(d).

358. *Id.* § 13.25(a).

359. *See* The Humane Society of the United States et al., Comments on the Animal and Plant Health Inspection Service (APHIS) Proposed Rule: Petition to Amend Animal Welfare Act Regu-lations to Prohibit Public Contact with Big Cats, Bears, and Nonhuman Primates (Aug. 31, 2016), https://www.regulations.gov/document?D=APHIS-2012-0107-21267.

360. *See* USDA, Inspection Report for License No. 33-C-0128 (Jan. 31, 2013).

revealed that Eickman's Processing (also in Illinois) slaughtered as many as twenty lions between December 6, 2009, and January 2, 2010, and that another exotic meat processor (Czimer's Game and Seafood, also in Illinois) was previously convicted of selling meat from federally protected tigers and leopards.[361] Restaurants have sold lion tacos and other exotic offerings, but consuming meat that was not raised for human consumption may pose a risk to human health if the animals are treated with drugs not approved for use in animals for human consumption, and consumers may not be aware that they are eating meat from an animal bred for exhibition and not for consumption.[362]

While not as common an event in the United States, captive hunting of lions in South Africa is big business, and American hunters have routinely traveled to South Africa to shoot lions that were often bred for photographic opportunities as cubs. A recent documentary, *Blood Lions*, explores the secretive industry and estimates that two to three lions per day are killed in South Africa's canned hunting industry, with hundreds more slaughtered annually to supply bones for use in traditional Asian medicine (in lieu of more prized tiger bones that are believed to possess therapeutic benefits, such as improving circulation, curing arthritis, and boosting energy).[363]

In 2015, the USFWS listed African lions under the ESA, with populations in Western and Central Africa listed as endangered and populations in Eastern and Southern Africa listed as threatened.[364] The rule requires American trophy hunters to obtain a permit for the import of any lion trophy, which can only be issued if the hunt is deemed to promote conservation. The rule also applies to captive lions in the United States, prohibiting the take of live African lions and the interstate sale of lion meat without a permit (and it is unlikely that killing a lion for meat, or the interstate sale of lion meat, would be deemed to promote conservation).

---

361. Born Free USA, Lions on the Menu: A Deadly Delicacy (Nov. 28, 2011), http://www.born freeusa.org/articles.php?p=3051&more=1.

362. Christine Dell'Amore, *Restaurant's Lion Tacos Renew Exotic Meat Debate*, Nat'l Geographic (May 11, 2013), http://news.nationalgeographic.com/news/2013/13/130510-lion-meat-taco -florida-animal-food-science/.

363. Blood Lions, http://www.bloodlions.org/.

364. 80 Fed. Reg. 79999 (Dec. 23, 2015).

The Future for Captive Wild Animals

This chapter has demonstrated that we hold captive and use wild animals for a variety of human purposes. Some purposes are more justified than others, and it cannot be disputed that many of the animals involved are subjected to pain and suffering that is necessarily caused by their captivity and related use. For many species, no amount of regulation can provide them the care and surroundings that satisfy their innate needs and allow them to engage in their natural behaviors and develop the relationships they would have living in the wild. The current legal regime is based on a utilitarian paradigm that weighs the costs and benefits of maintaining wild animals in captivity with little regard for the harms to the animals. As discussed, so long as the use is allowed, and the owner meets the minimal standards established, most harm done to the animal, even when it may be severe, may be deemed "necessary" and legal. Moreover, enforcement is inadequate with many violations going undetected. For those violations that are discovered, the fines are so small that many owners view them as a cost of doing business. In the end, the animals suffer without recourse because no private entity may enforce the AWA directly nor compel the USDA to enforce it.

Some may believe that the current state of the law is adequate, but for those who believe that animals, especially captive wild animals, deserve better, there are a variety of ways that the system may change to better protect their interests. First, and arguably least controversial, the current laws should be enforced aggressively. Additional resources should be allocated to the USDA, the USFWS, NMFS, and other state and federal agencies tasked with enforcement of the laws that protect captive wild animals so they may identify violations and prosecute and/or otherwise hold accountable the offenders. The standards set under the AWA are the bare minimum supposedly necessary to keep an animal from pain and suffering; animals deserve at least the minimum standard of care mandated under the law. Similarly, the accreditation bodies, such as the AZA and the Alliance, must regularly inspect and sanction members who do not meet their standards.

For many, this change, while sorely needed, is not enough. Many will argue that the laws must be strengthened to provide greater protections for captive wild animals. The first approach here is to remain within the utilitarian paradigm, but more honestly and accurately account for the harm caused by captivity and the specific use of the animal, to determine whether the human benefit from such use in fact outweighs the harm to the animal. For certain species, their care and treatment in captivity may be able to more closely reflect their natural habitat and social structure, such that keeping them in captivity may not severely harm them. Some argue that the benefit to humans and the animals may justify keeping such animals in captivity because they suffer relatively little harm. In these situations, the standards must be improved by amending AWA regulations to require that the environment in which captive wildlife is kept mimic as closely as possible their natural habitat, and that the regulations be aggressively enforced. In addition, laws should be enacted to ban certain especially cruel aspects of their use.

For some species, their physical, psychological, and emotional needs cannot be adequately met in captivity. The needs of a 12,000-pound, intelligent, socially complex orca whale who swims up to 100 kilometers per day and forms family relationships in pods in the wild cannot be replicated in captivity and the harm they suffer from captivity is significant. In contrast, the benefits realized by their captivity for public display (their primary use by humans) are relatively small and do not justify the harm caused. As such, some would argue that no orca should be kept in captivity for public display. In fact, steps have been taken to ban such use. For example, in 2013, India banned all dolphinaria finding "cetaceans . . . are highly intelligent and sensitive, and various scientists who have researched dolphin behaviour have suggested that the unusually high intelligence[,] as compared to other animals[,] means that dolphin[s] should be seen as 'non-human persons' and as such should have their own specific rights and [it] is morally unacceptable to keep them captive for entertainment purposes."[365] In the United States, in March 2016, Sea World agreed to stop breeding captive orcas and to end theatrical orca

---

365. Government of India, Ministry of Environment & Forests, Central Zoo Authority, Circular, Policy on Establishment of Dolphinarium, F. No. 20-1/2010-CZA(M) (May 17, 2013).

shows by 2019,[366] and legislation has been introduced at the state and federal level to prohibit the public display of orcas.[367] However, regarding canned hunting, the Sportsmanship in Hunting Act of 2011, which would have banned captive hunting of nonnative mammals, never made headway in Congress.

The most controversial cases are those where the wild animal suffers greatly yet humans believe that their use is essential to promote human health and well-being. Some argue that biomedical research on animals falls into this category and can be justified if the science is proven to be successful and there are no alternatives for achieving the same results through computer simulations or other technological advances. Nevertheless, primates used for invasive, deadly research in the laboratory suffer tremendously, and no amount of regulation can protect primates from such harm. In these circumstances, a utilitarian balancing under the current legal paradigm will allow the research. For those who believe that this situation is unethical and immoral, the law must shift to a deontological paradigm to protect the primates. In fact, such a paradigmatic shift was recently tested in the courts of the state of New York.

From 2013 to 2015, the Nonhuman Rights Project filed multiple unsuccessful petitions for writs of habeas corpus, asserting that four chimpanzees held in captivity in New York by private owners (Tommy and Kiko) and by Stonybrook University researchers (Hercules and Leo) should be recognized as "legal persons," granted the right to bodily liberty, and moved to an accredited sanctuary.[368] While the state courts declined the opportunity to revolutionize the legal status of these animals, the cases certainly generated substantial discourse about how we treat captive wildlife.

Of course, there are also nonlegal means to achieve greater protections for captive wild animals. In fact, the law follows societal attitudes

---

366. See David Kirby, *SeaWorld to End Captive Breeding of Killer Whales, Orca Shows,* TAKEPART (Mar. 17, 2016), http://www.takepart.com/article/2016/03/17/seaworld-end-captive-breeding -killer-whales?cmpid=tp-eml-2016-03-17-SeaWorld.

367. H.R. 4019, 114th Congress, 1st Sess. (Nov. 16, 2015).

368. Nonhuman Rights Project, *Court Cases,* http://www.nonhumanrightsproject.org/category/ courtfilings/.

and often is not amended until private efforts demonstrating a desire to alter the legal framework are successful. Thus, the decision of Ringling Bros. to go out of business[369] and the National Institute of Health's decision to retire all of their chimpanzees[370] have perhaps paved the way for other sea changes in the way we treat wild animals and ultimately for lawmakers to put an official end to the use of elephants and other wild animals in circuses or the use of any primate in research.

Associations and other entities also may help shape public opinion and ultimately the law. In February 2015, the American Bar Association (ABA) House of Delegates passed a resolution that urged "all federal, state, territorial, and local legislative bodies and/or governmental agencies to enact comprehensive laws that prohibit, unless otherwise exempted, the private possession, sale, breeding, import, or transfer of dangerous wild animals, such as big cats, bears, wolves, primates, and dangerous reptiles, in order to protect public safety and health, and to ensure the humane treatment and welfare of such animals."[371] The focus of the resolution primarily was to end the private ownership of dangerous wild animals by individuals so that another Zanesville massacre would never be repeated.[372] The House of Delegates further added "such laws should include reasonable exemptions, such as for non-profit wildlife sanctuaries, facilities accredited by the Association of Zoos and Aquariums, and research institutions."[373] Thus, while progress was made to alter the legal landscape with respect to the private ownership of wild animals as pets, it was clear that a mainstream association such as the ABA was not yet ready to suggest that the law require that zoos, aquariums, and research institutions change their approach to the captivity of wild animals.

Ultimately, only time will tell the fate of captive wild animals. Key to change will be technological advances that no longer require the use of primates or other animals in research, many of which are currently

369. http://www.cnn.com/2017/01/14/entertainment/ringling-circus-closing.

370. 81 Fed. Reg. 6873 (Feb. 9, 2016).

371. American Bar Association Resolution 105 (amended), http://www.americanbar.org/content/dam/aba/images/abanews/2015mm_hodres/105.pdf.

372. *See supra* section entitled Case Study: Zanesville, Ohio—Exotic Pet Tragedy.

373. American Bar Association Resolution 105 (amended), http://www.americanbar.org/content/dam/aba/images/abanews/2015mm_hodres/105.pdf.

available; private actors taking the lead to end other commercial uses of wild animals in the media; and public appreciation of the intelligence and complex social lives of the animals and the severity of harm they suffer in captivity, such as that accomplished by the film, *Blackfish*. Once society understands that the benefits from keeping wild animals in captivity are slight and/or can be otherwise accomplished, and the level of harm to the animals in captivity is great, we may witness not only greater protections for the wild animals in captivity but a paradigmatic shift in our views towards a belief, perhaps enforced through the law, that wild animals have a right to live free and with dignity.

Index